Explosive Preaching

'Ron Boyd-Macmillan has listened to more poor preaching than anyone should have to tolerate in a single lifetime. But he puts this experience to good effect as he considers the reasons for it, and introduces readers to some key issues that could make a difference. He tells it as it is, sparing no-one's blushes, and writes in a style that is entertaining and passionate, but also well informed. The accessible way in which he combines insights from Biblical, theological, historical and cultural studies is itself a model of effective communication at its best.'

John Drane, author *The McDonaldization of the Church*
(www.johndrane.com)

'Many books on preaching provide anatomies of sermons that examine their skeletons, or conduct autopsies of sermons that were dead on arrival or expired during delivery. By contrast, Ronald Boyd-MacMillan uses his journalistic skills to ensure that sermons are kept alive under his examination! The letter format of the book enables him to be engagingly conversational, humorous, and provocative. At the same time, this is a book of substance, displaying extensive research, theological reflection, a wide experience of Christian traditions and the world at large, and practical wisdom. He writes from both ends of the communication process: both as apprentice preacher and pencil-poised, pew-sitter. His contribution will help preachers burdened with having to say something become preachers who have something to say.'

Eddie Gibbs, Donald A. McGavran Professor of Church Growth

'*Explosive Preaching* vigorously exposes the scandal of poor preaching, diagnoses causes, prescribes remedies, and challenges preachers to rise to the majesty of their task. This is a highly readable book with an important message for all parts of the Church.'

Steven Wright, Director of the College of Preachers
(www.collegeofpreachers.org.uk)

'This is an impressively comprehensive and genuinely helpful guide to preaching! All preachers – from the novice to the expert (and especially the boring) – will find their preaching refreshed and renewed. Church members, buy this for your preachers!'

Stephen Gaukroger, Team Leader, Gold Hill Baptist Church

Explosive Preaching

Letters on Detonating the Gospel in the 21st Century

Ronald Boyd-MacMillan

Copyright 2006 Ronald Boyd-MacMillan

First published in 2006 by Paternoster Press

12 11 10 09 08 07 06   7 6 5 4 3 2 1

Paternoster Press is an imprint of Authentic Media,
9 Holdom Avenue, Bletchley, Milton Keynes, MK1 1QR, UK
and
129 Mobilization Drive, Waynesboro, GA 30830-4575, USA
www.authenticmedia.co.uk
Authentic Media is a division of Send the Light Ltd., a company limited
by guarantee (registered charity no. 270162)

British Library Cataloguing in Publication Data
A catalogue record for this book is available from the British Library

ISBN 1-84227-263-2

Cover Design by Design by James Kessell for Scratch the Sky Ltd (www.
scratchthesky.com)
Typeset by GCS, Leighton Buzzard
Print Management by Adare Carwin
Printed and Bound in the UK by J.H. Haynes & Co., Sparkford

Contents

Introduction:
Explosive Preaching

Only once in my preaching career have I physically hit someone in the audience.

I was speaking to a hundred or so pastors in Semarang, a large port city set amid the steamy jungles of northern Java, Indonesia. It happened while attempting to demonstrate that the act of preaching was just like bomb-throwing, which required four distinct elements to create an effective explosion.

First on the list was *dynamite.* I took out a handful of clay and said to them, "This is Semtex. You can't have an explosion without it. The preacher's explosive material is the Bible, the gospel." Indeed, the New Testament literally calls the gospel message, *dynamis,* from which we derive our word 'dynamite.' The gospel is an incendiary message. To an audience of pastors working in a society where Islamic extremists were rife, where five pastors had seen their churches firebombed and one had been kidnapped, there was no need to labor the point that it is the nature of the gospel to bring trouble!

But dynamite does not go off by itself. The second element required is a *fuse,* which enables the dynamite to be ignited, and also gives the bomb-thrower time to get safely clear. I took an incense stick and stuck it in the clay. "This represents the preacher. The truth of the Bible is not allowed just to sit in the Bible. It is proclaimed through the collision of our lives with the gospel. 'Preaching cannot occur,' said Martin Luther, 'without the mouth of a living witness to the truth – the preacher!'"

A fuse needs to be lit for the explosion to occur. That is the third element – the *spark* that lights the fuse. I took out a plastic lighter and lit the end of the incense stick. The smoke rose in sweet straight spirals, then scattered in the draft of the ceiling fans. "The spark is surely the Holy Spirit. Without the Spirit speaking through us, the gospel is not ignited, and we are left sounding – and sometimes looking – like a damp squib!" That is the terror of the preacher's call. The anointing can never be coerced.

These three elements can create an explosion, but not an effective explosion. "There is one more element to make sure the gospel explosion is effective," I said, picking up the clay with the smoking incense stick and hurling it down the aisle. There was a great "Whoa!" from the pastors who all ducked. I was aiming for the aisle itself, but my aim was off. One pastor must not have been paying attention because he rose at the time it left my hand. He was probably heading for the bathroom. He heard the shout from the other pastors and turned round to see what the fuss was all about. My "preaching bomb" smacked him squarely in the forehead.

He smiled, sheepishly, rubbing his reddened skin. I breathed a huge sigh of relief. If it had been California, he would have sued!

"My point being," I continued weakly after the hubbub had died away, "the fourth element is *placement*. Dynamite needs to be strategically placed for the explosion to be effective. If we are blowing up rock, it must be sunk deep into a seam. The preacher can explode the gospel in the pulpit, but then the explosion is only a spectacle for the audience. Rather, the dynamite has to be aimed, placed into the hearts of the audience, so that when the explosion takes place, it transforms the lives of the congregation and not just that of the preacher."

Perhaps it's an over militaristic image of what constitutes the preaching task, but the elements are valid as far as they go. This book is designed to assist preachers as they attempt to deliver an effective gospel explosion. The image does illustrate the contrasting skills and exercises the preacher needs to be successful. They need exegetical skills to go to the ancient yet living Scriptures and discern the word for the moment. They need spiritual disciplines to submit their whole life to the word and hear from God himself. They need faith skills to learn dependence upon the action of the Spirit, and great perseverance in prayer to beseech God to speak through an unworthy mouthpiece. And they need communication skills to get on the wavelength of their sometimes bewildering and diverse audiences, hold their attention, make their points memorable and, in the more advanced cases, actually read the audience during the sermon so that the bridge of connection is always built. It's not easy trying to be an excellent preacher. Nor should it be.

I should put my cards on the table though. This is not a book for people who are satisfied with preaching, or for preachers for whom the whole exercise comes easily, or are sure they are doing a wonderful job. Four convictions gave rise to its writing:

- It is a sin to bore for Jesus.
- Most preachers do.
- Most preachers bore because they fail to master the theological, exegetical, and rhetorical basics of the task.
- Yet most preachers really try to preach well, and most listeners appreciate them for it. These preachers don't deserve a hammering. Rather, they require encouragement to develop habits of excellence.

I absolutely accept that this is not a general perception that can be proved. If anyone is reading this and loves the preaching in their church, please put this book down. I have no desire to create dissatisfaction where there was none before.

But I have done an awful lot of listening to preachers, and have talked to literally hundreds of listeners, and I've come to this wearying conclusion: scratch a typical listener to sermons today and it's not blessing you find underneath: it's boredom.

Recently I was brave in church. Prior to the service I sat down beside a stranger and asked them a question. "I'm a new convert," said the young woman, after she had recovered. She was mid-twenties, with short hair and a nose stud, wearing a death's head T-shirt and wide black jeans that swept the ground as she walked. Everything about her screamed "alternative."

The service went on for a while, and then as the preacher was about to start she began to pack up and leave. "It's not over," I whispered. "There's a preacher now."

"Oh no," she said.

"Don't you like preachers?" I asked.

She darted a glance around, as if wondering whether someone was lurking to punish her for expressing an uncensored thought in a church. "No way!" she said. "They just make God boring!"

Outside over a coffee I probed her to expand on her view that preachers make God boring.

She puffed on a cigarette while the rest of the congregation looked askance. "See, preachers represent God. Can't help it! But the way they look and talk, I end up picturing God as male, overweight, middle aged, rambling and irrelevant. It shouldn't be. God is thrilling, but preachers make him sound so boring."

"Have you never heard a preacher that held your attention?" I asked.

She stopped, considering an answer to this as she flicked ash on the ground. "OK, there is another type of preacher I have heard. Young, handsome, flashy. All showy dynamism. When he points his finger you can't see his face for his Rolex glinting. He exudes used car salesman, and I end up picturing God as a rather predatory type who wants into my dress or my wallet, probably both. This kind of preacher doesn't so much make God boring as banal. You listen, but he's just like anybody else out there selling success. There's nothing particularly Christian about him."

"What would you do about this? To make preachers better I mean?"

"I don't know," she said, "but something should be done. Something pretty awful has happened here in church. The preachers sound bored with God. And the terrible tragedy is that they are probably neither bored with God, nor boring as people. It's just that when they get up into a pulpit, they can't run in any other rut than the boring rut."

She stopped, screwing up her face in concentration, then straightened and said in a voice that seemed to indicate sudden illumination: "Preacher's should choose their ruts more carefully. Because they'll be in them a long time."

I said, "I'll bet you read that on the back of a matchbox: *choose your ruts carefully, you'll be in them a long time!*"

She smiled. "It can be quite enlightening to smoke still."

I happen to share that young woman's perspective. I've been thirty-six years a Christian, and preached for twenty-five of them. I wonder how it got to this? How can such a thrilling God be represented by preachers that seem to make him sound so boring? The book must make the case. There are three obvious reasons that my friend at church hinted at.

1. Some preachers no longer find God thrilling

It's sad. There is a percentage of preachers that have lost the fire, for whatever reason. Some would like to retire, but cannot. Some wish they were in another job, but can't find one. Some would like to remain as pastors but stop preaching, yet are struck in structures that require it. Some awful things may have happened to make a preacher discouraged or disappointed. In many cases, it may be due to a discouraging church. But it doesn't help to go into the pulpit and reflect that discouragement back. The gospel message is not spread by expressing disappointment at God. Don't get me wrong. I'm not asking for glib "let's just praise the Lord" preaching. If a preacher is angry or disappointed with God, then let them express it! That isn't boring. That's biblical. Hans Walter Wolf in his wonderful *Anthropology of the Old Testament* tells us that the biblical definition of death is when the praise of God is no longer on a person's tongue. If a preacher – no matter what they are going through – cannot offer even the praise of a groan, or a fist of defiance, then they are dead, and cannot bring life to the sermon. A friend used to get me to take this simple test to see whether I had lost the fire. He said, "Repeat these words: LORD JESUS CHRIST." Then he said, "If you had an emotion as you spoke those three words, no matter how slight, you may preach." I know it's crude, but it gives a clue. Our attitude to God will always come out in our preaching. It cannot be hidden, anymore than we can keep sadness off our face. Some preachers do fall out of love with God. And when they do, it shows.

2. Some preachers are boring people

I know this sounds harsh, but there are a lot of preachers that just don't seem to have much of a life, or, oddly, even when they do, cannot seem to connect the faith to it. I used to be amazed at the typical person that put themselves forward for ordination for a certain denomination I was involved with. Usually they were early- or mid-twenties, middle class, reasonably well educated, and utterly devoid of life experience. In their sermons they would talk of fights with washing machines, of frustration at not finding the right book in the library, of failing to get an A on an exam. Congregations would titter and be nice, but these preachers had no conception of life lived under challenge. Strangely, they did not seem to sense the lack. They exhibited very little interest in the world at large, or in the church in other countries, where the faith is so much more vibrant. Amazingly, many of them seemed incapable of taking a genuine interest in other people, or at least those who could not help them up the church ladder. These preachers need to lick the underbelly of society. Set the taste of that on their tongue and their speech will be less boring because they have experience with real life. Encounter real struggle and real faith. Some preachers have just never left the library.

3. Some preachers are boring speakers

This is a far larger category than the first two. Many preachers don't know how to express their excitement about God in words that hold attention and move people. Many of them know it, too, and just put it down to the usual journey of a great idea in the world of thought seeming a lot less impressive when birthed into the world of words. Also, it must be true that we are living in days where it is almost impossible to learn the skills for powerful public speaking. Our forebears learned rhetoric – how to craft and speak words for effect. That element has dropped off the curriculum entirely, and this impacts all professions, not just preaching. Just yesterday I heard Andrew Marr, BBC political correspondent, lamenting the fact that the Westminster parliament today contained so few good communicators. He called it "a fundamental lack of professionalism in our politics." In the past, he argued, most politicians either came from an Oxbridge background where they had learned to debate or they were trade union leaders who had learned to speak at large rallies. Now they come from either academic or political backgrounds and have never "learned the habit of using strong, vivid, normal language." Homiletics should offset this, of course, but in practice it often fails to. Either it is taught by professors engaged to teach other subjects, who consider the basics of communication so obvious that anyone can run a course in it, or the focus falls too much on content rather than style. Great preachers rehearse skills like vivid storytelling, voice projection, and reading an audience. But it is not just in rhetorical skills that preachers struggle. There are also basic failures such as an inability to create theological synthesis, or to loose the imagination at the dramas of kingdom life, or to embed with authenticity the truth of Christ in everyday life.

Anyway, I may be wrong. Maybe most preachers are thrilled by God and sound thrilling about God in their sermons. I might have missed it, along with that new convert. Or perhaps being a homiletician has spoiled my ear. But if you think I might just be onto something, read on. This book is the attempt to find some new "ruts" to get stuck in, ruts that result in more interesting preaching.

My general definition of preaching is a simple one: *the oral proclamation and application of the Christian Scriptures in a worship setting.* Preaching is speech: it involves the use of words. Preaching is biblically based: there is a commitment to explaining how to understand and live by the book. Preaching is part of worship: even most evangelistic sermons occur in a worship setting such as a Crusade or a revival meeting. This definition is hardly exhaustive. I respect the "St. Francis of Assisi tradition" which defines preaching as any act that expresses the love of God to anyone. He famously is reported to have said to his aides, "Go into all the world to preach the gospel. Where necessary, use words." Fair enough, but every time the word "preaching" is used in the Scripture, it virtually always involves speech.

This book is in four sections. The first is called "The Crisis in Preaching – the Problems." The section examines a number of tributaries flowing into "Lake Crisis" for preaching today. These range from the fact that there is simply far too much bad preaching about, to the extra-defensiveness that many preachers feel today about the validity or impact of their profession. It's not all bad news though, and I also argue that preaching may be on the verge of a new golden age.

The second section is the heart of the book, called "Great Preaching – the Elements." I introduce six tests that the preacher can self-administer and use to improve their sermons. These tests are based on a specific definition of preaching: Reaching the whole person, where they live, with the word, from above, in love, which become the Oral, Experience, Reality, Exegetical, Grandeur, and Tenderness tests. It may sound complicated, but honestly, it isn't. Trust me…I'm a homiletician!

The third section, "The History of Preaching – the Forms," consists of telling the story of preaching through twenty centuries of church history using six paradigmatic forms. I am not claiming that this analysis is the only way to read preaching history. I accept that generalizing across such a large canvas will lack scholastic precision. My aim, however, is to expose preachers to the different types of preaching that have blossomed down the ages, and to urge them to experiment. Most preachers tend to preach in a single form, often the one taught at seminary or in their tradition. This is fine, but not every preacher is able to fit the prevailing style. This section suggests some options, as well as attempting to tell the wonderful story of how preaching has reflected and impacted society down the years.

The final section, "The Preacher's Life – the Issues," takes up a number of topics that are either timeless, such as "Criticism – What do I do when I get the bird?", or focus on proclaiming the truth amid the challenges of the twenty-first century, such as "Multimedia – to PowerPoint or not to PowerPoint?" The topics are varied, though hardly exhaustive, and have their origins in genuine correspondence with preachers.

The chapters are in the form of letters to preachers, a literary format that appealed to me as a journalist, and that allowed me to inject a little more pep into the pace and to let a little levity slide in here and there. The thoughts and guidelines in these letters are offered to the reader as suggestions, not rules. They are the reflections of a fellow preacher, not the wisdom of a master to a pupil. I am distilling the experience of twenty-five years as a preacher on three continents, and passing on the insights gained while tutoring other preachers. In 1997, I started a business in Hong Kong called Points-A-Cross Inc, a speech tuition agency primarily for preachers. One distinctive feature of the business was to come alongside the preacher and offer one-on-one guidance and feedback. This has privileged me to see into the personal struggles that many preachers face as they prepare and deliver their sermons.

I find preaching a struggle. It is the most agonizing and most rewarding activity I ever perform. Perhaps that goes with the territory. After all, the words we are handling are the heaviest words of all... eternal words. In my quiet time passage this morning were these words of Jesus: "Heaven and earth will pass away, but my words will never pass away" (Luke 21:33). Preaching is a crushing privilege – it is an invitation to speak words that will never pass away, to spin a strand or two in the fabric that forms and frames eternity. An old Brethren divine, Harold St John, caught this demanding joy best when he said, "Preaching is a happy labor, but I must give blood every time!"

Section One:

The Crisis in Preaching – the Problems

Letter 1:
Last-straw land

Or, why it's OK to get hopping mad at bad preaching!

You've snapped!

There was no mistaking the lethal cocktail of despair and anger in your letter. "I might not even go back to church any more," you wrote.

It would be a tragedy if you carry out that threat, for you have the makings of a fine preacher.

Look at it this way: It's good you have snapped! Without anger and disgust at the status quo, we have no chance of changing it. It is a mark of your ambition for good preaching that you are so fed up listening to terrible preaching. Just as it is impossible to be passionate about truth and indifferent toward evil, so the reverse side of a love for preaching God's word is anger when God's word is ignored, muzzled, or mangled.

Yes, the time has come to induct you into membership of the PAAP club. That stands for Preachers Against Appalling Preaching. I happen to be honorary chairman. It was decided that PAAP was a little less threatening than the other name proposed: SEAP – Society for the Extermination of Appalling Preachers.

It's for people that snapped because they heard one bad sermon too many. Just like you.

It's for people that suddenly stopped blaming themselves for hearing bad sermons. Oh, bizarre Protestantism that always blames oneself for others' failures: "Oh, I know this preacher is terrible, but I should have a better attitude and be getting something from it."

It's for people that continue to hold up an ideal for preaching, when all around them they are hearing, "Well, preaching isn't that important you know, there are other factors far more important: the Eucharist, for example, or the worship songs, or the fellowship."

It's for people that grew exhausted from the effort of always managing to get something from an atrocious sermon. Tolkien once started a letter to his son: "Sermons, well they are bad aren't they?" and goes on to list clever ways to make a silk purse from a sow's ear. Maybe you can do that as an Oxford Don, but most of us just can't keep it up.

It's for people who finally stopped being over-spiritual, believing that it didn't matter what the preacher said or how he said it, as long as the Spirit was in it. They shrank from the frightening theological conclusion of that position… the Spirit must be a very dull stick! No, as long as we are human, God asks us to develop skills, and preachers are not excused.

It's a club for a whole group of preachers and non-preachers who finally snapped. They face up to this fact: unless they are very lucky, most people hear pretty dreadful sermons. They face up to this challenge: it's time to do something about it!

*   *   *

We bring four items to our meetings: a straw, a scalpel, a black tie, and a garland. The straw represents the sermon we heard that pushed us over the edge. We did not despair because we heard one bad sermon. We snapped because, after years of hearing terrible sermons, one of them became the straw that broke our backs. The scalpel represents our commitment to cut out the cancer of bad preaching in the church. The black tie is brought to symbolize mourning, because we all have to live with an uncomfortable truth: bad preachers fill churches.

But we also bring a garland. It represents the truth that most preachers try their best. Preachers do not consciously set out to fossilize the faithful. Most are good men and women, standing with their people through rain and shine. They need to be honored, not hammered. They must be taught better habits of preaching in love, not anger. Hence the garland.

Each new member starts by telling their "straw story." You've told me yours. Let me tell you mine.

* * *

It was the early summer in 1999, in Santa Monica, California. My wife and I were visiting and we popped into a pretty looking little Episcopal church. The preacher was introduced as someone of note. He was a theological bigwig (let's call him Bill), and we were told what "an amazing privilege and honor" it was to hear him preach.

I licked my mental lips in anticipation. This was to be a sermon of theological substance then, especially as his passage was a juicy one: John 14:1–14, all that wonderful stuff about many mansions being prepared; no way to the Father except though Jesus; you will do greater works than I have done, etc. Bill shuffled his notes, fixed his eyes firmly on the lectern, and began to *read* his greeting! He read that he had been playing golf the day before, droning phrases like "We had such a lovely time" and "It's a privilege to be here."

Well, all right. Some preachers have no confidence to look an audience in the eye. Some have no fluency without a script. Some have no time to learn their script and have to read it. It makes for less power, but there's always Jonathan Edwards, who launched revivals reading in quavering tones from sheets held six inches from his face. In preaching, you don't have to sound like a lion to be one. And to be honest, Bill's opening questions on the passage were very promising. He asked the questions occurring to most of the audience: What are many mansions? Is Jesus the only way to the Father? Is that not a rather exclusive claim today? Can we really pray for anything and we'll get it?

Too right! I crouched forward with excitement. I'd love someone to have a pop at responding to that lot. But no sooner were the questions hanging temptingly in the air than he was back to his golf swing... and never left it again. Bill made two points that morning in his fifteen-minute sermon, which would have been better titled as "My golf swing as the exegetical key to the universe."

Point 1: Trust your swing! "Don't lift your head and look ahead," said Bill. "Trust Jesus... he'll take us." Point 2: Let the club do the work! "This requires us to be a little out of control," he said mysteriously. I'm not sure to this day what he meant. The only pro-golfer I know whose swing is a bit out of control is a portly genius called John Daly, and his swing goes out of control when he's been nipping at his hip flask. He doesn't win tournaments in that state. Non-golfers, like my wife, floated off to other mental heavens. For high handicap golfers like me, still hanging in with Bill, the overall point was, "Jesus is in control."

Bill had a stirring conclusion for us, read from his notes with all the passion of a dead haddock: "So don't lift your head and see. Just relax and trust Jesus."

Now that kind of preaching makes me mad. For one thing, *it cheats the listener!* He raised great questions, but made no attempt to answer them. He set us up to let us down. More importantly, it cheats the passage! That sermon represented a criminal neglect of his passage, and what a passage to neglect! Verses like "No one comes to the Father except through me," and "I tell you the truth, anyone who has faith in me will do greater things than these," and "You may ask for anything in my name, and I will do it." They all scream PREACH ME, PREACH ME!

But Bill preferred to tell us about his golf swing, and how it illustrated the heart of the passage as he saw it, which was to relax and let Jesus.

We left to the usual Episcopalian welcome. Those who eagerly grasped our hand at the passing of the peace fled the building without a word. My wife and I walked over to 3rd Street promenade, sat down in Starbucks, and burst out laughing. It was less embarrassing than crying. We looked at each other and said, "And people pay money to go to conferences puzzling why the churches are emptying out?"

*   *   *

Am I being too harsh? Tell me if you think so. For years I thought I was, and kept my mouth firmly shut. It is only after twenty years that I have found the freedom to see anger about poor preaching in a positive light. I would be careful not to sound harsh in person, and I would certainly be oblique with

Bill should he ever come to a seminar of mine. I might start by mentioning that preaching is subject to the same religious delusion that we have to fight in every area of life, namely the substitution of something merely worthy for something infinite. The biblical attitude toward "religion" is negative, and so, I believe, should ours be. Religion is all about deadly substitutions; rituals for God instead of relationship with God; programs on behalf of God instead of fellowship with God; and so on. The pharisaical spirit lies at the heart of us all. Our ego works hard to keep us from true encounter with God. And you and I will find, if we keep corresponding, that every problem in preaching is a reflection of a more general problem in our spirituality. To discuss preaching and its aspects is to explore the faith and its challenges.

Not for nothing did Melville write: "The world is a ship on its passage out, and the pulpit is its prow."

As we discuss the pulpit, the pain of the world splashes against the heart of Christ, unifying every issue of Faith and Life in the most dynamic way possible. Apply this to Bill. His specific failure was – and it sounds absurd to state it so baldly – his golf swing actually displaced Jesus Christ. His sermon was more about his golf swing than his Lord. The substitution was unconscious and subtle. He did not intend to displace Christ. And his thought was not unchristian. As far as it goes, it is not the world's worst image to liken Jesus to a golf club and let him do the job.

But is it the reason Jesus gave us John 14? He came from heaven to give us these words. They are his impassioned words of comfort to his disciples that he is The Way, and even though they will be bereft when he leaves, he is still there for them, able to answer prayer; able to send them power, safe in the assurance that he has made the way to God. Come on Bill. Get excited about those staggering claims. They are specific, concrete, not abstract and vague. What a passage. What a person!

According to Martin Luther, a sermon has to be *a heart to heart talk about Jesus Christ*. This is not so easy in practice. We are all like Bill. We are inclined to talk about everything else *but* Christ, even when we are talking *about* Christ. We fool ourselves that we are glorifying him when we are actually glorifying ourselves.

That's sad. That's bad. That's worth getting bothered about because Jesus must be at the center of everything – the universe, foreign policy, a nation, a church, even an individual sermon.

Otherwise, religion triumphs and not Christ. And we are left with vague principles, or legalistic rituals, and not the love of Christ. The stakes could not be higher. Don't you agree?

Letter 2:
Bad preaching up close

Or, yes, it *really* is OK to get angry at bad preaching!

You feel guilty with this new emotion of anger at preachers who bored you! It's there in those questions you volley at me: "What right have you to feel so angry at preachers? Could it be that your attitude is a bitter one? Preaching may not be as uniformly terrible as you imply? How do I know that the PAAP club is not really the BARP club – for Bitter and Angry Reject Preachers?"

Ha, the BARP club! We raised our glasses to that one last night at the chapter meeting. Your gift for acronym shows the preacher in you. No, we are not going to lose you to the guild.

That's quite a question starburst there. I will take up the issue I regard as most urgent: Is anger a legitimate or even helpful response to the state of preaching today?

I suppose anger is the most ambiguous of all the biblical emotions. That God gets angry a lot in the Bible does not necessarily justify our feeling the same way. Even Jesus' periodic outrage may not be for us to imitate. But if we have to parse it, anger in the Bible is really jealousy for the name of God. So the key issue becomes, is my anger of this holy caliber? I will give you three examples of when I was angry at what I felt was bad preaching.

My first example

Early in 2001. England. Ordained clergyman goes to the pulpit. Through half glasses, he reads a complete script in a flat, academic monotone. He has no stories, no structure, just loosely connected thoughts, rather badly phrased. There is no challenge, and he ends with a vague bromide delivered in a tired hiss, "Let's just all try to be more mindful of the positive power of our Eucharistic calling and find God within us."

Afterward, I was talking to a friend at the church. She was a professional singer. "What did you think of the sermon?" I asked. She pulled a face, then said quickly, "Well, there were a couple of phrases in there that got me thinking, so it was good."

I asked, "What if we had been at a concert instead and someone stood up to give a singing recital. But they had a very poor voice. Nor had they any training in projection. In fact, it was clear that they were clueless that there was even an art to singing. What would you say?"

She replied tartly, "I'd jolly well go up to them and say – look, you have a voice, it's a great thing, but you have to receive some training if you are going to do this in public."

I reacted by saying, "Oh, don't be so hard. There were a couple of true notes in there – I was happy with his performance."

She got it: "I see what you are saying. Preaching is an art that has rules of excellence too."

I felt anger at that preacher. What really bothered me was that this priest went up to the pulpit without the slightest awareness that this is an activity he should train and continually re-train himself for. The greatest minds outside and inside the church – Aristotle, Cicero, Augustine – all took the trouble to write us manuals on how to speak with effect, and he mounts the pulpit steps unaware they ever wrote a word.

That's arrogance! It's as arrogant as putting yourself forward for a singing recital when you have no clue how to sing. To preach well you need three things: a gift for it, skill in it, and the anointing on it. The point is, preaching is partly an art, and like all the arts, it demands skills. There are rules to the development of this skill. What on earth is the advantage of ignoring these rules? Let him read just one book on preaching. Just one! Let him learn how to be vivid rather than vague in his storytelling. Or, let him learn how to allow his personality to animate his speech. Or, let him learn how to structure the talk so as to hold our attention for the time.

Let him try just one technique a year. But no! He doesn't even believe he needs them. All he thinks there is to preaching is to look at his passages Saturday night, write out a few thoughts, and read them to the congregation in the morning.

And what was the result? The gospel – the world's most exciting drama – was rendered dull. Do you know what his text was? "And they will pick up snakes in their hands," (Mark 16:18). We all preach a dud from time to time, but this man actually thought, "If I read a few thoughts on a Scripture passage, I have preached!" Pity!

My second example

Mid 2002. Scotland. I could not help sitting with some excitement in the box pews of this historic church. The noise of an anarchic arts festival could just be heard from outside, but the space was hushed and sacred. The passage was Luke 13:10–17, where a Pharisee objects to Jesus healing a crippled woman on the Sabbath. This preacher knew how to speak. He could string words together with effect. Unusually for a British preacher, he actually looked at us, and even was versed in the old classical gears of rhetorical style – simple, middle, and grand. He had no problem holding our attention throughout his twelve-minute talk. He began by ribbing the Pharisee and showing how he was symbolic of a churchy, ritual-obsessed mindset. Then he posed his great question: Why bother with church and all these rituals? Why not just go away and form your own radical religion? This was a great set up and question. He had us on the edge of our very uncomfortable seats. His answer was – in a nutshell – we need the church because we need the rituals; we need the rituals because they make us less selfish. For once his elegance deserted him. This was his wind-up sentence: "Rituals teach us to identify with the whole of the universe, so we see ourselves no longer at the center of the universe – and that's what faith is all about."

Then he sat down.

Again, I was left feeling an angry sadness. There was not a word about who Christ was, what Christ did, or what Christ can do for us. The faith had been turned from a personal relationship with Christ, into a series of rituals that in his ugly term "relativized the ego." We need the rituals to be less selfish. That was his gospel.

This is hardly Christianity. I felt sorry for Jesus that morning. He wasn't there in the solution. He'd been edited out as too particular. He'd been melted into a one-world spirituality goulash. Christianity had been neatly eviscerated of its greatest and most distinctive element – a knowing of the Personal Being of God in Christ.

Ultimately, he gave us no compelling reason to be a Christian. Any religion would do for this preacher, as long as it had rituals that assisted the process of ego-relativization. Better not to bother with the church at all. We don't need Christianity to make us less selfish and embrace creation. Better to be a Buddhist, I think. There's less baggage and more exotic ritual. You don't even need to subscribe to any proposition about the divine being.

Ask yourself this question frequently: What one characteristic must my faith always possess? For me, faith has to be personal. I'm not interested in vague mystical experiences, or in-dwellings by mysterious archetypes. I want a God I can talk to and who talks back. A person like me in form and yet unlike me in power. I want a God that can feel and understand when life is just "trouble" and who comforts in the pain. And that's what Christ does. And that's… well, everything really. Now when I get to church and the most exciting and unique aspect of my faith is hidden, or even denied, I get angry, because that is literally anti-Christ.

My third example

Early 2003. United States of America. There are four thousand people sitting in plush seats in this warehouse style mega-church, and this is only one of four services in a typical weekend. The preacher is Pastor Tom, a young, hip-looking guy in his early forties. A good friend of mine said, "You've got to hear him – I've never been so moved by a preacher before."

He spoke for an hour – this was evangelical territory. His text was the third commandment. He starts off by holding up a newspaper clipping. It was an article about the recent Winter Olympics. The coach of a gold medalist was quoted as saying "Oh my god," over and over again. "This is not trivial," warns Pastor Tom, "it's terrible," and he takes us to Leviticus to justify why, in ancient Israel, youths were stoned for this. For the next forty minutes, through the use of brilliant illustrations, he trampolines around the Bible giving us a series of mini-sermons on the theme "Don't curse or your goose is cooked." As a sermon on restraining the tongue, it was OK. But the third commandment is not primarily about casual cursing. It's to do with the role of the oath in ancient Israel. Every transaction, to be legal, had to be sworn on by the name of God. Failure to take that oath seriously meant that one was saying, in effect, "I refuse to abide by the rules that Yahweh has set for us." To take the Lord's name in vain in that ancient context was to refuse to accept that he knew best. Is that a little more than casual cursing, or what?

Pastor Tom should have known this. Any good commentary will rescue him from a trivial application of a mighty truth. What does it really mean to take the Lord's name in vain? Pastor Tom will never know, because he's off giving us cute little stories and neat little mini three-pointers on taming the tongue. And thirteen thousand people over that weekend will never know either, because the preacher did not do his homework!

* * *

Well, three experiences and three disappointments. You will notice they are all from distinct church cultures: Anglo-Catholic, Liberal, and Evangelical. Preaching should be better... for God's sake. He gave us the gift of speech. The least we can do is use it well. He gave us the gift of his Son. The least we can do is center the faith upon him. He gave us the gift of his word. The least we can do is study it properly. Surely this is not too much to ask of the average preacher?

We are not to accept this state of affairs. Whether anger is a gift or a curse depends on our reaction to it. I know anger could make preachers bitter, and that would be a curse. Yet it can also be an energy to make preaching better, and that would be a blessing! A fair preacher by the name of Augustine once wrote, "Hope has two daughters – anger and courage; anger at the way things are, and courage to change them."

But come back to me. Am I too harsh? Tell me if I am and I'll repent. The important thing is that whether you think preaching is good, bad, or awful, we can always improve it. Let's go for excellence! God deserves it!

Letter 3:
How fed up are the listeners?

Or, Is the crisis in modern preaching something the homiletics professors made up to sell books?

Is the crisis in modern preaching something homiletics professors made up to sell books? This objection had to come from you. With any post-modern soul, suspicion soon becomes the central feature of any intellectual enquiry. You are right to be suspicious. Homileticians would not be the first caste to create a pretend-crisis in order to boost sales. If you observe your local church, the preacher is rarely besieged by an angry mob in the vestry complaining that his exegesis was off, or his alliterations were forced. We do have to address this paradox: *Those who teach preaching seem to think the entire enterprise is in crisis, while those who listen to preaching seem to be satisfied with what they hear.*

Call it the *sad quotes vs. smug surveys* debate. If you glance at homiletics textbooks from any age, you will notice that they often start off with a set of damning quotes from some luminary about the dire state of contemporary preaching. To write such a book today one could start with this broadside from the American novelist, Garrison Keillor:

> Most of the sermons I have ever heard in my life could easily have been dispensed with and the congregation would have been better for it. The sermon is, I think, one of the terrible failings of the church. And they're doing it to their own people. They are punishing the faithful with this querulous exercise in piety, the terrible harangues that nobody is entitled to deliver.[1]

It's an OK tactic for a homiletics textbook to parade these sad quotes at the start and then launch into "Well here's how to preach better!" The trouble is, instructive and challenging as these quotations are, all they end up telling us is that a few famous people heard some awful sermons, and were inclined to assume everyone else felt the same way. But that's not an assumption borne out by congregational polls. Hence the counterweight in the debate – smug surveys.

Do the listeners left in church today think that the preaching they hear is unacceptable? The answer has to be no – on paper at any rate. There is no study to show that a majority of listeners are seriously dissatisfied with the standard of preaching in the church today. Mind you, that's partly to do with the fact that there are very few such studies in existence. In Britain there was one recently – an attitudinal survey of 100,000 English church-goers conducted in April 2001.[2] Listeners were asked to respond to this statement among others: "The preaching I hear in this local church is usually very helpful to me in my everyday life." Of the respondents, 25 percent ticked the "strongly agreed" box, and 57 percent ticked "agreed." A measly 3 percent "disagreed" and only 1 percent "strongly disagreed." That's a resounding 82 percent of respondents saying that they found the preaching really beneficial. In other words: Crisis? What crisis? The findings prompted the Archbishop of York to claim that this gave "a clear indication that people find preaching helpful, rather than boring or oppressive."[3]

The problem is that these surveys – like the sad quotes approach – prove inconclusive with respect to our question about whether there is a crisis in preaching. In the case I quoted above, an extensive questionnaire is handed out to a group of people asked to wait after a Sunday service. The roast is in the oven at home, and they are hungry. The preaching question is only one of scores. Add in the psychological pressure to be "positive" that such surveys engender; add also the pressure coming from a church culture that frowns on any sort of criticism, and you have virtually set it up to get rave responses. They tick a box, but what does it really tell us? In so far as it measures satisfaction, it's useful. In so far as it measures whether preaching is effective, it's useless.

The good preacher really wants to know only one thing: is my preaching changing people into the likeness of Christ?

But these surveys answer only the much more trivial question: do people like my preaching? When I was pastoring, I set up focus groups each week where some of the congregation would talk back to me about my sermon. This was on a Wednesday night, long after all the politeness of Sunday had vanished. I discovered this: those who expressed the most admiration for my sermons were – in my opinion – the least changed by them, and those who reported high levels of dissatisfaction were most changed by them. If you want to put percentages on it, my approval rating was probably about 80 percent, but my effectiveness rating was about 20 percent. And I viewed changing 20 percent of the congregation to be a good success rate, and still would. So much for smug surveys.

The sad quotes vs. smug surveys debate does help us a little. The sad quotes warn preachers not to be complacent. The witness of ex-listeners must be respected. For every Garrison Keillor who opines publicly about the state of preaching, there are probably 100,000 others in church who think that way deep down, but would never dare to say it out loud. And how many people have left church because of poor preaching? We have no way of telling, but it may well be a substantial contributor to the exodus from the churches in Western Europe.

The smug surveys also force homileticians like me to come to terms with this incontrovertible fact, that most church-goers seem to be satisfied with the state of preaching today. Now the obvious response is to say, well, if you have never really been exposed to good preaching, then you are unable to discern good from bad. You just put up with what you get. It simply does not occur to most listeners to demand a better sermon. Fair enough, but there is also more to it. There is a whole culture and history to the relationship between preacher and listener that is broader than their interaction through the sermon slot.

For one thing, Christian listeners are unusually generous. A stand up comic friend of mine in Los Angeles once said, "You preachers have a wonderful job." I said, "How so?" He said, "Because if I bore anyone in my routine, I get booed off the stage. If you folks bore anyone, you get to continue in reverent silence, and at the door afterward everyone will still murmur 'nice sermon pastor' in your ear." It is true that the feedback that preachers hear – if they get any at all – is usually polite and positive. But that is the culture speaking. It has nothing to do with the effectiveness of the sermon. Church cultures are such that listeners often feel it is wrong to criticize the pastor, or they take responsibility themselves for a poor listening experience, or they may even feel unqualified to pass a critical judgment on a spiritual "professional." In other words, most listeners are not going to be honest when they hear a bad sermon.

Second, Christian listeners appreciate the *character* of their preachers quite regardless of their *competence*. They are primarily people who experience the pastoral care of the preacher, and are only secondarily consumers of the preacher's sermon. In most churches there is a pre-existing pastoral relationship between preacher and congregation, and happily it is one of respect. When the preacher presents the sermon, it is into this context of appreciation and love. The listeners hear the words of the sermon, but more deeply they are appreciating the man or woman who visited their sick mother, baptized their child, buried their grandfather, testified on behalf of their troubled teen, and so forth. The sermon preached may be a dud according to any homiletical criteria, but the *sermon* is still appreciated because the *preacher* is appreciated!

Thirdly, we have to recall what most Christian listeners are really listening for, and these are what I call *reinforcement bells*. Most Christians attend a particular type of church in order to experience a reinforcement that their understanding of the Bible, and their particular practice of the faith, is correct. They want *pats on the soul's back*. They want to hear that they have made the right choices. They want to know that they belong to the right group. When they hear the preacher, they are listening for these bells that enable them to relax, nod their heads, shout "Amen," and know that they are on the right track. Each subculture has a distinct peal, and the preacher's job is to ring these bells. For example, if one is in a charismatic fellowship, they want these bells rung: power of the spirit; promise of total healing; end-times trouble; latter-day outpourings; spiritual warfare; dominion prayer; and so on. The point is that you can ring all the bells in a terrible sermon, and people will love it because you rang *their* bells!

These are the reasons why the listeners are not fed up with poor preaching. There is, of course, the other side to the crisis: is preaching really all that bad? Maybe the listeners are right after all? Does bad preaching really matter?

Letter 4:
Why sweat it if the Spirit gets the word out anyway?

Or, On whether Balaam's ass is eloquent enough

Hmmn. "There is no such thing as bad preaching so long as the Spirit is in it!" you say, and I fancy I can discern a bit of stiff bottom lip with it.

Of course, the Spirit can redeem anything. I've even heard it put like this: If Balaam's ass can speak the word of God, anyone can. But if the implication is that there cannot be a crisis in preaching because the Holy Spirit always ensures that the word gets preached, no matter how poor the preacher, then just a minute please.

It's not a doctrine of preaching. The short answer to the Balaam's ass syndrome is to have the courage of your convictions: send a donkey into the pulpit! See how clear the message is then!

There is a longer answer, namely that this idea denigrates God's amazing invitation to be human. This world is a garden of God's making. He lets it run wild so that we may cultivate it, bring discipline to it, learn skills to manage it. God invites our cooperation, and has given us the skills and confidence to be creative as we tend his world, cut his flowers, and do his will. It's called... dominion! He is not satisfied with passive submission. When preachers start by saying, "It doesn't matter what I say or how I prepare, God will bless the word anyway," they are guilty of a catastrophic failure to be human. God didn't make the world to run on his emergency spiritual interventions. He made it so we could run it with him to his glory. Learning the craft of preaching, even the pain of parsing, is a form of worship.

Let me make a simpler point. Why do people think it's a boxing match: "sermons as technique" in the red corner vs. "sermons as God-blessed speech" in the blue corner? Who forced them to make the choice? The great Welsh preacher, Martyn Lloyd-Jones, talked much about the unction of the Spirit, but he warned very explicitly that the fire of God only falls on preachers who have prepared well.

> Some men fall into the error of relying on the unction only, and neglect to do all they can by way of preparation. The right way to look at the unction of the Spirit is to think of it as that which comes upon the preparation.... Elijah... built an altar, then cut wood and put it on the altar, and then he killed a bullock and cut it in pieces and put the pieces on the wood. Then, having done all that, he prayed for the fire to descend; and the fire fell. That is the order.[4]

In the Bible, the sheer rhetorical skills of preaching – by which I mean the skills of organizing, shaping and delivering the material – are never a threat to the unction of the Spirit, but are always complementary to it. Sure, Paul warns us not to trust in rhetoric to make the impact, and that is a good warning. We do all we can, but God must communicate or the preacher is a fool. That is the terror of the call. We offer nothing but air puffs if God does not speak through our efforts. But this does not excuse us from the burden of proper preparation. So let's put to rest the idea that to focus on technique is somehow unworthy or unspiritual. Technique and anointing – as well as many other aspects of preaching – are all peas from the same pod, and what God has placed together, let us not seek to tear asunder. Some skills just need to be learned. I never met a preacher who just prayed and – presto – they could read Greek and Hebrew. We'll give the last word on the subject to Watchman Nee: "The water of Divine deliverance depends upon the provision of human ditches."

There is a more refined version of your point of view to consider, one that makes important sense and is one of the big confidence-drainers for preachers today: successful preaching is nothing to do with the sermon or the speaker, but with the hearing and the listener. Preaching is a community exercise.

Words are spoken to be heard. Say the preacher gives an awful sermon? No matter, because in the words of George Herbert:

> Do not grudge
> To pick out treasures from an earthly pot,
> The worst speak something good; if all want sense
> God takes a text, and preacheth patience.[5]

There is much truth to this. I remember a discussion with a distinguished professor of theology. I was contending that a sermon which makes too many points works against itself. The preacher, I argued, should strive to have one main point to maximize the chances that *the point the preacher makes is the one the congregation gets*. At the very least, that is a definition of an act of successful communication. Sticking to one essential point is an important feature of all speech.

The professor completely disagreed, saying that in his church, "I like the preacher to multiply points. We use the lectionary, so let the preacher get to each of the passages [there were usually three] and make as many points as they like so that we can all find something." He added, "Every person is different so the more points the preacher makes, the more people can latch onto something. I love it when lots of people get points that the preacher didn't even intend to make. It's more creative and impressive."

There is merit in the grapeshot approach, but the underlying point is more radical. The professor was arguing that *what* the preacher says is far less important than where he is saying it. Preaching succeeds primarily because it is a community activity, speech given to committed listeners. In his particular church, many members read the Daily Office, and come to the service aware of the passages that are to be read. The preacher takes the passages, tosses a few random thoughts about, and everyone takes something from it. Growth occurs because these people are living in the word week-by-week, and they enfold the hearing of the word in a service into that ongoing process. They know what to do with the nourishment. For him, the sermon itself is largely unimportant. The "preacher" could just as easily get up and read commentaries on the passage and have the same effect. This professor was quite dismissive of the efforts of homileticians, since the sermon is not the key determinant in how people live by the word.

I think the professor had a shrunken understanding of preaching. Homiletics is not confined to the mere production of a sermon. It does focus on the spoken word to a congregation, but it includes a realization of the dynamics of congregational growth, and takes its place in this process. No preacher would argue that only listening to a sermon brings spiritual growth. Many Christians live by the word in ways quite independent of listening to sermons. In fact, in this preaching "dark age," they have to.

My quarrel is with the implications of the professor's view. Many use his argument to dispense with preaching altogether. Why not read the lectionary passages followed by complete silence, or a bit of music? If what really matters is that the listeners are ready to take something from what they hear, then the competence of the reader/preacher – short of a severe case of laryngitis – is irrelevant. As long as some words are spoken, or even just read, the same effect will occur.

Readings with silence are valuable – I love Taize style services – but if we let that replace the sermon, then it seems to represent a counsel of perfection. Are listeners in churches really that committed to listening and applying the word? Perhaps the concept would work in a community of monks, but for ordinary people? Hardly. In fact, I attended the same church as the professor and, contrary to his assumption, very few said the Daily Office during the week. It just asks too much of the modern-day disciple.

The professor's view also downgrades preaching as an act of communication. If his views had "won" in history, then Augustine, Whitefield and Luther-King, Jnr., should never have bothered. What a sad world it would be if they hadn't. Hearing a gifted preacher in full flow, masterfully arranging and delivering the message of God, is a thrilling and disturbing experience. We need these disturbances. Otherwise, it all gets too smug.

The biblical pattern seems to be against it. Israel and the early church set people aside to teach powerfully. They didn't only repeat liturgies or recite past Scriptures. They brought messages for the moment, and labored long and hard to put their messages into new and memorable forms. Look at the poetry of Isaiah. The dramatic structuring of Job. Or, the beautifully crafted parables of Christ. Or, the classical rhetoric skills of Paul. Thank God they worked on their presentation, or the Bible would be a prosaic litany of fossilized rules.

* * *

Perhaps behind the view that the Spirit does it all no matter what the speaker says is a fear of teachers. No one likes to be judged. A way of reacting is to say, "But the Spirit ensures that we get the word out." I understand. But it's a bad teacher of preaching that expects perfection. The vast majority of preaching is what I call "imperfect speech." Most of the time, preachers have to give a "good enough" sermon. They can't help it. It's been a busy week. They made some sketchy notes on Tuesday morning but the week is gone because Mr. Thwaites died suddenly, and a new member had a crisis when her boyfriend walked out without warning. It's Sunday morning and the poor pastors just have to preach whatever is in their hands. That's OK. An essential feature of preaching is that it is really a love letter from one sheep to the rest of the flock that says, "What a wonderful Shepherd we have in Jesus!" Love letters do not have to be perfectly phrased to make the heart glow.

In this respect, collections of super-sermons, like the book *A Chorus of Witnesses*,[6] can sometimes paralyze rather than energize the preacher. The average preacher simply cannot measure up. There's a sermon in that collection by Lewis Smedes entitled "The Power of Promises." This sentence is in it: "I want to say that if you have a ship you will not desert, if you have a people you will not forsake, if you have causes you will not abandon, then you are like God."[7] I could not produce a sentence like that in a month of Sundays. But listen, neither could Smedes! The sermons in this kind of book are mainly masterpieces produced by professional homileticians or pastors who took months to polish up a *beaut*. All these sermons lack the essential quality of the weekly sermon – imperfection!

Indeed, I would go so far as to say that if a pastor produced a sermon in one week as good as any of these he or she were either (a) a genius or (b) neglecting the congregation.

We must judge. It's a scriptural command (1 Cor. 14:23). God does have standards. But we love preachers! When they get to heaven the angels will not say, "I loved that illustration on the mating rituals of Patagonian hamsters in that great inductively structured sermon of Trinity Sunday, 1999." They will say, "You pointed to the Lamb... very well." Preaching is a lot more than technique, but it has to involve it. Let's move on and put all we are and have into the making of a sermon that lifts Christ high.

Letter 5:
Why preaching is always in crisis

Or, How the God who speaks became a sphinx

Yes, we did get a bit sidetracked there in our last letter, but that's the fun of correspondence – we don't have to be systematic. I was – until so rudely distracted – starting to make a case as to why I think there is a crisis in preaching today, and began by showing that a crisis in preaching could well occur without the average listener being aware of it. Before we proceed to examine the nature of this crisis, I must beware of being too "Westocentric."

All over the world, the church is growing, except in two places: Europe and liberal-Protestant North America. In Africa, Asia, and Latin America, it's the Evangelicals and Pentecostal/Charismatic Christians that are growing exponentially, and, in most cases, their services are structured around a lengthy sermon.

Europe is the only continent in the world where preachers have seen their congregations virtually disappear. What a dispiriting experience it must be to preach in, for example, Great Britain, where church-going dropped from 30 percent in the fifties to less than 8 percent today, and where historic denominations like the Church of Scotland release gloomy reports predicting their own extinction in thirty years. Indeed, it's official! Homileticians as a caste are extinct in the UK. Not in a single theological or Bible college, or university, will you find anyone whose full time job is to teach homiletics. Makes you think that there ought to be a *homo homileticus* on display in the British Natural History Museum, the skeleton of W.E. Sangster perhaps!

In the US, congregations have dwindled, but only in the mainline churches, where members deserted in droves for the more independent Evangelical or Pentecostal manifestations of church life. This decline spawned most of the writing on homiletics today, with men like Craddock, Buttrick, and Lowry reacting from a defensive liberal position. Craddock wrote his classic *As One Without Authority* in 1971, suggesting the replacement of the deductive form of the sermon with an inductive one because the preacher was no longer viewed as an authority figure. While his comments on form are universally stimulating, the concerns that prompted them are far from universally applicable, even within the US. The preacher is still a major authority figure in most of the Evangelical/Pentecostal churches, or visit an Afro-American church and the preacher is next to God. Go to a mega-church like Willow Creek or Saddleback Community Church and you will find upwards of 3000 people attending a service that has an appetizer of praise lasting ten or fifteen minutes and then a great big juicy T-bone steak of a sermon, lasting forty or fifty minutes. Crisis, what crisis?

It's a great story, really. Everywhere else today the church is growing phenomenally, and solid – even lengthy preaching – is warmly appreciated. The contrasts still stagger me. In China, the church grew from 2 million in 1979 to over 60 million today – that's more than the population of the entire UK. When I visit the house churches there, I am pressed to preach for four-hour blocks. In Indonesia recently I preached in a Pentecostal church in Semarang, Java. "Don't you dare preach for less than an hour," warned the pastor as I mounted the steps to a packed church of 1500. And all this at six-thirty in the morning, the first of four services. Oh, it's heady stuff preaching in Africa, Asia, and Latin America. The Christians are hungry for teaching, and entire societies are open to the possibility of embedding Christian principles in law and practice.

How can we seriously talk of a crisis in preaching after all this good news? Well, we must make the argument in stages. First, preaching is always in crisis because, by its very nature, it is a crisis-driven activity. Second, preaching at the beginning of the twenty-first century has some massive challenges that are causing great defensiveness, mainly in the West. For example, the arrival of the television and digital age has preachers scurrying to find new image-based languages, or to learn computer software to attempt a multi-media spectacle out of a deep and genuine fear that the half-hour sermonic monolog is already a boring anachronism. Non-Western preachers cannot afford to be indifferent either, or accuse Western preachers of imperialistically assuming that their own problems today will be everyone else's tomorrow. Chinese and Indian households are already beginning to exhibit the same television viewing addictions as their Western counterparts. Not every Western challenge will come to the two-thirds world preacher, but some definitely will.

First, preaching is always in crisis because that is the nature of it. No wonder homiletics manuals from every age start by worrying that the art is in decline, because preaching is always hard to get right. There is the *on-going crisis of connection*, for example. The preacher's task is always to connect faith to a target culture, but this culture is a *moving target*. What worked for the last generation will not work for this one. John Stott calls this "bridge-building." In every age, a new bridge between word and world must be constructed. It's never easy figuring out who your audience is, how they listen, and how to hook them. Some American mega-church preachers commission expensive professional PR firms to profile their typical listeners. Stott recommends forming a fortnightly focus group to reflect on contemporary novels and films. At any rate, it ain't easy. The language of crisis is never misplaced.

Next, there is the *on-going crisis of understanding*. The preacher has to face the often agonizing process of understanding what the word of God is for a particular situation. It's not easy: Partly because God's thoughts are higher than our thoughts, partly because the personhood of God is, in a very real sense, beyond articulation, and partly because it is such a difficult task to still the riot of our own lives in order to hear a God that, in Craddock's terms, prefers to whisper than to shout. He writes intriguingly, "It is the position of the theology of preaching… that the New Testament, which carries the word as both a whisper and a shout, is best interpreted if one understands God's word as being heard as a whisper and spoken as a shout."[8]

Following the shattering events of September 11, 2001, I made a point of visiting seven churches in the city where I lived to hear how preachers attempted to understand and apply the word of God in the light of the tragedy. That the congregations were traumatized by the event was not in dispute. Churches were fuller than usual with people trying to gain some discernment and perspective. However, out of seven preachers, only one even attempted to bring a perspective upon the event. Five of them refused to preach at all, and instead said, "We are all so shocked by this that the only appropriate response is silence." Some led the church in prayers; another showed images of the tragedy and played Celtic harp music. That five out of seven preachers never even made the effort to understand what God might want to say about the terrorist attack was disappointing.

Donald Coggan, a former Archbishop of Canterbury who held to a very high view of preaching wrote, "Christians believe in a God who speaks. Ours is not a silent God, a God who sits, Sphinx-like, looking out unblinking on a world in agony."[9] Silence is surely appropriate in certain settings, but silence never constitutes the whole word. Tragedy, no matter how shocking, does not absolve the preacher from the burden of speech in God's name. Quite the contrary. It demands speech all the more! But it is not easy to find the words. That's always a strain, in every age.

Then there is the *on-going crisis of competence*. Preaching is always in crisis because the bad preachers always massively outnumber the good. How can the church ensure that enough preachers preach well? That's the constant crisis.

Of the two hundred and twenty attendees of the 2002 UK College of Preacher's conference, I managed to interview forty. All were regular preachers; thirty-three were full time ministers in various denominations. I asked each of them, "Do you think preaching is in trouble? And if so, why?" To a man and woman, they all agreed that preaching was in trouble. What they meant was that, in the words of one participant, "The twenty-minute sermon in the context of a worship service is really losing ground." Even more interesting, however, was the almost total unanimity (two exceptions) as to why preaching was in trouble, namely, *because most preachers are not very good at it!*

In other words, the problem was located in the realm of competence. For them, preaching was not under pressure from outside forces, like sociological upheavals, but from a poor level of excellence in the art and craft of most preachers. They all made comments like "Preachers are unable to tell stories," or "Some just cannot hold attention," or "We don't know how to do the essential spadework on a passage of Scripture any more."

I used to think it was simple to describe what was wrong with Western preaching. After all, only two things can go wrong with a sermon. Either the preacher has nothing meaningful to say – *a failure of content* – or something to say but cannot put it across – *a failure of craft*.

There are some simple and some sophisticated ways to explain these most basic catastrophes. Failing to have something to say is, in my view, most often linked to a failure to use the Bible. This is due to three things:

• ignoring the text;
• using the text as a pretext for your own remarks;
• an inability to exegete the text competently.

Of the three, I would say that the worst was the first. I remain continually amazed at how many preachers pass up the chance to preach a biblical text. Last week, I was in a famous Anglican church in a big university city. The preacher announced his subject: Some thoughts on the crisis over the ordination of homosexuals in the Anglican Church. One often needs to look no further for a failure of content than this – the preacher just doesn't pick up the Bible enough! I'm not implying that reading the Bible on controversial issues dissolves every crisis. But, as journalist Ann Monroe, in her trawl through America, observed of liberal churches, "Everybody I met insisted that the Bible was important. None of them read it."[10] At least wrestle with the texts.

If the failure of content is a more Liberal failing, then a failure of craft is more an Evangelical one. The main problem is usually that the face of Christ in the text gets hidden by a huge scaffolding of propositions, contextual explanations, and off-the-point guiding imagery. In a word, "multiplitus" kills the clarity. The average Evangelical preacher invites his audience to a ten course meal. Every course is a sizzling steak, with four roast potatoes, buttered broccoli and carrots, a huge dollop of sour cream on the spud, and a creamy béarnaise sauce with extra onions and mushrooms on the side. If Liberals take the Truth and keep it secret, Evangelicals take the Truth and make it indigestible. The point they often forget is that the prime goal of preaching does not consist in putting across the "original" meaning of the passage, but the contemporary significance of it.

Yes, that is a bit simple, but it's a way toward describing the crisis. Failing to have something biblical to say, or having something biblical but failing to articulate it, are the twin tragedies of the modern pulpit.

Letter 6:
Old distinctions with modern consequences

Or, How Kant and Ramus shrank the gospel

Oh, it's all a bit too sweeping for you, is it? You always want to know the philosophical roots of things. Very well, here is a more sophisticated take on these two basic failures we mentioned before, which I first glimpsed in a wonderful book called *Elements of Style for Preaching*, by William H. Kooienga.[11] The failure to have a message of substance can be traced to a distinction made by Immanuel Kant (1724–1804); the failure of craft can be traced to another distinction made by Petrus Ramus (1515–72).

Kant divided reality into two realms, the phenomenal and the noumenal. The phenomenal is the realm of reality we can know something about definitively, because we observe it through our senses. The noumenal is the world which lies beyond the apprehension of our senses, beyond our understanding. We can get glimpses of it. We know it's there. But since it lies beyond the ability of our body to observe, (for example, our eyes are incapable of discerning spiritual substances,) we have to be very doubtful about the veracity of our conclusions. Kant carried the day, and left the preacher in a bit of a pickle. If you want to convince people about God, you have to stick to what you can prove – the phenomenal realities. But those are never enough to prove that God or even a spiritual realm exists, because that's out in the noumenal realm, beyond our powers of observation. Here's the bind then: if you stick to the phenomenal, you always say too little; if you stick to the noumenal, you always know too little.

From this distinction two sermonic animals are birthed. First, the *phenomenal factual* sermon. A good example of this was a Cambridge University sermon preached by a famous Harvard scholar recently. His text was Psalm 42:1: "My soul yearns for the living God." He set out to prove that religion was something many people yearned for. If you are going to stick to what you can prove, then you have to make modest claims. The whole sermon was a litany of reasons why humans in many situations seem to long for faith, and, as far as his argument went, he probably showed that, at least in William James's definition of religion, many long for it. James said that religion involved an awareness that something is wrong and that an outside force is needed to fix it. Fine, as far as it goes. But does it go very far? Our preacher ended up preaching a sermon that mentioned God once, Jesus not even once, and recommending faith in the vaguest sub-Christian terms because if you limit your reasoning to empirical points, then you cannot make transcendent claims! He didn't use the Bible because it doesn't have any empirical validity. It can't, under Kant's rules.

Then there is another animal, the *noumenal glimmer* sermon. This is where the preacher tells stories that carry intimations from the beyond, a mixture of testimony and deep mythological truth. It's about the use of metaphor that grabs us emotionally and awakens a glimmer in us that recognizes what lies beneath, or beyond, or above, or within, or wherever, because we're not too sure. Many preachers trade in the biblical imperatives and become little more than storytellers of epic but ambiguous tales. If they have the skills of a novelist, they succeed in painting attractive word pictures tinged with the numinous of other worlds. But again, it's not the Bible that is helpful to them here, or if it is, it's the Bible only as an epic myth alongside other classics, and it's a long way off from the kind of language New Testament audiences were likely to hear from their preachers who told them of "that which was from the beginning, which we have heard, which we have seen with our own eyes, which we have looked at and our hands have touched – this we proclaim concerning the Word of life" (1 John 1:1–2).

Don't get me wrong. These sermons have their uses. Proving that most humans yearn for God in a world suspicious of all religious claims has some value, even if it's only a move useful in a Western context. Skillful storytelling can transport us to experience the mysteries of religion in a way that makes a propositional sermon seem crude and clumsy. But there is a critical downgrading of the role of the Bible involved in both sermon types because the category of revelation has been evacuated by the buying of the Kantian distinction. Reason and intuition have replaced revelation as the grounds of persuasion.

Well, if Kant has played his part in the modern sermon curiously giving up on the Bible, how has Ramus caused preachers with a biblical message to fail to project it?

Peter Ramus was a teacher of rhetoric in the sixteenth century when that was the keystone discipline for getting up and getting on in society, teaching students how to think, talk, speak, and write for maximum effect. A Catholic, Ramus converted to Protestantism and then died a martyr, thus enabling his system of logic to attain near cult status among the Puritan preachers, who still define the modern evangelical forms of the sermon.

Ramus is famous for dividing everything into twos, and he divided the five canons of classical rhetoric into two – logic and style. Classically, the study of rhetoric was divided into five parts: invention, arrangement, style, memorization, and delivery. The latter three Ramus split off, calling them "style," the first two were "logic." Come the Puritans with their dark coats and plain churches, and they think to themselves, "Style, that's for those who go in for pompous moralizing." They made a huge deal out of conducting sermons in the "plain style," which, in effect, meant no style, just the logic. Thus, the critical skills of using words pleasingly and tellingly fell into disuse, as did the disciplines of delivering words with memorable force. The sermon became like a human being who was all bones and no flesh.

In practice, a typical Puritan sermon starts with a text, then the context is explained, then a series of propositions deduced are announced, the reasons for these are then given in greater detail, and finally each proposition is applied. In this way, we get to the modern evangelical sermon – text, context, points, and practical applications.

But it's all bones. And as Warren Wiersbe once famously warned, "If you take a skeleton up into the pulpit, you end up with cadavers in the pews." The problem is that the evangelical preacher puts all their effort into producing a logical structure, so that they end up failing to connect us to the living God. They don't have the tools to be vivid, or powerful, or even emotional. I recently heard a pastor in Kansas City preaching on that wonderful verse in Colossians 3:16 which ends, "Sing psalms and hymns and spiritual songs to God with thankful hearts." Here was his outline:

1 We have to train ourselves in thankfulness
  • It's not dependent on personality.
  • It's not a passive response.
  • It's not a switch.
  • It's not impossible in certain circumstances.

2 Understand the benefits of gratefulness
  • We find pleasure in gratefulness.
  • We find protection in gratefulness.

3 The elements of gratitude
  • Gratitude grows as we reflect on our relationships.
  • Gratitude grows as we recognize God's riches.

4 Understand the impact of gratefulness

See what I mean about a ten course meal that is all steak? That's really four sermons, over twenty separate points, and he told maybe eight stories. I've got indigestion already. That's just far too much to retain. The logical structure has taken over, and people can't retain that amount of information. More importantly, for all his logical structure, he missed a central point of his passage, which was not the power of being grateful, but how Christians can let the words of Christ dwell richly in them to produce a spontaneous gratefulness. The process of how that happens was completely overlooked, possibly because the structure is so massive that it sucks in all the time just to explicate briefly and apply each point.

I don't know how often I say this after listening to conservative evangelical preachers. I come to drink of the bottle of life. They hold it up, smash it, and show me the pieces. I'd rather drink of it.

* * *

Anyway, that's a longish excursus on why there is a major crisis of content and style in the pulpit today, stemming unintentionally from distinctions made by Kant and Ramus.

But the crisis in preaching is not only to do with poor sermon production, or the on-going issues of competence, connection, and understanding. There are bigger blizzards blowing far beyond those that have to do with just the preacher and his sermon. Bonhoeffer once mused in a prison letter: "Our church, which has been fighting in these years only for its self-preservation, as though that were an end in itself, is incapable of taking the word of reconciliation and redemption to mankind and the world."[12]

The point being, preachers don't preach in a vacuum. Writes Frits De Lange, "The failure of Christian proclamation is not located by Bonhoeffer in the content of proclamation as such, but rather in the pragmatic context in which the church speaks."[13] De Lange divides that context into three: the persons speaking and the persons spoken to; the institution of the church itself; and the historical culture in which the church is located. For Bonhoeffer, preaching died because the preachers no longer believed in their message, the church no longer stood out against tyranny, and the society no longer cared to hear a religious message anymore.

This much is clear – and this is what we must move onto next – the crisis in preaching is also caused by four revolutions that began far away from the sermon itself, but causes many preachers to feel greatly defensive today.

Before we move on, you asked me for my most embarrassing preaching moment. OK. One Sunday morning I was preaching with some liberty, and feeling something shift in my nose, plunged the hand into my trouser pocket for my handkerchief. As I started blowing my nose – still in full flow you understand – the titters from the front rows started up. I stopped to gaze at the object in my hands: my Union Jack underpants! I had left the house in a tearing hurry, reached into my dresser drawer and stuffed what I thought was a handkerchief into my pocket. I just stood there, trying to think of something funny to say. One always wishes one were Groucho Marx in these situations. All I could muster lamely was, "Well, I seem to be revealing more than I intended this morning." Anyway, it was enough to give permission to those who were stifling guffaws at some risk to their health to let it rip. At the end of the service a little teenager came up to me and said, "You know, you never did get the smut off your nose!"

Letter 7:
The four contemporary confidence drainers of the modern preacher

Or, Why many preachers feel defensive about preaching today

Never has there been an era like ours for preachers uncertain of the worth of their profession. There are four main revolutions that have sapped their confidence.

1. Sociological revolutions: the preachers have lost their audience!

The sad fact is, in the last fifty years in Europe and mainline North America, the gospel is a drama played to an increasingly empty theater. It's probably not the preacher's fault. The population has moved on to find other activities more exciting and profitable than church-going. But it is soul destroying nonetheless. You can't hide from it. From all quarters, one hears that preaching is passé. In *The Tablet* today, there's an article calling on all preachers to give it up.

> Preaching is not a medium of communication that is much liked or effective today. There was a time when thousands would gather in the open air to hear a famous preacher; today everyone wants to be heard, and attention spans are decreasing. Telling people what is good for them to hear, without giving them a chance to express their views or even ask questions, is about the worst attempt to communicate imaginable in our culture.[14]

Under this barrage, the preacher digs a trench, and reads wistfully of those preachers like Fosdick and Spurgeon who were the talk of major cities, whose sermons were published in the local papers and sent as far as Australia to be pored over before the week was out. Even politicians came to hear them. Now, the preacher has been excluded from public discourse.

What's it all down to? Who knows? The sixties must have had a big impact, bringing an anti-authority mood that evolved into postmodernism. Ah, the big PM word. Forget those French academics who ramble on interminably about what postmodernism means to the intellectual realm. What really matters is how it shows up on the street. Practical theologian John Drane says that postmodernism really means three things, which, crucially, are at the forefront as people listen to preaching:

- an awareness that things aren't working any more;
- an increased knowledge of the world and of different ways of doing things;
- a search for more spiritual ways of being.

That's the impact of postmodernism at street level. Preaching, then, is seen as something that doesn't work any more for two reasons. One is ideological – the preacher is a religious expert, and all experts are now distrusted. The other is communicational – people learn differently now. They want to speak themselves – dialog, question – and find preaching too non-interactive.

Or, so the explanations go. It's the emotional sense of humiliation that many preachers feel that is so telling today. The empty pews mock them. I was up in the north of Scotland attending a Presbyterian service. The church was shaped like a T, the pulpit was at the top and middle of the T, and on each side were large galleries, where the youths of rival villages used to face each other. Not within spitting distance though. Now these galleries are empty. The youth are not living in the towns anymore, let alone attending church. That morning, there were barely twelve worshipers, and all over sixty. The harassed minister had driven post haste from another town. He plays the organ, his wife reads the prayers, and the congregation shrinks at the back of the church like he has bubonic plague. He preaches a standard off-the-peg three pointer on Psalm 19: See God in the skies; see God in the Scriptures; see God in the soul. All delivered in a rapid, disinterested fashion. He can't hide it – he's dying of discouragement. Who wouldn't be... with all that polished wood glowering back?

2. Ecclesiological revolutions – the sermon has become liturgically overshadowed.

In the latter part of the twentieth century, there has been a much vaunted liturgical revival, yet in many cases this has fueled a certain *logophobia* among some groups in the more liturgical traditions. An Anglican vicar solemnly counseled me not to worry about the sermon, but "just let the liturgy do its job." This devaluation of the sermon is a historical fact in Roman Catholicism, when at the Council of Trent the sermon was explicitly downgraded in response to Reformation claims. The view, in essence, was "We've got the Presence in the Eucharist, so who needs words... that's a mere sign." This theological myopia afflicts the Orthodox traditions also. Despite an attempt to correct this imbalance at Vatican 2, many Catholic priests still struggle with preaching because they see their main role as celebrating the Eucharist.

Even in parts of Protestantism the sermon is eucharistically overshadowed, due either to a loss of a sacramental understanding of preaching, or an overrating of the language of symbolic enactment.

In the first case, the sermon is seen as too prosaic relative to the more magical Eucharist. P.T. Forsyth foresaw this at the end of the nineteenth century, writing, "The Catholic form of worship will always have a vast advantage over ours so long as people come away from its central act with the sense of something done in the spirit-world, while they leave ours with the sense only of something said to this present world."[15]

Forsyth was quite right, and went on to teach that a Real Presence was mediated through the sermon as much as through the Eucharist. One rarely hears about that today.

And despite Ricoeur's famous assertion that "the symbol gives rise to the thought,"[16] many maintain that the language of symbol is sufficient, even that words only distract or muddle. A Methodist leader recently told a group of preachers, "Jesus spoke about the kingdom by breaking bread with sinners, not by using words." It's absurd to set up this *words-vs.-action* fight. This same preacher went on a walk from Sheffield to Number 10 Downing Street carrying a letter to the Prime Minister protesting the treatment of asylum seekers. This walk he called a "symbolic action." Fine, but what was he doing on this walk? Giving countless interviews with the media, explaining why he didn't just stick a stamp on the letter. Hundreds of thousands of words, without which his symbolic action would make no sense. Otherwise, he was just a clergyman taking a hike in the country. On similar grounds, Erasmus argued for the primacy of speech over all other sacraments: "What good is it to be baptized if one has not been catechized," he wrote, "What good to go to the Lord's Table if one does not know what it means?" Jesus uses words to supplement and explain his actions. To drive a wedge between the two is foolish. Some clergy are scared to preach. They play up the liturgy as a way of hiding from the people. A sermon is the best barometer of the spiritual life of the minister. Some fear that it is too accurate an instrument.

It has been said that the history of the church is the fight between the pulpit and the altar. There's no doubt that the altar is winning in certain areas of the church, but really it's a false fight. The two are twins. I'm a big fan of preaching in a liturgical setting, if for no better reason than it keeps preachers humble. They are not the main event, taking their place in a larger worshipful action that is God-centered rather than preacher-centered. Three cheers for liturgical preaching – as long as the sermon is an equal participant with the Eucharist. Last word to the late great Bishop Lesslie Newbigin: "Words without deeds are empty, but deeds without words are dumb."

3. Intellectual revolutions – the preachers have lost their confidence!

Three areas form the bricks and mortar of preaching: truth, words, and text. Intellectual earthquakes have occurred in each of these in the twentieth century that have left many a reflective preacher shell-shocked and defensive.

Take the text for starters. Before I went to seminary, it was easy to interpret Scripture – too easy mark you, but the Bible was fun, and God had a reassuring habit of speaking in simple three point outlines, usually alliterated. For example, take Isaiah 40:31, about soaring on wings of eagles. I would have minted a sermon like this: *Christians never flag – Eagles never flap – God never fails.* You can bung in anything you like in a three pointer like that. Then I hit Hebrew, Greek, philosophy of religion, systematics, and (gulp) exegetical method classes. Finding the simple meaning of the passage suddenly became the most complicated activity in the world. The burden of critical apparatus became overwhelming, and one despaired of ever finding the truth in the passage. The light always seemed to lie behind the next word to be parsed, the next article to be read, the next commentary to be consulted. Worst of all was actually reading the professional commentators, their vague "on-the-one-hand-this-on-the-other-hand-that" approach left one groping for a preachable point. That Isaiah text again. *Start with context?* No one agrees what the context is: you can choose from the 740s BC or the 550s BC – a difference of nearly two centuries. *Study the word itself?* Text needs emending they say. Might be a phoenix, not an eagle at all. *Get into the syntax?* It's an adverbial accusative. Hmmn, thanks for nothing. You parse and read, parse and read, until you reach this stirring conclusion in one august commentary series: "When a person who is greatly weakened suddenly begins to run, it is as if he sprouts wings."

Where did all the soaring like eagles go? After all this work, we are left with the quite unpreachable knowledge that this commentator has never jogged! No wonder the great Jesuit preacher Walter Burghardt half-jokes, "Preachers sympathize with the plaint of a priest echoing Mary Magdelene at the tomb of Jesus... the exegetes have taken away my Lord, and I know not where they have laid him."[17]

Crushed under the weight of this ever-heavier historical-critical method, I observed two preaching reactions. One response was to go *apologetic*. Preachers got up there and apologized for the complexity of the passage, stuttering through the minefield laid by the professional exegetes, and ending up with pitiful, trivial applications. Their key phrases were, "Well, I know others may not agree with me here," or "This is just a whimsical understanding toward..." The other response was to go *apocalyptic*. You know, "There's a lot of nonsense spouted by the commentaries on this. Let me tell you what God said – nay thundered – to me about this passage. This is the plain meaning of Scripture." Such dedicated anti-intellectualism does not last too long in a seminary atmosphere.

It is a dismaying discovery, particularly for the evangelical preacher, to find out how hard it is to unearth the biblical author's meaning, and even more dismaying to realize that many consider the whole attempt utterly naive.

So much for the exegetical revolutions and the text. What about the linguistic revolutions and words. Says Rowan Williams, "We live in an age where the covenant between language and reality has been broken." The deconstructionists have introduced an infinite suspicion of all words, seeking only to unmask the bid for power that lies behind them. The preacher then appears manipulative, that is, "You're just a representative of an institution that is out to create guilt and control us." The skeptic's response to a preacher becomes predictable: "Well, you would say that wouldn't you?"

There are further epistemological revolutions to do with truth itself, but I'm going to start to whimper if I begin that one. My point is not that all these revolutions utterly undermine preaching, or that, for example, you must give up on finding authorial intent, but merely to note that many preachers caught in the vortex of these revolutions have lost their confidence about the veracity of the preaching enterprise. Not all, but many.

4. Communications revolutions – the sermon has become outmoded!

It is fascinating to notice that preachers who slough off the first three revolutions rarely exhibit the same air when it comes to the communications revolution. Preachers suspect that the space between the preacher and the audience is radically different now from fifty years ago. Many speculate about these changes. For example, "Well, images are more important than words now," or, "The attention span has shrunk because of television," spawning new and demanding forms of sermon preparation to cope with the new dynamics, usually a rush to use PowerPoint, to incorporate film clips, or to beef up one's visual storytelling skills.

The value of these methods we will leave to another letter. Suffice to tempt your interest by saying that using PowerPoint could be disaster in the pulpit if it splits the consciousness of the listener between screen and speaker, depriving preaching of its most essential character – *embodied speech*. The communications revolution – whether one means the information revolution, the mass media revolution, or the technological revolution, or more – is reshaping our existence, often in ways we are quite unaware of. Remember McLuhan's warning, "First we shape our tools, and then our tools shape us."

The sheer all-pervasive size of the communications revolution prevents our understanding it fully, and preachers have a problem knowing whether their responses are adequate. At its broadest, the communications revolution brings a world-view that subtly reduces life to an information question: How can I solve this problem now? Everything in an information world becomes a question of gathering more information to solve the problem. Questions of spiritual meaning get edited out. Jacques Ellul, in a fantastic book, *The Humiliation of the Word,* calls this "The Technique." Lately, I heard a discussion of death on the radio. A scientist was called in to explain the biology of it and to give us hope that genetics can solve the "ageing problem" (note the technological redefinition). A psychologist was consulted on how to manage the "death process." But no one was asked about the meaning of death itself. Management triumphed over meaning, and the gospel of the preacher had been rendered irrelevant and invisible. How do you think that makes a preacher feel?

There is the more common concern among preachers that the sermon seems a dull form of communication in an age of special effects films, fast-paced television, and new languages of sound and music. When a preacher friend of mine preached with film clips he became shocked at the door when a listener said, "Wow, the clips are so exciting I wanted to see more, but then you spoke and it all got dull again."

Are preachers the dull ones? If so, then what do we do? We know we have to change our style, but we don't know what works from what doesn't.

OK, not everyone is equally affected by each revolution in society, but they do impinge on the preaching enterprise for the twenty-first century. They create great defensiveness among many preachers, and with good reason. That's the final installment of my argument that modern preaching is in crisis – which you denied at first. But defensiveness is not the same as despair. If there is one thing the history of preaching shows, it is that dark ages are always followed by golden ages. I believe we are on the verge of another golden age. If you want to know why, then you'll have to write me back.

Letter 8:
Why the twenty-first century may be a golden age for preaching

Or, In praise of Helmut Thielicke, master preacher of the atomic age

Yes, it's a historical fact. Preaching dark ages are always followed by preaching golden ages.

No sooner was the ink dry on Paul's letters than a "dark age" of preaching began with the *early* early church Fathers, the so-called Apostolic fathers, who lost sight of grace and left us worthy sermons full of moral finger-wagging. There was a good reason for this – they were still over-influenced by Christianity's birth culture, Judaism, and so the gospel was presented as the "new law." The gospel became a moral system. For example in the Shepherd of Hermas, regarded as Scripture for the first 200 years, salvation comes about "by your simplicity and innocence." This was less than faithful to the New Testament, where we are good because of what we have become (e.g. Col. 3:3–5), we are in Christ, so we act like it. Somehow this got reversed in the early Fathers, and law became emphasized at the expense of grace. See Tommy Torrance on this if you don't believe me (I know you won't).

In the fourth century, Greek rhetoric combines with Bible-based speech to create the likes of Ambrose, Chrysostom, and Augustine. They find themselves in a state sponsored religion, with huge cathedral buildings commandeered from the mystery cults, and with packed audiences corralled in by the authorities. These were the superstars of the preaching world.

After Gregory the Great, another dark age sets in, where preaching falls into disuse from widespread illiteracy. This is shattered in the twelfth century when the great Friars like Francis and Dominic found Mendicant orders designed specifically to rekindle preaching. And when their reforms degenerate into a barren scholasticism, along comes the Reformation in the sixteenth century and another golden age for the pulpit gets launched with a mighty splash.

Then much Reformation preaching itself becomes dry and contentious. Have you ever seen that famous *Punch* cartoon from the period, showing a learned clergyman leaning over the pulpit to his congregation of country yokels, one of them chewing a grass stalk? The preacher is roaring, "What's that I hear you say, *anti-sabellianism*?"

By the eighteenth century, the great Revivalist preachers like Wesley and Whitefield rode to the rescue, inaugurating a new style of preaching altogether – emotional, personal, passionate. We see the tail end of their comet in the evangelistic preaching of Billy Graham and Martin Luther-King, Jnr.

Yes, yes, I see your fingers drumming on the leather inlay of that eighteenth-century walnut desk of yours (oh the sermons I could write on that) as you think, "OK, but why does he think a golden age is coming *now*? After all, dark ages last for centuries, don't they?"

You need two elements for a preaching golden age: you need a society that clamors to hear the word of God; you also need preachers who will speak *to* the Age, rather than *past* it. The first is definitely on its way in the West I believe, and the second, well, that's why we're corresponding. I have high hopes for you.

Some ages just don't want to hear the word of God. Remember Paul warns Timothy that "a time is coming when people will no longer listen to right teaching" (2 Tim. 4:3). Ask any prophet... if you can find one. There are periods when the "hearing" is just not there. Maybe it's a case of when the living is easy the hearing is poor. But this is changeable, and the greatest change agent is always that ancient one – catastrophe. In Britain, we saw this recently in two events. When Princess Diana died in 1997, the churches were suddenly full as large swathes of the population came looking for answers. I remember one girl repeating in a daze, "But famous people can't die, can they? Not at thirty-six?" After September 11, 2001, the churches were briefly full again, and for a few weeks the essential questions of life were back on everyone's lips: "Where does evil come from? Why did God not stop this? What kind of future can I expect in a world like this?" I fear that the twenty-first century will be marked by catastrophes that will make 9/11 look like a match flare in a forest fire.

Don't take it from me though. A very famous English scientist and astronomer, Sir Martin Rees, recently released a book called *Our Final Century*. He has taken a bet (he hopes he loses it) with *Wired* magazine that by 2020, a major catastrophe from what he calls "bioterror or bioerror" will strike in a Western setting. His thesis is that in the twenty-first century, technology will put into the hands of the many – as opposed to the few – the power to destroy good-sized chunks of human life and the ecosystem. He writes,

> We are entering an era when a single person can, by one clandestine act, cause millions of deaths or render a city uninhabitable for years, and when a malfunction in cyberspace can cause havoc worldwide to a significant segment of the economy: air transport, power generation, or the financial system. Indeed, disaster could be caused by someone who is merely incompetent rather than malign.[18]

When the atom was split, humans knew that they had crossed a bridge. For the first time in human history, they held the keys to humanity's destruction in their own hands. But up until very recently, only those with a finger on the nuclear button actually held these keys: a tiny club consisting of the Presidents of the USSR, US, China, and France and the British, Indian, and Israeli Prime Ministers. No more than ten members!

With the advances in technology and science, these keys have been copied and handed out to many thousands of individuals. Creating a chemical weapon to poison an entire city is doable with low tech tools. Some may be terrorists, some may be nasty clerics, some may be well-meaning types, and some may just be anti-social. But technology has handed them this power, not to launch nuclear havoc probably, but chemical and biological havoc. Martin again:

> Conceivably, ordinary citizens could command the destructive capacity that in the twentieth century was the frightening

prerogative of the handful of individuals who held the reins of power in states with nuclear weapons. If there were millions of independent fingers on the button of a Doomsday machine, then one person's act of irrationality, or even one person's error, could do us all in.[19]

This is what convinces me. If one person's act of irrationality, or even one person's error, could do us all in, then, knowing what the Christian knows about human nature, can we really think that *one person* will not act irrationally, selfishly, stupidly, madly? On what a wobbly pillar the security of this century depends – on all scientists being ethical, all terrorists being sensible, and all experiments working as planned. The future of large tracts of humanity are going to be held hostage to the likes of the Unabomber, Bin Laden, Saddam Hussein types, the greedy scientist, or even the committee of well-meaning scientists who make an error. Welcome to the new world.

The question is: how do we preach to this? The twenty-first century might see many 9/11 moments. The only difference is that the death tolls will probably be far greater, the environmental fallout possibly irreversible, and the economic impact shattering. Yet the preacher will perhaps find a more attentive audience because the essential questions will return to everyone's lips. The idolatries of sport, fashion, foreign holidays, the frenzied striving for bigger and better homes – will be cruelly exposed as trivial pursuits. The preacher will have a vital opportunity.

This is my biggest fear, however: preachers will not be ready to speak the word of God in this apocalyptic era because they are locked in to preaching a self-fulfillment gospel in a prosperity era. A common type of preaching in America's growing mega-church movement is concerned with empowering the Christian individual to function better in an advanced capitalistic society. The gospel helps them fulfill their potential. To put it more crudely, it's about how to enlist your faith in sending your kids to Ivy-league schools, increasing your income to get a bigger home, and living the American dream to the glory of God. However successful a message this is for the prosperity age, it won't work in an apocalyptic age because you can no longer take a future for granted.

As an exercise, I urge every preacher to prepare their "catastrophe sermon." Preachers need to be ready to speak to their age. Mine is based on 1 Samuel 2:8b: "For the pillars of the earth are the Lord's, and on them he has set the world." The main idea here would be to say, "Look, it seems as if the pillars of the earth are mad and wobbly, pillars like

- sustaining peace by over-producing weapons that cannot be destroyed;
- maintaining prosperity by a consumerism that rapes the earth;
- relying on terrorists and madmen to refrain from killing through technological warfare."

These are not the pillars of the earth at all. The pillars of the earth are the promises of God – his desire to save us, help us, and even use history for his consummate revelation and reign. To end the earth is not in our hands, but God's. Whew!

What preacher can one turn to as a model? Apart from Jesus – the preeminent apocalyptic preacher – I would suggest the great German preacher Helmut Thielicke, who preached to thousands during the catastrophe of the Second World War.

Thielicke is the preacher of the atomic age par excellence. No one grasped better than he that when the atom was split, the gospel had to be proclaimed differently. He has a searing sermon called "Floods and Fires." It's on the flood of Genesis 6 – 9 and he starts off by asking if it is just a fairy story from a primeval age. He goes into the "floodgates being opened" language and the belief that the sky held back water. After all, it was blue. Then he says:

> These are quite modern ideas, here expressed in terms of mythical conceptions. The igniting of the atom-bomb has made us familiar with the idea of a 'critical mass' – even though in this instance expressed in a different language... The powers of destruction are still present in the midst of creation. The atoms – did God not create them? – need only to be split, the bacteria let loose,

hereditary factors played with, genes tampered with, and poisons need only to be distilled from the gifts of creation – oh yes, the powers of destruction are still with us and the heavenly ocean is still heaving and surging behind its dams.[20]

After establishing that the flood story is relevant, he suggests that it is only the grace of God that holds backs the floodgates, and that there may come a time when he won't any longer:

> And therefore this world, which we think we govern by our own power, may one day come crashing down upon us, because the thing we play with so presumptuously has gotten beyond our control, and because God is not to be mocked. He may suddenly cease to hold the ocean in check and the unleashed elements will sweep us into their vortex. The Bible always has in view the possibility that this is the way our human history could proceed and finally be shipwrecked, and it is for this very reason that is has so much to say about the end.[21]

Boy was he on it! It's like he was reading Rees's book, giving the preacher two planks to preach on in response. First, catastrophe is always imminent, but second, it is ultimately in the hands of God whether it happens or not, and not merely a consequence of hubristic technology. Thielicke had an amazing grasp of the threatening times in which we live. Maybe it was because his preaching was formed during the Blitz.

Thielicke's sermons are organized around a theological insight of mercurial density. You really get your money's worth with Thielicke. He gives us a monster thought, usually of great freshness. His sermons are not expository. They dance around a central theological insight of great weight. What's the biggie with the "Floods and Fires" sermon? It's this: "Noah sees more than the waters. He knows that new life will spring up deep beneath him. He knows that the day will come when God once more will utter his 'let there be' across the wasteland…"[22]

The grand insight is that the story of the flood is not the story of the flood at all, but the word. God calls a family, and promises them safety. It's the story of how God ensures that what we think is the end is never the end. "God can never be a God of the end of things," says Thielicke. Is that big enough for you? Catastrophe becomes grace, and the world is re-described in its true terms – held together by the grace of God alone and humans will live for ever by the word of God alone.

What a preacher, and what a message! Thielicke sat on all the mythic furniture. By the time he was finished you knew that he had given you the most profound solutions to the world's – and the heart's – biggest issues. That's what all the great preachers do – they raise grand questions and answer them with the full 12 bore gospel. They are never afraid to be epic in scope. That kind of preaching is needed for this coming age.

Unfortunately, preachers will look in vain to the current discipline of homiletics for help to preach like Theilicke. Homiletics often consists of puerile "how-to" books of mind-numbing simplicity, or abstruse tomes of bewildering complexity, intelligible only to other professional homileticians.

How will we create the kind of preacher who is bold, skilled, and worthy of God's gigantic gospel in this catastrophic century? You'll have to write me back.

Letter 9:
The four unconscious questions everyone asks of the preacher

Or, The wounds of homiletics

I'm giddy from the experience of starting a letter confirming that we are of the same mind on at least one subject – the general uselessness of most homiletics textbooks!

It's not just that most books on preaching are unnecessary, it's also the fact that *no book* really does the job. If you want to help preachers, putting a book into their hands is not going to work, because they read the advice on how to preach and say to themselves, "Well, I do that." Or, they look at the lists of "don'ts" and they say, "Yes, but I *never* do that." It's like trying to see the curve of the earth from where we are standing. We're too close. We can't see our faults or our strengths half the time. It takes a friend to point out the faults. And a book can never be a friend in that sense, because it has no knowledge of the preacher as an individual person.

As for homiletics books themselves, well, they do seem to split into two types. The first are the puerile how-to's. These books are useless because, if you will pardon a British colloquialism, they all deal in *the bleedin' obvious*. At seminary, the book we were given in our preaching class would list, for example, the marks of an effective sermon title, to wit: "(1) stimulate interest, (2) succinct, and (3) contemporary." Well, why didn't I think of that? The whole book was full of lists of stunning banality. Here are the marks of the preacher: "A called person; a healthy person; a disciplined person; a compassionate person; a humble person; and a courageous person." Gosh, thanks!

It's all the fault of this "wedding planner culture." When my wife and I married in a Los Angeles church, we were assigned a "wedding coordinator." This woman actually taught us how to walk down the aisle. "Always lead off with your right foot," she said, and watched our stately progress. Being thirty four at the time, and fairly steady on my pegs, I really didn't need anyone to tell me how to walk slowly down an aisle. Lots of preaching books are that way. They are full of the most obvious advice, stuff you could come up with yourself after five minutes' scribbling. Forget them. These books just give preaching a bad name. Preaching can be simple, but it's not that simple!

The other types of book fall into the opposite trap: they make preaching sound so complicated that we end up bemused, even discouraged. After all, if you can't understand a book about preaching, how on earth can you actually venture to preach? There's a book called *Patterns of Preaching,* and it lists nine traditional patterns to structure the sermon ranging from "puritan plain style" and "bipolar preaching" all the way to "sermon as theological quadrilateral." Then there are ten more contemporary forms to choose from, including "sermon as plot and moves" and "preaching from oops to yeah." What does all this mean? Do I really have to select from nineteen different sermon forms for my Sunday sermon?

I suppose, like everything else, homiletics becomes an industry, and a small band of famous homileticians are pressed – maybe against their better judgment – to flood an eager marketplace with a steady stream of books, which, in the main, contain little that is new or important. One should cut them a little slack though. Their books are like those concept cars at motor shows, shaped like spaceships and full of gadgets that would befuddle an astronaut. We wonder why these cars never get into a local showroom where we can buy them. But they are never meant to go into production. They are pure experiments of design and engineering and are of primary interest only to a coterie of other car-industry engineers. Yet some benefits and breakthroughs do filter down to become part of our less glamorous family saloon. It's the same with these homileticians. We need them to write books to each other assessing the impact of deep epistemological fissures, or proposed changes in the human sensorium – issues that are not of pressing concern to the average preacher, harried as they are by more pastoral concerns. But the odd insight may well drip down from this erudite conversation that the preacher will need to communicate to a new age.

The terrible failure of modern homiletics is the impression that form is the critical determinant of effectiveness. Ninety per cent of the writing zeroes in on the question: How do I structure my sermon? This is a tragedy. Remember that an absence of form never troubled great preachers of the past. Hark at Yngve Brilioth – one of the most distinguished historians of preaching – writing about Augustine of Hippo:

> It is indeed curious that the most obvious defect of the Augustinian sermons… is the neglect of inner logical unity and a systematic structure. A preacher who has so definite and so rich a message can afford to pay little attention to these things. The case is different with lesser spirits. They have great need of an external technique in order not to fail entirely in their enterprise.[23]

If Augustine never needed to bother about form, why should we? Is it because, in Brilioth's words, we are *lesser spirits*, or that we lack a *rich message*? Deal with form by all means, but surely an overemphasis on form is symptomatic of a collapse of content. Augustine himself begins his book on preaching with these words: "There are two things which all treatment of the Scriptures is aiming at: a way to discover what needs to be understood, and a way to put across to others what has been understood."[24] The problem with modern homiletics is that the "discovery of what needs to be understood" was wrenched away from it, and handed to a new discipline called "hermeneutics." This forced homiletics to make the most of what was left: how to put the content across. No wonder the discipline is overburdened by an endless obsession with form. Form is all that has been left to it. The discipline should never have surrendered hermeneutics to the biblical scholars, who after writing 500 page commentaries leave us a little snack-sized message to preach where once we had steak and a salad.

Don't get me wrong. Working on form is important. Even Augustine advised it, and his lifelong training in rhetoric gave him an ability to hold an audience's attention that is mostly quite beyond us today. But I don't believe that preaching is ineffective because one is being deductive in an age when one should be inductive, or inductive when one should be using narrative. Form is not the critical determinant of effectiveness. Most preaching is terrible today because most preachers neglect a set of principles that are far more basic than the trivial focusings on sermon design.

A friend of mine is a pro-golfer, and people pay US$50 for fifteen minutes of his time if he will cast an eye over their swing. He told me, "Everyone expects me to ask them to swing hard a few times so that I can spot the glitch, and they expect it to be some subtle adjustment of weight transfer, or wrist cock, or even something like, you've got the wrong shoes. But I usually ask to see their grip and the way they address the ball." He said, "Ninety-nine percent of what goes wrong with a golf swing for most golfers is an incorrect grip and an incorrect stance. Get those two wrong and you will never hit the ball where it is supposed to go."

It's the same with preaching. It's the neglect of certain basics – that most preachers are already aware of – that kill the effective sermon. I'm going to give my six basics that most preachers, amazingly enough, neglect. The best way to start is for you to send me a sermon, and I'll apply these tests to it so that you can see better what I mean.

But consider this for now. I used to do quite a lot of qualitative surveys of listeners. I've done research among listeners to preaching as far afield as Hong Kong, Los Angeles, London, and Jakarta. I discovered that when a preacher spoke, the listener was actually asking – not always consciously – four questions in the first five minutes of the talk. If the preacher answered wrongly, then the listener decided not to pay the cost of listening. Here were the four:

1. Is the preacher alive?

Most preachers sound like the living dead. It's so obvious that preachers overlook it. Here's how one of the listeners put it: "He talks about this glowing, wondrous gospel, about how it will change your life, but he sounds half dead. You want to ask, well, if it's as good as he says, then why hasn't it livened him up?"

The passionless preacher contradicts the excitement of the gospel. I remember an Easter Service with a preacher telling us, "This is the most dramatic story in the universe." He told us this while squinting at the stained glass windows, reading a script with a clipped academic detachment. Everything about him – voice, face, stance, demeanor – oozed the same message: "Don't try what I'm talking about."

People pick up on non-verbal signals. Preachers should ensure their bodies send out the same gospel as their sermons, and if it doesn't, ask themselves why it doesn't. If you are happy, tell your face about it! If you are mad at God, then let that emotion come through! Only... for the gospel's sake... resign from the "ghouls for God union."

Joseph Campbell, that influential scholar who tried to reduce the world's religious mythologies to a few gnostic nostrums, knew how to make converts to his cause. He was a riveting communicator, alive with his discoveries. George Lucas fell under his spell and the Star Wars trilogy was born. He made one of the most challenging statements about preaching I have ever heard: "Preachers err in trying to talk people into belief; better they reveal the radiance of their own discovery."[25]

I love that. That is the key question: What does the preacher radiate? The listeners can hear what the preacher is saying. But they are asking themselves, What is this preacher radiating?

People are not asking for a frenzied jolliness. That's just tiring to watch. There is a place for sobriety in the pulpit. Indeed, I wish there were more of it. I heard a famous US pastor – constantly on the radio – literally joke his way through the book of Jeremiah. No, what we want is for the messages of the preacher's body and voice to confirm – not contradict – the majesty and importance of the life-giving gospel message. For some, that takes more work than others. But it has to be done.

2. Does the preacher care?

Listeners are looking for the reassurance that the preacher actually cares whether the individuals in the pews are listening. Church should be the place where people are named again. In the world at large, they are weary of being treated as a statistic, a number. The preacher is the one who takes the words of God and gives people back their dignity, their worth, and their names. We are the only creatures in the entire creation that God speaks to by name. In that fact is our whole sacred identity and preaching's greatest role. If the preacher isn't actually interested in the listener as a person, the whole enterprise falls down.

People are asking, "Does this preacher care about me? Is there any love emanating from her? Or, is she just going through the motions? Or, more interested in getting a laugh, or building a career? Is she preaching for herself, or me?"

Early on in my preaching life, I fell woefully short on this. My attitude was, "Well, here's the truth in all its glory, make sure you live by it and you will grow; fail to, and you will wither." I knew something that I dared not admit to myself: I didn't care whether they grew or withered! I saw my job as simply to proclaim the truth! I was doing it for God, not for them. It didn't work. Only a loving preacher communicates the love of God. A competent one, a brilliant one, a persuasive one, without love, communicates all right, but communicates a different God – a wintry, calculating God. Brrr. I remain continually saddened by how few ministers actually demonstrate a love for people from the pulpit.

3. Is the preacher wounded?

Too many preachers project an image of themselves as successful, and this spills over into presenting the gospel as a success-making formula. A chairman introduced a speaker recently like this: "Dr. So-and-so is the son of a famous industrialist, and oversees his father's charitable trusts all over the world. He was educated at Harvard, Yale Divinity School, and the University of Cambridge, England. He has written four important, best selling books, and is a much sought after speaker throughout the world." On and on the chairman went, and the speaker was finally ushered to the podium to thunderous applause because, well, you bunch of losers should feel really privileged to hear from such a winner.

All we really heard about this man was that (a) he had been raised rich, (b) attended elite schools, and (c) continued to be rich and influential. In what way, I wanted to ask the chairman, did that qualify him to preach the gospel? In fact, might it not disqualify him? With all that success, and all those advantages, is this man in the position to know anything about a gospel that only works when we die to ourselves and offer up our emptiness to him who died on a cross, and builds – by stealth – a kingdom through the weak, the poor, and the broken hearted?

Inside every listener is a pride-policeman. They know that pride is an anathema to the gospel. Any preacher that comes off as a complete got-it-all-together person is repellent, and rightly so, because the gospel is for broken people. Each preacher ought to be broken by the passage every week, and that experience should be reflected in their sermon. Every genuine encounter with the word of God must result in a greater sense of our own emptiness, foolishness and unworthiness. Thus emptied, we can be used; that's the whole thrill of it! This brokenness is what listeners are straining to see and hear, because it creates a fundamental union between themselves and the preacher. We are all in the same boat before God – the empty boat! Our weaknesses drive us to God, and he builds his kingdom on the only raw material we can offer: our brokenness.

If that brokenness doesn't come across, then the gospel doesn't come across. It's just basic humility, that's all. No magic formula to it. It doesn't mean the preacher should catalog their failings, heaven forbid! Brokenness is a lot more obvious than that. It is the right attitude of dependence on God. If it's there, then it comes across as brokenness. If it's not, what's left also comes across... pride!

4. Is the preacher talking about God?

Does the preacher talk primarily about God? Not about life – we can read any novel showing how complex life is. Not about church – most of us aren't interested enough in religious institutions that God himself probably feels quite neutral about in any case. Not about themselves – of what interest is the life of the preacher, *per se*? Not even about the Bible – how many sermons have degenerated into information *about* the Bible. No. The preacher's job is to point. To point in one direction only – to God!

Listeners come to church for a blindingly simple reason: they want to know what God is up to. A preacher who makes no attempt to tell them is a real let down. The preacher is unique in all the world of words in attempting to proclaim and explain what God is doing. Of course, God's ways are often inscrutable, but I'm not meaning the preacher has to give a detailed report of how Ezekiel 28:7 applies to the Middle East peace negotiations of the week. Saying what God is up to is primarily about drawing inferences from hat *God has already done*. Our Bible, whatever else it is, is an interpretation of God's action in history that gives human beings the opportunity to be actors themselves. They are invited up onto the stage of history and given roles that – depending on how they play them – alter the shape of the plot itself. We preach God's intentions, and those are seen in God's dealings with the nation of Israel, the sending of his Son, and his superintending of the early church. God has kindly embedded his will not in the vague beyond, but in the historical world.

Yet so many preachers just don't talk much about God. Strange.

There's a wonderful Donatello sculpture of John the Baptist in Sienna Cathedral. What a preacher he was. He is shown in rags, with his fingers pointing out. I want to share with you a poem that I wrote while gazing at that sculpture one day on a visit to Tuscany. I imagined John speaking to me, and then me speaking back to him. That sculpture, as you will see, spoke to me of the central task of being a preacher... pointing!

> Lose your shame. Lose your fear
> All that matters is that you point... to
> Another.

*   *   *

Clothes don't matter – see how my coat hangs in lumps.
Looks don't matter – see my matted, greasy beard.
The point is
To point to
Another.

Say you lose your certainties?
Say you lose your tongue?
Say you lose your head?
Look. See. Watch.
I am the man who points... still.
My head is gone.
My bones are dust.
My disciples are dead.
But still I point.
Still I point.

I get your point.
But
Your *utterness*
Shrivels my
Pointing finger.

Not for me the
Sexless, menu-less life,
One coat on the peg,
A stone for a pillow
And body odor to fell a charging rhino.

Yet, a drunken fool
With power
Severs your neck.
And as your tongue bulges out
Of slack cheeks,
Still you spoke.

If a headless corpse
Can testify
Then my own
Death of a life
Can point too.

I will point...
To Another!

Letter 10:
The six elements of great preaching

Or, as <u>Warren Wiersbe might say, "Be memorable; be moving; be real; be biblical; be epic; be loving"</u>

Ah, we are back to normal… starting with the latest carp. You say those four unconscious questions have all the appearance of a list from the *puerile how-to* school of homiletics. Well, touché I suppose, if they had *already* occurred to you. But had they?

Remember, my beef with modern homiletics is that it either makes preaching too complicated with a lot of trivial piffle about sermonic form, or misses the point entirely by listing a bunch of points we already know! I have more sympathy with the latter school, because most preaching flounders when the basics are neglected. However, as a teacher of preaching, I find I have to pour all my energy into showing preachers *how and where* they neglect these basics. You can't just tell a preacher, "Preach the main point of the passage" for example, *because most think they do, yet, they don't!* It was never about *knowing* the basics; it's about *doing* the basics!

Take that sermon you sent me on Psalm 107. It's a lovely sermon, and I got such a blessing reading it. Thank you. What great skills in illustration you have! But let me apply an exegetical test to it. The test is simple: Did I preach a sermon consistent with a major thrust of this passage?

Your message was: "Whatever your problem, let God speak a word into it, and he will heal you now." Verse 20 was your key verse: "He healed them with his command." You finished by calling on people to come up for prayer and experience that healing.

I would not dispute the truth of that, but here is a question for you: *Is that how God saved these people in this*

Psalm? Is that a fair application of the deliverance they received?

The context of the Psalm is just after the exile. This tells us two crucial things. First, the deliverance is corporate. It's the people as a whole who are delivered, not individuals primarily. Israel, *plural*, is restored to the land. If you want to apply this to individuals, well, we know that most of the individual Israelites did not come back at all. It was just a trickle. Second, the deliverance occurred over 70 years. That's the length of this exile. How many people died during that time? How many individuals did not get deliverance?

So, I'm suggesting that to imply that every individual is going to get a short-term deliverance may never have been the point of this Psalm. The message is, rather, God hears the cries of his people and restores them according to his promises! The application to us is as a "kingdom body." It's long-term. This deliverance could spread over three-quarters of a century.

How do we make the application focus on that? We would have to challenge the individual to connect with a greater social-spiritual group. Most people get their identity from living for themselves, but that's no good. We're going to die. Many are going to die without seeing the promises of God fulfilled, like thousands of ancient Israelites did in exile. Yet we are part of a kingdom that will always be prospered. Simply to be part of it is enough. God is working out his plans.

Track the amazement of the Psalmist. Israel was taken captive by the world's most powerful man, Nebuchadnezzar. Yet in a mere 70 years, the world's most powerful empire had fallen, replaced by a new empire of which the leader – incredibly enough – was disposed to allow the Jews back to their homeland. What a litany of miracles! It's time to whoop and yell!

There is an epic dimension of deliverance here. God intervenes in the world of international politics to ensure that a promise he made to a tiny tribe over 2000 years before is still on track. Think of the hope that releases to Christians trapped in "exilic situations," our persecuted brothers and sisters for example, who look and see a government in control that they despise, and the promises of God mocking them as they huddle in underground house churches. It even applies to us in the West who are so prone to despair of our political leaders and often counsel a detached pietism. No. God is in charge of world affairs, and can still work his purposes out even if you think the antichrist has just been elected.

I can think of no better illustration of this than the contemporary Chinese church. Mao Tse Tung prosecuted the most systematic large-scale attempt to annihilate Christianity of the twentieth century in his so-called Cultural Revolution (1966–76). Sweeping away the government controlled church, the "Three Self Patriotic Movement," he closed every church building, banned all worship, banished Christian symbols, and jailed all known pastors. Bibles were burned in the streets, crosses torn from the necks of Christians by ever-vigilant Red Guards, and everyone forced to undergo ideological retraining. There has never been another attempt like it in spiritual engineering. The church disappeared from view. Certainly from his view. But did he succeed in his actual aim, namely, did he finish off the Christians?

Not at all! The bald statistics tell the story. In 1949, there were 750,000 Protestant Christians in China and two million Catholics. In 2001, thirty years after the Cultural Revolution, there were officially 13.3 million Protestants and 5 million Catholics. And this figure is a lie, partly to save embarrassment to the Communist party. Unofficially, there were over 60 million Protestants and 10 million Catholics. Far from neutralizing the church, Mao's campaign revived it on a scale unseen in 2000 years of Christendom. Mao kicked off the greatest revival of faith the world has ever seen while thinking he was destroying it. He is history's fool. Under Mao, China moved from having one of the smallest churches in the world to one of the largest. Smart work. Can you hear the Psalmist starting to boast?

How did this happen? How did he get it so wrong? There's a story (possibly apocryphal) told of a Protestant underground leader called Watchman Nee. He was due to speak at a meeting when the authorities were beginning to close the churches. Hundreds of leaders from his movement (called "Little Flock") were coming to the meeting to receive guidance from the great man. Yet Nee had been ordered not to speak. Police got wind of the meeting and arranged to attend in plain clothes. The moment Nee spoke would be the signal to rush the platform and arrest him. Nee knew of this, but wanted to go. He desperately wanted to give some leadership to his followers at this critical juncture, and had vital truths to impart. If he spoke, then he would fail to communicate anything. Tough choice. He solved the bind in a way that would make even Mao applaud in admiration.

On the night in question, the church was packed. There was a frisson in the air you could almost have bottled. Over a thousand leaders squashed together under whirring fans. People looked around playing spot-the-spy. Suddenly, Nee appeared and strode to the lectern. He opened his mouth to speak. The policemen all tensed, ready to charge the platform. Not a word came out. He just looked at them… for five whole minutes. Five minutes. Hitler would stare down an audience too, but only dared to do so for a minute and a half, maximum. People began to mutter, "He's lost his nerve." But as he held the audience with his gaze, his features began to mottle, eyes narrowing with rage. He picked up the glass of water by the lectern, and with a look of deep hatred dashed it to the wooden floor. Not content with smashing the glass, he jumped onto the bigger pieces with both feet, the crunching sound searing the shocked silence. Then, he walked around the platform, arms folded, looking smug with his work, the glass crunching like fresh snow under his tread.

By this time there was a puzzled buzz of conversation, which stopped as he looked up at them again. As they looked, they saw his facial expression changing from hatred and cockiness into one of shocked horror. He looked pained, agonized, drawing his lips back in a grimace as if to say, "How could I have been so stupid!" He got down on his hands and knees and began to pick up the tiny shards of smashed glass. Returning to the lectern, he tried to put the glass back together. Of course it was futile, but he continued trying for nearly ten minutes. He gave up, throwing the pieces into the air in disgust. And walked off!

Not a word crossed his lips. The police could not act. But the leaders that night had heard their message. Nee had mimed it perfectly. One of those leaders interpreted it like this, recalling it fifty years later as if it was yesterday:

> Nee was acting out a parable. He represented the state, and the glass represented the church. A time was coming when the state would smash the church. It would look for a short time as if it had succeeded. But soon the state would realize it had made a terrible mistake, because in smashing the church it would find it had not destroyed it, but merely dispersed it. Instead of being able to hold the church in its hand, the church was now out of its control. A time would come when the state would try to bring it back into its hands, but it could not, because the smashing would be too thorough.

So it proved. Mao smashed the institution of Christianity in China, but the Christians went into the homes, and there it became rubbed in to Chinese culture, embedding itself in families, sitting rooms, and apartment blocs in a way missionaries only dreamt of for centuries. Said one Shanghai pastor, "Before the early 1960s, we practiced Christianity in churches, and hardly anywhere else. After the persecutions, we practiced it in our homes, and *therefore* everywhere else!" That's why the vast majority of China's Christians call themselves "house church Christians."

That's the kind of deliverance this Psalmist is talking about in Psalm 107. But all you said was that an individual who comes to God for healing prayer will get delivered. Surely the Psalm is more fecund.

I know what you are saying, "But I read the commentary, and just didn't see it." That's perfectly understandable. You came to the passage with the question – inevitably in an individualistic age – what is it saying to me? All the information you read about it gets funneled through that grid. But a key exegetical consideration was overlooked, as it is so universally, that the Bible is primarily a message from God to a *people*.

Now having said that, your sermon did not fail. No one can ever say that! Indeed according to my criteria, you did well. When I started to derive a basic checklist system to help me help preachers, I was struck by five major failings in these specific manifestations:

1 **Multiplitus** – Using too many points until the sermon becomes a starburst that dazzles rather than communicates.

2 **Elephantine introductions** – Huge ten or even fifteen minute introductions that contain the guiding imagery to control the rest of the sermon. Trouble is that the imagery is either tiresome, prosaic, or just misleading.

3 **Vague phrasing** – Preachers seem hardwired to eschew all vivid verbs and concrete nouns, with the result that they sound vague and uninteresting.

4 **Sub-Christian resolutions** – There is not enough gospel-insight.

5 **Trivial applications** – The gospel is shrunk down to an individualistic technique that we can use on a Monday, all in the name of relevance, but the grand scope of the gospel as a message that speaks for all time, to nations and tribes as well as individuals, gets lost. I actually heard someone starting a sermon: "The toothpaste squirted out all over my jacket, my alarm failed to go off, and in the shower I used rubbing alcohol as shampoo. I was having a bad day." This was to introduce a biblical twosome who were having a *similar* bad day – the Emmaus pair. Come on!

Of course there were others, but these were the specific ones that kept coming up as I listened to many preachers. They are not useful as criteria, since they are too specific. I came up with a definition of preaching which eventually became my six elements or tests of effective preaching:

PREACHING IS: REACHING THE WHOLE PERSON, WHERE THEY LIVE, WITH THE WORD FROM ABOVE, IN LOVE!

1 **The oral test: reaching** – as opposed to missing. Preaching is an oral event. You must use your voice and body to communicate a message. One of the most basic implications of this is that preachers must be careful to make a singular point in their sermons. David Buttrick points out that group consciousness cannot handle more than one main

point, yet most preachers tend to multiply points. Does my sermon have a singular thrust, or possess organic unity? Am I looking at the audience? Am I using oral English? Am I speaking up? These are the communicational basics that come from preaching being an oral activity. You have to know how to reach a listener with words! You would be amazed how many preachers do not realize that the voice is a muscle.

2 **The experience test: the whole person** – as opposed to just the mind of the person. Preaching is not out merely to inform the mind, but to move the heart. It hopefully reaches the affective as well as the intellectual side of the listener. We should look for preachers to reproduce the *performative* sense of Scripture; namely, are they actually *doing* during the sermon what the text was designed to *do*, as opposed to merely saying what it means? Does my sermon attempt to produce in the hearer what the sermon is about? Or, do I treat them as a computer, a mere information processor? As Harry Emerson Fosdick famously remarked, "People do not come to church to hear about the history of the Jebusites." We do not have a mere informational objective, but a transformative objective.

3 **The reality test: where they live** – as opposed to where the preacher lives. To have credibility, preachers must demonstrate an understanding of the reality in which their listeners live; otherwise they come across as well meaning, but irrelevant. How well does the preacher know and describe the real world? Is there an awareness of the complexities and ambiguities of human nature? Or, is the world unfairly simplified in order to preach to it? Am I aware of the human binds and ambiguities in which my audience find themselves?

4 **The exegetical test: with the word** – as opposed to our own word. Preaching ultimately is not merely relating the thoughts of the preacher, but the giving of the time-transcendent word of God as revealed in Scripture. The issue here is to ensure that the preacher is truly preaching the meaning of the text in question, or at least being biblical in their assertions. Is the divine perspective

properly represented in the sermon in a way consistent with Scripture? Am I really preaching what is central to the passage?

5 **The grandeur test: from above** – as opposed to from below. Am I preaching the greatness of God and dealing with the constant universal questions of life? We're not talking about anything trivial here. We are dealing with the most important question of all: What's God up to? As Elizabeth Achtemeier maintains, "Great preaching talks mostly about God." We are located in the Person of God, who has loved us before the world's beginning, and even now is working out his perfect will in the midst of history. We are the eternal people. Does the preacher bring this epic dimension into our lives, so that we are part of this great, grand drama?

6 **The tenderness test: in love** – as opposed to out of duty. Do I really love those to whom I am speaking? Have I a heart of compassion for them? Is my attitude like Jesus, who had compassion on the crowds, "Because they were like sheep without a shepherd?" Only this heart of love communicates the gospel.

These are the six, and they give me a method to home in to help the preacher. It's a checklist and shows me where to start. All can be cultivated and improved. With you, for example, I would start in with the exegetical element. With a young Chinese lady I am helping at the moment, I am starting off with the oral element: she has a penchant for lists of ten. And no one hits all six at the same time… least of all me. I fail all the time. Your sermon was one I would have been honored to preach. But the six tests just gives me a useful way to assess where a sermon has been successful or not, and a way to assist the preacher – if he or she wishes it – to produce a better sermon.

I suppose I need a snappier way to present them. After all, the acronym OERGRT smacks too much of a shadowy group trying to take over the world, like Ian Fleming's SMERSH. They might go more easily into Warren-Wiersbe-speak: Be memorable; be moving; be real; be biblical; be epic; and be loving. I'll have to keep working on this.

Let me go on to deal with each of these elements, but before that happens, you must answer me one more question: How important an activity do you consider preaching to be? I'm of the opinion that if a preacher does not think that preaching is the most important activity in the entire universe, then he or she should find another job, fast!

Letter 11:
The biggest bang in the universe

Or, Why preaching is the most important activity on the planet

The devil may not be original, but he can be effective. And when it comes to tempting, his first temptation is always the same – *Ask them to value bread more than words!*

He came to Jesus in the wilderness and said, in effect, "Turn these stones into bread and you will become the most sought after person in Israel because you will solve the hunger problem, and when you die, everyone will bless your name."

Jesus answered (roughly speaking), "No, nothing is more important than to preach the words of God, because we are creatures that live by words first and bread second."

This was how Jesus realized his deepest and greatest identity – to preach a message!

Since every preacher continues this work of Christ, so every preacher faces this same temptation. Wouldn't it be better to be useful? Wouldn't it be better to be powerful? Wouldn't it be better to be relevant?

There is no sight more distressing than a preacher who really does not believe that what they are doing is the greatest and most needed activity in the world.

I urge this exercise upon all preachers to help with this. Answer this question: Why is it more important for me to be a preacher than a _____?

Fill in whatever you are tempted to be or do instead. Remember, whatever you are tempted to do is not an intrinsically inferior call, but it would constitute an inferior call for you if your main purpose in life is to preach.

Why is it more important for me to be a preacher than a lawyer?

Boy, do we need lawyers. The profession is not diminished just because some fat-cats use their expertise to defend silly celebrities. After all, there are some preachers who ride in Rolls-Royces and use the profession for self-aggrandizement, but that does not invalidate the profession. Lawyers, in criminal cases, protect society by prosecuting criminals and defending the innocent. In civil cases, they help us to comply with the law and settle disputes as a matter of last resort. We need them. We don't like paying their rates, but we do need them.

The preacher is needed in a very different way. Much of the law as we have it in the West is sourced in the word that the preacher handles: the Ten Commandments, for example. More importantly, the preacher speaks to the whole person in a way a lawyer cannot. We live by words and the values of those words, not by law.

A friend of mine is a Communist, quite high up in the Chinese government. He was raised with the anti-religious rhetoric of undiluted Marxism. Nonetheless, I remember him leaning over to me during a Beijing banquet in 1999 and saying, "I wish that all of China was Christian." After I spat my prawns across the table in surprise, he explained,

> The government does not know how to keep order any more. In the past, people were good out of fear. The state was coercive, the penalties severe. Now we are liberalizing, and becoming capitalistic. The whole system will only work if people are hardworking and honest. But, they don't want to be good. We can threaten them with the law, but the law doesn't scare them. We need people like you who inculcate moral values and give people a motivation to be good for its own sake, for the sake of pleasing God, I suppose. Only then will we truly prosper.

He's right. It is the message of the preacher that creates people who make, respect, and keep the law. Without those values, law and civilization are doomed. Preachers build those values directly in a way that lawyers cannot.

Why is it more important for me to be a preacher than a doctor?

Doctors, like lawyers, have a very particular focus – the health of our bodies. In recent years, they have been learning to see the person not merely as a biological organism, but as a whole person with psychological and spiritual dimensions that must become part of the treatment plan for effective healing to occur. But their focus has to remain primarily physical. By contrast, the preacher remains the one person who gives an individual a message that mends body, soul, and spirit at the same time, even giving hope to a dying body soon to be exchanged for a better one.

I'll never forget working for three months as a hospital chaplain in Arcadia, California. One day, I came into a ward where a doctor was bending over a patient. "Oh, sorry, I'm the chaplain, I'll come back later," I said. The doctor straightened up and said, "Don't go. You matter more than I do. I can only work from the outside in, with crude tools like pills, scalpels, and needles. You work from the inside out, with tools like faith, hope, and love." As he left the room, he said one more thing: "I can't do anything about death. Only you can."

I wish I could have bottled that doctor and taken him on a world tour with me.

Why is it more important for me to be a preacher than a psychologist or a therapist?

Psychologists offer essential support for those of us who can admit that we need it. They help us break out of destructive thought and behavior patterns. They help us work through problematic relationships with ourselves and other people. They can help people to function again in "normal" society. But, here's the question: What if normality is mad?

The preacher has a message that identifies the madness in society, and helps people gain and hold a truer perspective on life. Ultimately, what has the therapist got to offer? A way to function again? All too often, this is only dealing in two dimensions when four need to be involved for transformation to take place. Practical theologian and therapist James Loder calls these four dimensions the Self, the Lived World, the Void, and the Holy. Most therapy seeks to strengthen the ego's capacity to cope with the lived world, but what if the primary route to growth is to face the Void – all those existential dilemmas that the ego tries its hardest to distract us from. It is as we look into the Void that we find not only darkness, but a place where the Face of God can become visible. I don't want this to sound flip. There are forms of therapy that do incorporate all four dimensions; however, it is the preacher who is the dealer par excellence in these dimensions because the gospel incorporates them all. We refuse to let the ego think that it can manage life. We deny that life is a simple negotiation between pleasure and pain. We respond to the fact that we all begin to die the moment we are born and the ego cannot guarantee our survival. Only the preacher specializes in proclaiming a message that says, "The Void is your friend. Keep looking and you will find God there."

Why is it more important for me to be a preacher than a Fortune 500 CEO?

No one gets happy being wealthy. The more wealth you have the less you enjoy it. The preacher holds up a treasure that can never fade or spoil, nor destroys us in the process of accumulation. My favorite quote from a business banquet: "The problem with the rat race is this: even when you win, you're still a rat!"

But the challenge needs refining. What can I give to the world that Bill Gates can't? After all, he does a lot of good. No one should sniff at the generosity of the wealthy. Their interventions can save millions of lives. Here, it is the eternal dimension of the preacher that sets them apart. Ultimately, we talk of true wealth that lasts for ever. We have the pearl that is beyond price, yet so freely available – it takes only a humble heart to embrace it. And for those who do, the world goes on for ever!

Why is it more important for me to be a preacher than a president or a prime minister?

There was once a British prime minister called James Callaghan. I happened to hear him reflecting on his two years at the pinnacle of power. He said, "The one thing that you realize about being PM is how little you can change. I think that the only difference I have made in this society has been to pass the law that required country lanes to have cat's eyes – reflectors to show where the middle of the road was." This innovation did indeed save thousands of lives, so no one would say that PMs and presidents have no power to do good, however limited. But it was a strangely humble reflection, and he was quick to share the "glory" with a hundred others who (a) invented the cat's eye, (b) proposed it and gained the funding for it, and (c) actually installed them into the roads.

Political solutions are so useless sometimes. For example, a report on street crime in St. Louis discovered that most criminals plied their trade purely to keep up with their peers. They were not Freudian calculators, weighing the rewards of crime against the drawbacks of detection. They thieved, pimped, and pillaged without fear of jail. They did it because they needed lots of cash to look and act cool in the culture. Being cool was defined in terms of spending on cars, sex, and drugs. It was the attitude on the streets that drove the crime. Think how irrelevant political solutions are in the face of this. The Democrats say, "Let's give them jobs." But they don't want the jobs because they do not generate the amounts of cash in hand to keep in with the cool culture. The Republicans say, "Let's increase the jail sentences," but that is useless too because the criminals don't fear jail. Only the message of the church can change this street culture where politics fails, and it starts with a preacher!

Why is it more important for me to be a preacher than a top TV presenter?

Because TV only looks at the surface story – the antics of human beings. Preachers reveal the deep and eternal story – what God is up to underneath all this evil, stupidity, and foolishness. Preachers can "keep hope alive" instead of opting for a detached cynicism.

Why is it more important for me to be a preacher than a Nobel Prize winning scientist?

Scientists cannot understand this universe fully because it is not built to human scale. Our powers of observation will never be sufficient to construct even a surface, physical explanation. And, after you have speculated on the how of it all, you are no nearer answering why it all is! But God has revealed the purpose of it, and only a person with divine revelation knows what the universe is for. How did Einstein put it? "Science without religion is lame; religion without science is blind." The best scientists even admit that the preacher has the floor when it comes to the "pre-eminent mysteries." This is how Martin Rees starts his book *Our Cosmic Habitat:* "The preeminent mystery is why anything exists at all. What breathes life into the equations of physics, and actualizes them in a real cosmos? Such questions lie beyond science, however: they are the province of philosophers and theologians."[26]

There is also a slightly less high-faluting reason why preaching is more important than science: it meets our deepest emotional needs. There's a website called "The Edge" which asks distinguished scientists to answer the question "What is your dangerous idea?" The site was originally designed to canvass reactions to a book that argued that Darwinism was a universal acid that ate through virtually all traditional beliefs. Yet amazingly, many scientists admit that as science grows, so too will religion. Anthropologist Scott Atran writes that "science treats humans... as incidental elements in the universe, whereas for religion they are central."[27] He adds, "Science is not well suited to deal with people's existential anxieties, including death, deception, loneliness or longing for love or justice. It cannot tell us what we ought to do, only what we can do. Religion thrives because it addresses people's deepest emotional yearnings."[28]

*   *   *

Again, I'm not arguing that these are all inferior calls. And if you cannot think of a good reason to be a preacher as opposed to being a _____ then for God's sake go and be a

_____! But if you are called to be a preacher, then they would constitute inferior calls for you!

Here's another exercise to get this across. Every month, write a poem on the theme "What preaching is." Let it come from within. It's often when preachers reconnect with their imaginations that they see how important their work is again. Here's my offering for this month to get you started:

Searing fire
Dazzling light
A compass in the fog
A chart showing the reefs
Gentle fatherly advice
Mother's goodnight kiss
Lines to God
Towers of refuge
A needle lancing the boil of hypocrisy
Microscope of the heart
Wisdom of the elderly
Peace of the icon
Relentless as a running brook
Menacing sulfur
Trade winds to eternity
Party hats for the end of time
Cool water on a parched tongue
Skulls that speak
Politics unmasked
The brain examined
The heart dissected
Deep sewers of pain plumbed
Enchanting fragrances from a heavenly world
The invisible unveiled
Infinite value spread around freely
Everyone dipped in love
A deafening cheer from God for every soul

Or, try this – preach a sermon on the importance of preaching. Here are six points in respon se to the question "What does the word do?"

1 **The word starts.** The word starts everything. John 1:1–3: "In the beginning was the Word..." All things came into

being through him. It was at God's word that the world began, and every blade of grass grows as a result of that word. G.K. Chesterton said, "The sun does not rise in the East and set in the West because it has to; it does so because it has been told to."

2 **The word finishes.** Isaiah 40:8: "The grass withers, the flower fades; but the word of our God will stand for ever." The word was there at the beginning, and it will be there at the end. It is eternal where everything else is temporary, and makes eternal what is naturally temporal, like our existence.

3 **The word sustains.** God's word sustains this fragile world. He intervenes to guide, judge, and direct history. It's a fragile world, but ultimately it depends on God's words. Our lives, and our nation's destiny, all hang on a word. As preachers we reveal this sustaining process.

4 **The word informs.** It is the "information." It locates you in the world, answering those essential world-view questions: Who am I? Where am I? What's wrong with the world? and, What's the solution? These questions cannot be answered by searching. It takes the word to answer them. For example, there is nothing in nature that assures me that I am loved by God, or that my nature is sacred. Only the word enables me to place an infinite value on my humanity. What an impact that has on people. The American poet Maya Angelou once told an interviewer in her smoky baritone why she didn't believe in violent protest, "Why, because my grandmother told me that everyone was a child of God."

5 **The word connects.** It is the way that we connect to Jesus Christ, the living Word, and therefore enables our religion to be transformed from a series of disciplines to an exciting personal relationship. Sure there is prayer, fellowship, the Eucharist and so forth, but these are all as a response to, and a celebration of, the word. That's the unique essence of Christianity – it's personal, and it is only personal through the word and with the word. Christianity is more than a coping religion, full of disciplines like meditation and ritual that enable us to bear life's suffering. We are a religion where we are beckoned to speak to God as to a Father, where a

human being who is also God talks to the Father on our behalf. That's all the word's doing. If it wasn't for the word, Christianity would be just another self-help philosophy.

6 **The word guides.** Psalm 119:105: "Your word is a lamp to my feet and a light to my path." It's the torch that gets us home. That's why the Magi can only make it to Jerusalem by the light of the star. They know the Christ has been born, but they don't know where. It takes the words of the prophecy to light their path to Bethlehem. Thank God that we are not left to deduce his person from nature! How do you get to a loving God from a world where the big animals eat the smaller ones? If it were not for the word, then we might conclude that the big gods eat the little ones, and we would always be wondering whether our god had been gobbled.

See how vital this word is – it began everything beautiful, sustains everything wonderful, and outlasts everything temporal. Proclaiming it simply must be the most important activity in the universe.

Besides, what other form of speech has these five effects: to delight God, to astonish angels, to discourage devils, to encourage saints, and to restore sinners? I've done my time preaching to virtually empty halls and churches, and it is a great fillip to remember that three of the five audiences of a sermon are unseen.

This is the speech that does the most, and that is why preachers must be convinced that this is so, otherwise they will fail to live up to the full glory and influence of their calling. All great preachers realize that what they are doing is great. Admittedly, it is harder in a world that says, "That's only words," and has no understanding that to speak a divine word is an event of shattering power. The preacher should realize that the "Bigger Bang" occurs every time the word is proclaimed.

We have a universe not because the Big Bang took place. We have a universe because God spoke first, and then the Big Bang took place.

Now onto the elements of this "bigger bang."

Section Two:

Great Preaching –
the Elements

Letter 12:
The oral test – "reaching"

Or, Do I have a central focus?

I had no idea you wanted to be a scientist. I always took you for a frustrated naturalist when you led those thrilling hill walking excursions in the Lake District. I treasure my memory of ascending Skiddaw on a balmy June afternoon. It isn't often one gets the privilege of walking with someone who can name virtually every flower and bird, and also knows the story of how the rocks got to be the shape they were.

Ah, one must be so careful not to perpetuate this false "science vs. religion" fight. The preacher must do better than the tabloid journalist here. I absolutely agree with you: the battle never was between science and religion. What nonsense! Galileo got it right: "the church teaches us how to get to heaven, not how the heavens go." Therein lies the problem and the solution. Where the church tries to tell us how the heavens go, there is a clash. And where scientists try to tell us how to get to heaven, or assure us that heaven's address cannot be empirically verified, we again have a clash. But the clash occurs only when science or religion overstep their bounds.

The clash that people think is science vs. religion is really between two worldviews: theism vs. naturalism. Both are faith positions, and impossible to prove. One puts faith in God to bring all this design. The other puts faith in chance. Personally, I could never muster the towering levels of faith in chance to bring about all this glorious diversity in unity. As someone said, it's a lot easier to believe the phone book resulted from the mind of a printer than from an explosion in the printing works!

I once heard a wonderful sermon on Genesis. It was called "Why I baked the cake! Signed, God." It lifts off from an old illustration you probably know. Auntie bakes a cake. She brings it to a scientist and asks, "Why is this cake so delicious?" He can answer according to chemical compositions and taste buds. But if she asks the scientist, "Why did I bake the cake?", he cannot answer. He has no information pertinent to the answer. So what is the book of Genesis but God telling us the answer to the one question the scientists can never answer: *why I made the world!*

You gave me some favorite quotes on this tension. Let me return the compliment. My own is from John Lennox: "The existence of mechanism is not an argument for the absence of agency." I love that. It defines one of the great intellectual blind spots of our age. How many scientists have you heard say that Darwinism does away with the need for God? Darwinism is a mechanism in nature that leads to the natural selection in species. That's it. Saying that it disproves God makes about as much sense as saying the combustion engine proves Henry Ford never existed. Or take those people who are always telling us that because spiritual states can be explained by brainwave patterns, then God's gone! How many more *TIME* magazine cover stories do we have to endure from gushing journalists thinking God's been edited out by the scientists? The confusion of mechanism and agency really is one of the great foolishnesses of our age.

Anyway, talking of scientists, and attempting clumsily to segue into our first preaching test – the oral test – I went to a lecture by a famous scientist recently. I remember two things: his tie, which was a revolting pink with orange spots, and his introductory statement, which was, "Why can't we understand the universe? Answer, because it isn't built to human scale!" He was a fine communicator, and it is a triumph for his skills that, three months later, I can remember that much. But in the course of his talk, he made no less than forty-two separate points. That's fine for a lecture where we are all writing down information, but this was a general talk to the public. We were overloaded, and the brain went "warning, warning, about to blow fuse, shutting off temporarily." The point is, we remember very little over time of a speech, and knowing the parameters of an oral situation is essential to communication.

In a nutshell, being oral is the way we organize our speech so that the point we make is the point the audience remembers!

Orality is a strange abstract term, and many abstruse musings have accompanied it. What I mean is that before one gets too spiritual about preaching, the fact that it is an oral event must not be overlooked. On an oral level, three things have to happen for good preaching to occur:

- To be heard, you have to be audible.
- To be followed, you have to be interesting. Otherwise people will tune you out.
- To be remembered, you have to be memorable. Otherwise no one will retain what you have said.

These are the oral dimensions of preaching, and they are overlooked at our peril.

Picture yourself back in the Stone Age, before alphabets and books. All the knowledge that was important had to be carried about in the human brain. Forgetfulness spelt death. Forget how to make fire and your ability to survive is compromised. Fail to remember that the plant with the red leaves and yellow thorns is edible but the one with the red leaves without thorns is poisonous, and you are in for trouble. That's life in an oral age. Everything important was imparted by the storyteller in the light of the camp fire. Did he or she drone on with propositions and lists? Of course not, for the simple reason that propositions and lists would not be remembered. This is the age of Homer. The storyteller's job was to impart crucial information in such a way that it would never be forgotten. This required them to use words memorably. They used narrative structures to hold attention, vivid phrases that sparkled and stayed in the mind, vital characters that the listeners could identify with, and a story of mythic dimensions so that the world was described and the individual placed within it.

When we preach, there is a sense in which we are back in the Stone Age. We are the heirs of the ancient campfire storytellers. We are the new Homers, only with a greater story to tell, not of gods with human failings, but of a God who became a perfect human. We have to be memorable or the people, and the culture, will die. Some churches try to overcome the oral dimension by introducing other technologies than just the voice, words and the brain. They provide outlines for the listener to write on and take away. But I wonder how well this works. The vast majority of Christians do not review the sermon notes afterward. Indeed, the vast majority have a problem bringing their Bibles to church, or even reaching for the pew Bible by their knees. Like it or not, better to accept that when you preach, you are back to the oral dynamics of the Stone Age.

This is fine. Nothing to be bemoaned if we can adapt. The aim of preaching in an oral setting is to be (a) heard, (b) followed, and (c) remembered. This links to the three essential elements of being oral: voice, words, and brain.

- With the voice, it is the failure to be audible that results in us not being heard.
- With words, it is the failure to be interesting that results in us not being followed.
- With the brain, it is the failure to be memorable that results in our message not being remembered.

The brain

Let me take the last of these first, for our target is the listener's brain, their center of consciousness.

Here is the best piece of advice you will ever receive on preaching:

SPEAK UP.
KEEP ONE FOCUS.
MAKE IT MEMORABLE.
SIT DOWN!

Here's what you have to know about the human brain: *the more points you make to the audience, the more points the audience make up.* Humans have a poor retention rate, so that when you multiply points, so do they! If you want it in Meyers Briggs terminology, only INTJs (that's the ultra cognitive professorial left-brain types) test out at remembering a three-point structure twenty minutes after the sermon is delivered.

At most, they will be only 12 percent of your listeners. The rest can't remember, but rather than admit that to researchers, their brain creates three amalgam points that you never made at all. It's the same with stories. If you tell a multiplicity of stories, people run them all together to make a new story. So get this – *if you want them to get your point, confine yourself to one point!* Or more specifically, make as many points as you like, but make sure they all serve one overarching *point*.

Some might ask, what's wrong with the listeners making up their own points? Well, why give up so easily on preaching as an act of communication? If we have a message that must be heard, we should take the pains to ensure it is understood. You don't just put something out and then, to parody Mao, invite a hundred interpretations to bloom. Do you think Paul would have been indifferent if the philosophers at Athens came up to him and said, "Your gospel message is just like mine, but I don't need Jesus at the center!"? No, he would find a way to make his good news clearer. If our point is important, life-saving even, then we have to take care that *the point we make is the point they get.*

Saying one thing is easier than it sounds. If you are wedded to a three point structure, don't despair. I remember Carol Anderson, the gifted rector of All Saints Episcopal Church Beverly Hills telling me one of her sermon secrets: "I love the three point sermon – it lets me say the same thing three different ways!" A sermon should have a single focus. You can make many multiple points within a single focus. For example, I preached a five point sermon last year. The five points were the five sources of persecution in the New Testament – rulers, priests, mobs, merchants, and families. Five points, but there was only one main focus: *wherever you are, there is a source of persecution near you!* That's the one overarching point that all the other points served. It's the prime meaning of 2 Timothy 3:12: "All who want to live a godly life in Christ Jesus will be persecuted." That was my biggie. The other points were organic developments from this trunk, either roots or branches.

The greatest killer of orality is the fear of saying too little, so the preacher packs the sermon with more points, more information, more illustrations. It's a terrible fear. I know it well. Many times I have sat looking at a sermon and with a sinking feeling said, "It's too thin, too insubstantial," and then loaded it down with more points. This probably reflects a misconception about the true balance of the sermon. Perhaps preaching should rarely be primarily about what a truth is, and more about how much that truth *weighs!* Should we major less on explaining the truth and more on applying it? Here's an insight from Charles Kraft which has helped me enormously: "The amount of crucial information involved in Christianity is, I believe, quite small. The amount of Christian behavior demanded in response to all that information is, however, quite large. We have, however, given ourselves over to a methodology that emphasizes the lesser of the two ingredients."[29]

In other words, our focus should fall more on how a truth is used, than how it is explained. Not what it is, but how it weighs. This isn't easy to learn. It's hard to stop at just one truth and then make it count. We feel like we haven't said enough. Perhaps because we have not felt the weight of the truth we are expounding.

Take God's answer to Job. Here's one way to see the essence of it: God says to Job, "I'll run the world; you be a creature. Question me by all means, but not to the extent that you try to do my job." Now that's the truth of it. It's huge. In that truth lie all the problems of humankind, our insane desire to run the world and our refusal to accept our creaturely status. We must apply it carefully so that Christians don't just say, "Well, I'd better not question God any more." Rather, they are given permission to question, and that questioning is placed in a context where God can give replies, as opposed to answers. The profundity is not just in the truth itself, but in its outworking. The preacher really assists the Christian in practicing the most obvious truths. The more obvious the truth, the more forgetful we are of it. In our Bible study last week, a fifty-year-old Christian said wistfully, "The most important truth to me is this: God loves me; but in thirty years of Christian living, I've never found a way to live by that truth daily. If I did, I'd be so different."

It's these simple, obvious, yet profound truths that are the hardest to live by. Eugene Peterson translates the parable of building one's house on the rock and not the sand, as *work the words into your life*. Just examine how basic the truths of art are. Mel Gibson's film *The Passion of the Christ* focuses on just one truth – see how he suffered! What's a central truth of Tolstoy's Anna Karenina? That passion between lovers is dangerous and a good marriage is its happiest context. It is not just a great novel because of its truth, but because of the craft that is brought to bear in making that truth memorable as a story. We preachers have a similar task: to make simple yet profound truths memorable in a sermon.

That's the brain and how to be memorable. Now onto the other two more briefly – the voice and how to be audible, and the words and how to be interesting!

The voice

As an African preacher once said, "You can put your mind into a speech, you can put your heart into it, but if you don't put your diaphragm into it you've got no speech."

He's right. It all about air. Your voice is about how well you manage your air. Most preachers cut off their air supply by leaning toward their audience, crouching forward, drawing their shoulders down. This posture hampers the voice. It happens easily. There are two culprits. First, the energy of the audience draws preachers forward. Second, sermon notes are often on a lectern that is set too low, so that the preacher one has to look down to read them. True audibility requires a counter-intuitive posture: leaning back and arcing your voice out and over the listeners. That stance gets your air flow right, your voice in tune, and your words heard. The microphone has vitiated this technique somewhat, though the whispering preacher is still a common enough scourge, especially for elderly listeners, who – bless their hearts – will insist on sitting in the back rows.

The old masters were alive to these dynamics. In the transept of Iona Abbey, where Celtic Christianity first took hold in Scotland, there is a face carved in the fourth stone of an arch just opposite the pulpit. The face is in torment. Why it is there is a mystery. There are three schools of thought about it. One says that it is symbolizing Luke 19:40 about how even the stones cry out in witness, but that doesn't explain the torment. Another says that it is a reminder to keep the sermon short lest the audience end up in a similar torment. A third view says that it represents the perfect point of projection for the preacher. All the great preachers of the past used a "pitch point" – a spot for their eyes to light upon in order to keep a correct posture. It kept their bodies straight, so that their voices could arc out over the people, supporting the weight of the words. Try it. Much more can be said on the voice, but in my view that is the most important element. If you struggle with voice projection, or get a hoarse throat from speaking often, it's a good investment to get some lessons from a voice coach.

The words

Finally, there is the failure to be interesting with the words themselves in order to hold the audience's attention. There's an important little factoid in connection with this – we speak at 80–120 words a minute, but we hear at 1000 words a minute. That's why we can hold so many internal dialogs while the preacher speaks. The preacher's challenge is to still this riot of thought. I offer some simple remedies in a complex area:

1. The way to hold attention is to create a tension!
Start the sermon with a conflict, make that conflict count to the listeners, and they have to tune in until the conflict is resolved. It is a physical impossibility for a human to tune out a speaker if they have been hooked.

2. Use words better
Most preachers just fail to use words in an interesting fashion. They are boring because they are banal in their use of language. Now this is not easily remedied, but let me give you two words to get started: *stakes* and *jewels*.

First let's take *stakes:* spend the first five minutes (or more if you have over twenty minutes) of the sermon explaining why this material is so important. What's at stake here with this sermon? Why is it worth listening to? Why should the audience bother to tune in?

Martin Lloyd-Jones was a past master at this. Notice how he introduces a sermon about the first words of Jesus in Mark 1:15: "The time is fulfilled, the kingdom of God is at hand; repent and believe the good news." Lloyd-Jones starts, "I am calling your attention to this passage because it is such a perfect summary of Christianity and of what the whole message of the Gospel really is. And I do this, because there is, perhaps, nothing that is so sadly needed in this modern world as just to get a simple, direct, unvarnished statement as to what the Gospel is about."[30] He doesn't stop there. He goes on to muse about many modern people rejecting Christianity even though they have no idea of its essence. Then he quotes from a book called *Soundings,* published by a group of Cambridge scholars in which they maintain that "it is a time for taking soundings, not charts and maps."[31] He has a go at this, claiming that if he has a ship, then he wants a pilot that knows the currents and reefs, not one who has merely taken soundings. He establishes the sense of confusion and crisis around in the modern era – the world in which his audience is living – and then says: "I want us to consider these verses together because I am not taking 'soundings.' I have a chart; I have a map and I want to tell you something about it as simply and as plainly as I can."[32]

Now that's what I mean by "stakes." Lloyd-Jones starts by claiming this verse of Scripture will clear up one of the biggest issues of modern confusion. You have to pay attention when the scene has been set like that. What's at stake? You can either heed the gospel, or continue in confusion.

Secondly, *jewels*: sentences that sparkle! In bygone days, it was part of an education to study and produce what were called "schemes and tropes." These were patterns of sentences minted for effect. A student would learn patterns like parallelism, antithesis, ellipsis, and antimebole, the latter where words are repeated in successive clauses, in reverse grammatical order. These are still used in the modern world. Remember Kennedy's famous phrase, "Ask not what your country can do for you; ask what you can do for your country." That's an antimebole!

One need not be particularly fastidious about it, just get some sentences together that sparkle, then sprinkle them throughout the sermon. The fastest way to do this is to get some good short quotes. I visited a church where I had preached six months previously. A woman approached me and said, "I remember still that sentence about how the Christian should always be in trouble." I had used a quote from William Barclay, who once said that a New Testament Christian had three characteristics: "One, they were absurdly happy. Two, they were filled with an irrational love for their enemies. And three, they were always in trouble."

Mint your own epigrams, or steal them. Here is one from a sermon on Job: "There are two problems with suffering; one is that God goes silent; the other is that God's *people* don't!" I remember a sermon at a funeral which contained this quote: "Because we are human we want to know why; because we are human we *cannot* know why." It was brilliantly put, and so appropriate to the occasion, which was the death of a child. But be sparing with these jewels. Put too many in and you will just dazzle. A good rule of thumb is one every five minutes.

Speaking *written* English kills the oral element. Perhaps this is where most of us go wrong. We write our sermon, then read it in the pulpit, but it is a form of English that is too dense, too convoluted and too stilted, for the ear. We have written words for reading, not for hearing. Most disastrously, our ability to establish eye-contact with our audience is fatally compromised. Oral speech is different. Sentences are shorter, plainer, and argument is developed more slowly. Speaking in public requires a slowed down logic. Group consciousness cannot handle rapid shifts of subject matter. You cannot become oral just by being conversational.

Here we are touching on the myriad answers to the issue of "to script or not to script?" My advice is to write a full script, if you have the time. It's best for clarity. Then learn it by preaching to the wall a few times, until you can do it virtually without notes. With some practice, you may find yourself throwing the script away before you enter the pulpit. With or without the script, you will at least be able to look the audience in the eye, because you have generated a fluency that can depart from the script as the Spirit so prompts. By all means take up a full script to steady the nerves. As long as you have practiced it, you will be able to look at your audience.

At least take up an outline. I often take a sheet or two that has the first and final paragraphs fully scripted, and the rest just in outline. Always take something up because a section of the audience never gets over being wowed by an ability to speak without notes. When people remark in awed tones, "I loved what you said, but I'm just blown away by the fact that you never used any notes at all," I feel I have failed. Anything that detracts from people concentrating on the actual message should be removed.

Of course, for every rule there is an exception. I once heard the great black American preacher Samuel Procter preach at Princeton Seminary chapel. He used a full script, and somehow managed to read it and look at us the whole time. And, it was oral English! But that's not easy. Proctor was a genius.

Anyway, preaching is an oral enterprise. Forget that and you will never succeed in it. And if you forget everything else in this letter, don't forget this:

SAY ONE THING, SAY IT WELL, SIT DOWN!

And let me say one more thing (ha ha!). There is a lovely Muslim story that urges the oral test on their preachers. It's called the "Mullah and the Groom." I first came across it in India. A famous mullah enters a hall where he was scheduled to give a sermon. Expecting a huge crowed, he was crestfallen to see only one young man, a simple groom who looked after the horses of the rich men in the town. The mullah waited five minutes, but no one else came, so he leaned over the pulpit and asked, "Do you think I should speak or not?"

The groom answered, "Master, I'm just a simple man, and do not understand these things. But if one day I went to the stables, carrying fodder for all the horses, and I saw that all the other horses had run off, and only one remained – I would feed it all the same."

The mullah thought this was a good reply, and began his preaching. He had prepared a scintillating talk, and the more he got into it, the freer he became. Intending to preach for an hour, he preached for three. It felt wonderful. At the end of the sermon he leaned over again and addressed the young groom. "Well, what did you think of that?" he asked, with a glint of triumph in his eye. "Did you like the sermon?"

The groom replied, "Master, I told you I was just a simple man, and don't understand these things very well, and I know I told you that if I came to the stables and found the all the horses had bolted except one, I would still give fodder to the one left."

He stopped, hesitated, and then said, "But I wouldn't feed the one all the fodder that was meant for the many!"

Letter 13:
The experience test –
"the whole person"

Or, Does my sermon enable the hearer to experience the truth I am preaching?

I commiserate. Reminds me of a friend who used to say, "I had a couple of GCMs in there." GCM stood for "gawping-carp-moments," when you can't remember the script and you just stand there, mouth opening and shutting, nothing coming out. I wish we preachers didn't spill so much ink on this question of whether to speak with or without notes. I suppose we worry about it so much because, for most people, it is enough of a terror to speak in public, let alone speak without notes in public. Terror, and its avoidance, makes us loquacious.

I used to preach without notes, but no longer. For three basic reasons. One is that I feel enough pressure trying to speak the word of God. I really don't want the additional and unnecessary pressure of remembering the words in the stress of sermon delivery. Two, I found that I blathered too much. It wasn't that I had GCMs; instead of gawping like a carp I would blether like a washerwoman, all the while trying frantically to remember what I was supposed to say. Finally, I realized that I was unaware of forgetting key material. I was preaching in an Anglican church a few years ago that was very "high up the candle," and went up without notes. Foolishly I thought that because it was a short sermon I didn't need notes. It was one of those places where the liturgy went on for two hours but woe betide if the preacher took more than seven minutes! The preacher played second fiddle to the incense! Anyway, I had my sermon well learned (or so I thought), and did my stuff in the pulpit. Something odd happened as I mounted the steps to the pulpit. I ran my hand up the banister into a splinter of oak. The blood flowed and I staunched it with a handkerchief, keeping the sight of the blood below the pulpit rail so no one noticed. Perhaps because of all this, when I heard a recording of the talk I was appalled to discover that I had utterly omitted some key phrases that provided essential linkage and structure. The sermon didn't make sense, and I didn't even know it! It happened again also, without a splinter experience to blame it on. So now I use the Campbell Morgan method: introduction and conclusion fully scripted, and the rest in outline, with key phrases and story cues.

Let's bury it. Being oral is very little to do with to script or not to script. It is to use words in such a way that they are most likely to be remembered. Rather, focus on having a single thrust, and on using words powerfully and evocatively.

I've just invested in the complete set of the sermons of St. Augustine of Hippo, which are issued in a new translation. What a joy they are to read. He's incapable of a dull sentence, and he is the master of the beautiful idea. When you read Augustine, you realize that God in Christ has given us the most dramatic, most beautiful, and most amazing faith. So it pays to read the masters. But I came across this paragraph recently, and it leads us nicely into our next test.

> Because he had fallen from himself, and gone away from himself, he first returns to himself in order to return to the one from whom he had fallen, in falling from himself. You see, by falling from himself he had remained in himself. So in the same way, when he returns to himself he must not remain in himself, in case he again goes way from himself.

Now, remember, Augustine's powers are so great that when he wishes to be clear, he is. So when he is being this unclear, he is out to *do* something to his audience. I think he wants to confuse them, because he is talking about the natures of Christ, and the blending of the two is a mystery. So his audience experiences mystery as Augustine speaks of mystery. Said another great preacher: "A preacher's task is to create in his congregation the thing he is talking about." Thus spake a bygone master of the art, Harry Emerson Fosdick. It's a superb observation, and contains a good chunk of what I mean by the *experience test*.

Jesus showed the way. Remember when he is reading (and possibly expounding) the Scriptures in his home town of Nazareth? He rolls up the scroll, and then says to a shocked audience, "Today in your hearing this text has come true" (Luke 4:21, REB). In other words, the truth of "good news to the poor... release for prisoners... recovery of sight for the blind" is happening now. The truth starts here. Can you see it? Can you feel it? The truth is experienced *in their hearing!*

Ask this question of any sermon that you are about to deliver: Will it create in the heart of the listener the very thing that I am talking about? Or to put it another way, what is the sermon going to do to my listener?

Say you are to talk on the love of God. Is the sermon designed to produce an experience of the love of God as the audience listens? If expounding on the wrath of God, will the hearer feel an appropriate emotion, like godly fear or reverence?

Perhaps the question is more profitably asked afterward. If our subject was the greatness of God, did the listener experience wonder? If we were talking about God's sense of humor, did they laugh, or – if you are in Britain – chuckle? If you don't know, ask! You want the sermon to enable the listener to *experience* the truth. Because if they experience it – if they have feelings as well as thoughts – then the chances are that their whole person, not just their mind, has been engaged, and the likelihood of transformation increased.

Remember, preaching is still a sacrament, despite what some people say, and a sacrament traditionally defined is something that *effects what it signifies*. It does something to the person. It changes them by its action. So a vital element of preaching is to enable the listener to have a transforming experience of the truth, as opposed to a disengaged comprehension.

The last thing you want is for the audience to say at the door, "Hmmn, interesting... I'll have to go away and think about that." Fat chance. They'll never get the time. Try to create the transforming moment during the sermon itself. This can never be achieved if your goal is to impart information *about* the text. No. Let the goal be that they actually *encounter* the text.

Preachers sometimes divide into two opposing schools in this respect, either the *information school,* where the sermon is conceived purely as a means of instruction, or the *experience school,* where the sermon is seen as producing an experience. The information school sees the job of the sermon as providing as much clarity about the meaning of the text as possible, so that the individual will later incorporate the ideas into their daily life. It's a good school. I'm not rubbishing it. But it does tend to overrate the human mind as the seat of transformation. In contrast, the experience school – which quite possibly was best articulated by Fosdick – sees the sermon as creating an experience of the power of the truth during the sermon itself. Fosdick achieved this through his inductive structure. He began every sermon with a description of a particular need in the lives of the congregation, creating tension, and then applying the truth, creating release. Thus the listener feels, as well as hears, the truth.

Actually, it's a lot easier than it sounds and happens quite naturally a lot of the time. This is partly to do with the fact that preachers frequently use "performative" language, a category of words where the utterance constitutes the action. For example, if you say "I love you" to your beloved, the words create an experience, a reaction, hopefully a positive one. Shout "fire" in a crowded theater, you also create a reaction. So when the preacher says "God loves you" to a group of people who have a tough time even respecting themselves (probably includes most of us), that creates a feeling, a reaction, an experience, maybe of disbelief or gratefulness. There's nothing sillier in the world than to say "That's only words." Words are actions! When it comes to the gospel, we do not speak, then act. Speaking the gospel is an action. The utterance of the good news *is* the good news! God said, "Let there be light, and there was light." In the same way, when we proclaim the gospel, then the gospel event is underway!

There's another reason why this concept is not so alien – we've all seen it used by evangelistic preachers. Take the most famous evangelist of the twentieth century, Dr. Billy Graham. He freely admits that every sermon he preaches has the same essential elements – he tells people they are sinners and are going to hell; he tells them that God loves them; he tells them that God has made a way in Jesus to be friends with him and avoid hell; and then he asks them to make an act of repentance and welcome Jesus Christ into their lives. Graham learned preaching from the books of turn-of-the-century homileticians who believed in "tripartite man," the idea that a person was made up of three parts – emotion, volition, and intellect. While they addressed primarily the intellect in their sermons, they were under no illusion that the mind controlled the will or the emotions. That kind of romantic rationalism was best left to the liberals. So when they preached, they had three targets, and all three had to be hit for transformation to take place. Thus we see Graham, in addition to addressing the mind, targeting the emotions of the listener by deliberately creating anxiety about the consequences of their sins. He targets the will by asking them to get up from their seats and make a commitment to follow Christ. By the end of the evening, the whole person – intellect, volition, and emotion – has been confronted with the gospel and the "experience" of new birth occurs for many. Millions of "Billy Babes" throughout the world insist that this was no fickle experience.

Perhaps it might be fairer to ask, what kind of experience are you giving to your listeners? Are you going to try to structure their experience in the direction of the truth that you are speaking of or not?

That's the theory. What does it look like in practice?

Let's look generally at the principle in action in the world of art before we apply it to the sermon. It is here that preaching most closely resembles art. Good art sets out to move the onlooker to feel the truth being shared, even to somehow enter into it, to experience it.

Not so long ago, there was an exhibition at the Royal Academy in London called "Apocalypse," and it contained a piece of art entitled "Hell" by the brothers Jake and Dinos Chapman. Seven cases mounted three feet off the ground held fields of sculpted figures, five thousand in total. Each figure was no more than three inches high, and intricately detailed. We looked down on carnage. There were heaps of bodies and horrific acts of torture, and grotesque distortions of human forms. The general theme seemed to be Nazis being tortured by mutants in a kind of revenge Holocaust. One of the cases contained a broken down church. An ape stood in the pulpit. Bodies hung in clusters from the beams. Heads impaled on poles surrounded the church, vultures waiting for the bodies to rot. Perhaps we were being invited to view the scale of the slaughter from a God's-eye view. One quickly tired of it.

The experience element ran like this. You started off feeling astonishment and revulsion, looking with disgust on all the maimed bodies and bestiality. After a few minutes, you began to become blasé. There were too many figures. You couldn't keep looking at all the individual dramas. You started to move from case to case, and one pile of bodies began to look much like another.

Suddenly it hits you like a blow in the face: my reaction to these figures is exactly how a holocaust gets tolerated – we get used to it so fast. It becomes so overwhelming we just shut down. We go numb, and refuse to feel the suffering. And so holocausts continue in our modern world… because we have a capacity to go numb when the scale of suffering becomes overwhelming.

The art leaves you with an experience. I am the problem. Humans cause the holocaust, not just Nazi nutcases. The indifference that started to well up in my heart as I skipped from case to case is the real root of human suffering in the world today. *The point is, we didn't just get a perspective on the holocaust, we got a revelation of why it happened!*

The sermon is just like art in that sense – it is designed to leave you with a revelatory experience. The master of experiential preaching in the Bible is of course Jesus. Remember when a religious lawyer comes to him and asks, "Who is my neighbor?" Jesus tells a story that contains a 5000 volt shock to the listener. Why? Because he puts "good" and "Samaritan" together. Samaritans were viewed by first-century Jews as traitors and blasphemers: traitors because they cooperated with invaders to snatch Jewish land, and blasphemers because a few years before the telling of this parable, they herded their pack animals into the holy places of Judaism, where they defecated over the sacred objects.[33] The idea that traitorous blasphemers could be morally right and thus do the will of God would constitute an incendiary combination for the original hearers. One might as well talk of the "holy Satanist," the "moral pimp," or the "virtuous suicide bomber."

Shock moves the audience. That is definitely targeting the emotions. But if that were all Jesus were doing, it would just be manipulative. After delivering the shock, what does Jesus convey through it? The parable is told in response to a particular question: "Who is my neighbor?" (Luke 10:29). As the story develops, the neighbor in the parable is the unconscious victim. So Jesus rephrases the question at the end of the parable: "Which of these men was a neighbor to the man who fell into the hands of the robber?" (Luke 10:36). Jesus changes the definition of neighbor from passive to active. The lawyer obviously came to Jesus assuming that a neighbor was someone he was to help in his quest for eternal life, but in the parable, the neighbor is the one who helps him. Douglas Adams calls this shift "a complete reversal of worldview, which can be compared to a shift from salvation by works to salvation by grace."[34]

Indeed this is the heart of it. The lawyer is unmasked. If he was wanting to score points at Jesus' expense, it is over. He is undone. But more importantly, his world is fundamentally shattered. Salvation for him was doing good to those who were ritually regarded as a "neighbor." Now all that is gone. The ritual definition, if it is not universally embracing for all those in need, is insufficient to deliver what it claims. And what's worse – he has had to admit it publicly! He has lost his way of salvation. He either has to find a new one, or walk away.

Do you think the lawyer had an experience? Or, would he go home and say, "I heard an interesting idea at the temple today?" Not likely. And it only took Jesus 150 words or so. That's genius! Jesus determined to give that man an *experience* of how shocking the grace of God really was. The man also experiences the discomfort of *not* being a neighbor. We do not know whether the man became a follower. Perhaps the taste of grace was too strong. Better to sit in a world of safer rituals, where friends and enemies never mix.

Jesus uses a narrative device to create an experience for his listeners. Storytelling creates tension in the breast of the listener. Then the listener feels the resolution of the story as a physical relief. There are other ways. Acted drama is useful. On Sunday, December 25, 2001, in every Methodist church in the UK, there was a crockery smashing moment from the front, designed to draw attention to the virtual ubiquity of domestic violence. Here is a clear conscription of a shock tactic to drive the point home. The difference is clear between the sound of plates smashing and a minister simply asking, "Did you know that one in four women in this country are the victims of domestic violence?" The performative dimension gives the recipient the possibility of actually feeling what the communicator is trying to say. The smashing of the crockery actually delivers – for an instant – a tiny facet of the experience of being abused. It registers, not as information, but as experience. Film clips are another way of doing this. And as we have seen with Jesus, words can do it.

Start with having an experience of the text yourself, and then consider how to reproduce that experience for the audience.

Once I was asked to preach on the book of Daniel.

My first experience reading the book of Daniel was to say, "Lucky Daniel and his friends... they're always getting delivered." There are wall-to-wall deliverances in the book – from the King's wrath in Chapter 2; from the fiery furnace in Chapter 3; from the lion's den in Chapter 6. Problem: Daniel and his pals are always getting delivered, and I'm not!

Most of us don't get those remarkable deliverances in real life. We shuffle on in our unspectacular way. That very week a friend of mine went bankrupt in Australia. He had extended credit to farmers who had terrible harvests. He did the Christian thing. The families were grateful. Only one group were not grateful – the bankers – and they foreclosed on him. Why didn't God deliver him? Why is he now a ruined man... for doing the right thing?

Then the more I got into the book, the more I realized – with a start – that Daniel's basic problem is that he doesn't get delivered from his most important issue: he's sitting in Babylon, while wishing he was in Jerusalem. Worse, his God has been humiliated. It looks as if the Babylonian gods are more powerful since they routed his beloved Yahweh in battle.

Daniel's resolution comes in a staggering insight wrapped in an exhausting dream – his God has him in Babylon because the God of Israel's kingdom actually includes all the nations. He is not just the God of Israel, but of the whole world.

Daniel never goes home, and never needs to.

Now I want the listener to feel the relief that Daniel felt, and I felt. God seemed to be defeated, yet through the bitterness of the defeat, we realized that he is much bigger than we thought, and up to something far greater than we dreamed!

So I try to structure the sermon to create the same experience.

I start by setting up a tension like this – Daniel's always getting delivered, and we're not. We feel like second rate Christians.

Then I increase the tension by pointing out that in the Christian world there is a deliverance industry. All around us, the bookshelves are groaning with testimonies of how God healed Sandra from terminal cancer, or brought a million dollars into the life of Ted. And we feel like the only ones not getting delivered.

Then I switch back to Daniel with a story about the limits of deliverance. OK, you are healed. But you are still going to die. You're never really delivered… from certain things. The big things still loom up menacingly. Daniel may have been released from the lion's den, but he's not released from the pain of knowing that he is not free to return to Jerusalem. I went on to outline what this big issue was for Daniel, and how it might parallel in the life of the listener.

With all that tension piled up, I release the insight of the dream, creating the feeling that God is more sovereign than we ever thought, and only a "non-deliverance" experience can make us see that. I finish by asking, "What's your Babylon?" in the lives of the listeners.

The structure somewhat guarantees the experience. They feel the truth. They are not just informed by it. And they feel it because I felt it first. Most important of all, the experience has to be one Daniel had from the text. It has to be exegetically honest. It's easy to create an experience for the listener. It's much harder to create an experience of the biblical truth.

I must confess a great indebtedness to the thought of the Princeton Practical Theologian, James Loder, who posited a five-element logic of transformation. This logic is a universal structure for experience and insight, and one can pattern a sermon after it with great effect. His logic is split up into these steps though they are not necessarily sequential (for example, the insight frequently comes before the conflict is identified):

1 **Conflict-in-context:** There is incoherence, disequilibrium, and fragmentation. A problem needs to be solved. It weighs with us. We have to solve it.
   Example: Daniel's problem – his God delivers, but not from Babylon? Why?

2 **Interlude and scanning:** We search for solutions. Our whole being will work on the problem, including our will and the unconscious mind if we feel the conflict keenly enough. We try this solution and that. Most do not work, but it is vital in the process to make attempts.
   Example: Could God be less powerful than the Babylonian gods? Is God's power not so powerful outside Israel?

3 **Insight felt with intuitive force:** There is that breakthrough moment when the conflict is resolved. What brings it is something of a mystery, as the insight seems to come from the blue.
   Example: The God of Israel is also the God of Babylon, and his kingdom is universal, not national.

4 **Release and repatterning:** There is a release and redirection of the psychic energy bound up with the original conflict. The person who has just solved the puzzle literally feels the tension going, and is changed by solving it.
   Example: Daniel is a stronger believer for seeing how much greater his God is. And see how much God teaches us about himself and his kingdom by *not* delivering his people. We must redefine deliverance to include the insights of endurance. How often do we bend God to our system and miss his revelations?

5 **Interpretation and verification:** It is not enough simply to have the insight and feel release. The value of the insight must be tested and fully demonstrated to make sure it is genuine. It must also be tested publicly and subjected to the tests of the wider community.

Example: Look at how much more Israel discover about God's intentions and love during and after the exile, as opposed to before it? What does Babylon teach us that Jerusalem cannot?

This transformational logic, claims Loder, is universal in its application. It is of the essence of the human spirit, part of the image of God. Obviously, if it is universal, it should be visible everywhere. One cannot help it operating because if we are spirit, we have this logic. It even governs a human's developmental growth. It also reveals why we are storytellers, and the logic actually forms the structure of transformational narrative.[35] More radically perhaps, it is a complete episte-mology. It is, literally, a description of the way we know, and the way we gain breakthroughs in our knowing. Using it allows the preacher to structure a listening experience within the sermon, so that it becomes a real transformative event, involving all aspects of the human being.

Let me round up some of the key ingredients for this experience test:

- You must have a powerful outline that delivers an experience. Fosdick used an inductive therapeutic form. A more intense form is narrative. Actually the good old deductive form can do it too. Whatever your structure, it must ensure that you build up enough tension so that your insight – when it comes – is felt with real force. They experience the truth.
- You must see the transformation of the listener as beginning during the sermon itself. Don't just hope that they think about it later. See the sermon as the opportunity to be the beginning of the solution.
- You must have the faith to believe that words are actions too. Gospel words are not just words. They are bombs that

explode deep in the heart of the hearer through the power of the Spirit. Never say, "Oh, I haven't done anything, I've only spoken." To speak the gospel is to act, to launch the only solution the world will ever need to its problems.

- You must experience the text yourself first in order to know what experience you want to convey to the listener.
- You must not fear to have affective goals for the sermon as well as cognitive goals. There is nothing wrong with trying to move the listener. It is not manipulative to seek to engage their entire being with the truth. Manipulation is when the preacher overwhelms the emotions (or the mind for that matter), and creates a disorientation that actually takes the power of will away from the listener.

I commend the experience test. Seek to move the listener with the truth. Don't be content merely to inform them. Do something to them! Remember, you will move them. Try to move them toward Christ, not away from him. That is our awesome responsibility.

Letter 14:
The reality test – "where they live"

Or, Am I describing the real world of my listeners?

Yes, the experience test is tricky to get a grip on. I count it my biggest preaching failure that I took so long to waken up to the fact that it was a dimension of preaching in the first place.

Think of that specific preaching assignment you have coming up in a month – Habakkuk. All right, we both know that it is a book about how perplexity *at* the will of God ends with a greater faith *in* the will of God. So the experience test involves the attempt to reproduce this movement in the heart of the listener from perplexity to trust. You are too smart an exegete to make the common mistake of thinking that Habbakuk is perplexed as to what the will of God is. That's not really his problem in the book, although he starts in with it. One has to do justice to the specific nature of Habbakuk's perplexity. He knows what God is up to – God is sending the Chaldeans to judge Israel. His problem is, how God is working out his will seems indefensible to him. His God, who is supposed to love Israel more than any other nation, is, apparently, on the side of the Chaldeans, who are slaughtering Israelis at the rate of ten a second. Habbakuk asked God for justice, only to discover God is bringing it – courtesy of Israel's enemies. But if anyone needs judgment more than Israel, it has to be the Chaldeans.

So his issue is: *What's a God like mine doing mixed up with a bunch like that?* That's his perplexity. A more modern parallel might be a German Christian praying for revival in the 1920s and hearing God reply, "I've heard your prayers, and I will answer – I'm raising up the Nazis." I'm not saying God raised up the Nazis, only that the perplexity the German Christian might feel would begin to put him in poor Habbakuk's shoes.

So the task is to bring home to the audience – with some voltage – Habbakuk's experience of feeling that God is not on their side at all, but on the side of their enemies. Of course, not everyone will have the exact same perplexity as Habbakuk. I'm not suggesting that feeling betrayed by God is an everyday experience, but there are universal elements in it. Find these parallels in the life of the listener. Why did the foul-mouthed guy at the office who was always mocking Christianity get the promotion and the Christian was passed over? Why are the two elders making that pastor's life miserable at the moment prospering so much in business? Why does God allow Kim Jong Il, the leader of North Korea, to have power when he oppresses 22 million people so dreadfully? Why have so many dictators died peacefully in their sleep when they have deprived millions of the right to live? Why does God not deal more swiftly with the enemies of the faith? Make your listeners feel it, and you have brought Habakkuk's quest back from the seventh century BC to the twenty-first century AD. His quest deserves to be felt. Make the truth an experience. Then you must go on to give them an experience of relief as they attain a vision of God so great that they are content even "if the fig tree does not bud." That's going to be hard. It is a very difficult test. But please feel free to fail. It isn't easy. I fail all the time in this, but I still find it useful to try for this dimension in a sermon. At the very least, it deepens my own encounter with the passage.

Well, enough said. Time to move on to the reality test.

Maybe it's because I just saw the animated film *Finding Nemo*, but so much modern preaching makes me feel like a clown fish listening to a deep sea angler fish telling me how to live on a coral reef.

I live in a world of glorious Technicolor. Vivid purples, bilious pinks, dappled greens all shimmer before me. There are colors even Rembrandt couldn't mix on his palette. It's beautiful, and dangerous too. You have to know how to separate warning from welcoming coloration, distinguish predators from grazers, poisonous plant from nourishing plant. Along comes this grey ugly fish to give me a talk entitled "God's ten key principles for survival on the reef." I can't resist staring at his awful teeth, but he has an earnest air. He wants to help. Trouble is, he only knows two colors – the black of the deep ocean and the white light of his lure. He wouldn't know a bright orange sponge if it rubbed him on the underbelly. The miracle of photosynthesis is a mystery to him. He can't relate the principles to where I'm living. I need to know if that fish with the yellow and blue scales is my enemy or my friend. But he can't tell me, because his universe is only in black and white. He doesn't know my world, my reality.

Preachers often oversimplify life into black and white while their audience lives in color. They can't relate the gospel to people who live "on the reef." For example, when I was visiting a big Evangelical Anglican church in a southern English city, the female vicar got up to speak on the phrase "Do not be anxious" (Matt. 6:25). She began by warning us that we mustn't make Norman Vincent Peale our guide. "*Do not be anxious* is a theological truth, not a self-help principle," she told us sternly. Good start. What exactly the theology was, though, passed me by in a couple of mumbled paragraphs. Then she asked, "OK, so how do we stop worrying?" Three points: (1) Do what you can, then trust God. (2) Don't project anxiety into the future. (3) Readjust your perspectives. "We must realign reason with emotion. If you let doubts get out of control, you're in trouble."

Illustration time. She told us that she had doubts once. Big ones. About her future. She had been sleepless with anxiety. She leaned forward and gave us our prescription: "Just learn some promises of God, repeat them at night and you'll have a great sleep. It works for me. Whenever I wake up with doubts, I just repeat the promises of God, and I'm soon snug as a bug in a rug." I kid you not!

That's a failure of the reality test. She failed to describe where her audience spiritually lived. Most people were thinking, "What planet is this woman on? I'm glad for you, but that's not how it happens for me. I live on planet anxiety, and I can't find a simple way to conquer my fears." That vicar has crucially failed to describe where her audience is with anxiety, and so her solutions seem simplistic. Anxiety is more than just fretting about the future. There are deep roots of it

that are often not of our making. To suggest that the whole
gamut can be sidelined by Scripture memorization is just daft.
Thank God Job never followed her advice, or we wouldn't
have the book's profound treatment of suffering in the world.
There are forms of doubt that are healthy. Surely a more real
question is: when is a doubt useful to my spiritual walk, and
when is it destructive? Reality is a lot more nuanced. But she
oversimplified reality in order to preach to it. She cut down the
problem to preach a cut-down solution. The price is a failure
to connect God's reality to the listener's reality. If that vicar is
saying, "All doubts are bad, quote the promises and they will
go away," then what she has really said to her audience is,
"Just try harder, and remember, this only works for vicars and
super-saints!" She will never realize that this "gospel" doesn't
communicate, because she is completely clueless about life on
the reef. Yet the reef is where her audience swims!

By the reality test I mean that the preacher's job is to describe
authentically the real world of the hearer and plant the truth
into that reality so that the listener says, "Yes, that's where I
am, show me how to get out of this bind," rather than, "I'm
glad that *you* find it all that simple."

Is this vicar too extreme an example? The reality failure does
take more subtle forms. One way is when a sermon is loaded
with "musts." My first homiletics class was taught by an old
Scottish Presbyterian master called Ian Pitt-Watson, now gone
to the great Golden Pulpit in the sky. He had a number of
mantras, and one was: *The gospel is given to us in indicatives,
but we have turned it into a gospel of imperatives.* You have to
imagine him rolling his "r"s – imperrrrratives! The first time
he said this there was an uncomprehending silence. The fact is
that we didn't really know our grammar well enough to know
what he was on about. After digging out the old school text
book, I grasped his point, especially as I saw someone do it
the next Sunday. The preacher's main point – "We must sit
more at the feet of Jesus!" – was a predictable application of
the passage where Jesus visits the house of Mary and Martha.
The preacher gave us an imperative – we must sit. But in
the gospels there are no imperatives in the account. It is all
description. Everything is in the indicative mood. This is how

it was. Martha is cooking. Mary is sitting. And so it is with the balance of the whole gospel story. *You must be born again,* is the exception. *He entered Jericho,* is the norm. The way the gospel is written and spoken is primarily not exhortation, but description of the action of God in the lives of individuals and nations.

If the preacher just uses an imperative, we still don't know what that looks like in action. It has not been embedded into the world of lived life. The preacher said, "We must sit at the feet of Jesus." Well, I try to. But I have problems being a Mary. It would be a lot easier if Jesus came to my house in physical form. The preacher went further: "If it is important to us, surely we would do it." Well, I know it is important to do it, but I still fail more often than not. The preacher then clubs me with, "If you don't do it, then it shows that you don't really love Jesus deep down." Thanks for the guilt, but he is still not describing my reality, nor the reality for most Christians. Jesus has not come to us and said, "Would you rather cook the stew or sit at my feet?" That's not the choice as it comes to the audience. If it were that simple, that black and white, then sure, I'd sit at the feet of Jesus. But in reality – where most Christians are – we think sitting at the feet of Jesus is a great idea, but somehow we can't seem to do it often enough. Now why is that? How does that happen? How do we fail? Describe that process and you've got the hearer!

That preacher's reality assumptions were all off. He thought, "If I can tell them to sit, then they will sit." But we are *already* all agreed that it's a good idea to sit at the feet of Jesus; the point is, in real life, it ain't easy. Move onto that territory, describe it, and find ways to sit with Jesus, and the preacher just might have a chance of putting the gospel into the lived world of the hearers.

So what's involved in the reality test? How can we ensure that we connect to the real world of the hearer? Let's break it into three steps. It involves:

- a description of reality which is authentically complex;
- an explanation of reality that is genuinely insightful;
- a reframing of reality that is biblically liberating.

Now let's look at each of these in turn.

1. A description of reality which is authentically complex

The key here is to get a feel for the *human bind*. Life is complicated because our choices are not easy. The evangelist who asks, "Will you choose for heaven or will you choose for hell?" is surely wrong. What kind of doofus does he think I am? Of course I'll choose for heaven. Anyone would choose for heaven if you are going to put it in terms that stark. It's like asking a starving man would he prefer to eat or fast. But in life, most choices do not come to us that way. They appear as dilemmas. We choose between the bad and the bad, the good and the good, the hard and the hard. On the reef of reality, life is ambiguous and complex. Often the consequences of our choices are hidden from us, and we make our decisions in unfortunate ignorance. Often we make choices unaware.

Look at this with some biblical characters. Take that perennial baddie, Caiaphas. Was he really just a blood-loving psychopath who wanted to see Jesus suffering a gruesome death, as Mel Gibson's *The Passion of the Christ* depicts him? In reality, Caiaphas had a bind. Jesus was a known troublemaker coming to Jerusalem at Passover time, when rioting was common. One more riot and Pilate had his excuse to wipe the Jews out. That was Caiaphas's reading of the situation, and he was in a position to know the stakes. So he made his fateful calculation: it is expedient that one man should die for the people. You would – in other circumstances – call it a statesmanlike calculation. As J.K. Galbraith once said, "The art of politics does not consist in choosing between the good and the bad, but between the unpalatable and the disastrous." We now applaud Winston Churchill, who took the "Caiaphas option" in the Second World War. Told via a spy cryptographer that the Nazis were about to bomb Coventry, Churchill faced a hard choice. Should he warn Coventry, and save hundreds of lives? Yet if he did, he would signal to the Germans that Britain had cracked their communication codes. They would then change their codes and Britain would lose its intelligence advantage over the enemy. Churchill judged it better in the long run not to warn Coventry, and to let thousands die, in order to preserve an intelligence advantage that resulted in D-Day, the successful allied landing in Normandy. I'm sure he didn't sleep well when Coventry was taking a pounding, but he never regretted his action. Like Churchill, Caiaphas's calculation was successful up to a point – the Jewish nation did survive for at least another forty years. But within those alternatives, what was his sin? That's when it gets interesting!

That's Caiaphas's reality. Pilate had another bind: his job or justice. Not both. He couldn't let this innocent man go and hold onto his job. The gospel writers have an eye for the complexity of human behavior. Sure there are psychopaths, and not all of us exhibit the same complexity, but life as we live it is complicated, not simple. The preacher must develop a nose for how complex and ambiguous lived life actually is.

So when a preacher tells me to pray for healing, I also want him to acknowledge that probably 90 percent of his audience has prayed for healing and not received it. That's their reality. John Wimber shared candidly that only 5 percent of those he prayed for were healed. Don't oversimplify the world in order to preach to it, or you just make Christians simplistic. Millions of Christians the world over struggle with a critical disconnect: *the faith they are taught does not fit the world they find!* Instead of being allowed to talk of this reality gap, the preacher ignores it, or makes people feel guilty for being smart enough to see it. These people are then forced to begin searching for another context in which their issues can be aired honestly and understood in all complexity. Alas, for many, that is not in another church!

2. An explanation of reality that is genuinely insightful

Say you are talking about intercessory prayer. You can describe how difficult it is in practice to know when a prayer has been answered, or how to keep praying when it hasn't. That's description. But the preacher has to take this further, and deal with factors that explain this reality. For example, why don't I want to pray? What are the factors of resistance? Can the preacher help me here, to know what I don't know myself? Where's the insight as to why the listener might be in this bind? What is the element in reality that sabotages successful faith?

Think back to that preacher who was bidding us all to sit at the feet of Jesus. Instead of telling us that we should all be sitting there, what we really needed was an insight as to why it was so hard. Maybe the problem is really to do with the difficulty of sitting still. How, then, do I sit still? That might be the insight: we have lost the ability to still the spirit. So let's have some pointers on recovering stillness. The preacher might have taught us *lectio divina*[36] for that purpose. Or, maybe the insight is that we are afraid of Jesus. We're afraid he might judge us because we were raised in families where God was an angry, kill-joy deity. No wonder we don't want to sit at the feet of a God like that. Our job is to recover a God of purer love. Or maybe the insight is more to do with not finding the feet of Jesus in our fragmented lives. Scripture doesn't cut it as the feet of Jesus. How do we make Scripture into a body of flesh and blood that speaks to us?

See what I mean about getting to the insight that explains why their reality might be the way it is? But many preachers persist in saying, "There's the principle, now go and be obedient." They miss the essential point: many Christians want to be obedient, but they don't know how to be! No amount of telling them to be more obedient is going to help.

3. A reframing of reality that is biblically liberating

Reality is catastrophically misdescribed by the world. It is shrunk down. Fallen humans wish to manage life without God, so whenever they face a problem, they are careful to re-define it in such a way that it can be solved through material or merely human means. We don't ask, "What is the meaning of death?" Rather, we ask, "How can I manage the dying process?"

There was a radio program about prostitution a few weeks ago. The audience was invited to participate in the discussion, but the presenter warned them, "We are not going to make moral judgments here… we just want to solve this." The discussion then focused on two issues: the use of condoms and police procedure. The behavior of prostitution, and its causes in "grooming," drug abuse, sexual abuse, lovelessness, and lust, were ignored. This limited approach will never get to the causes of prostitution. When preachers get to a subject, they have to re-extend reality back to its fuller biblical dimensions.

A helpful method for doing this is one I heard first from Richard Mouw, since 1994 the President of Fuller Theological Seminary: look at any issue through the four acts of God's story with us – creation, fall, redemption, and consummation. Place each issue in its fullest theological context. In this way, we consider what was originally intended, what has gone wrong, what will put it right, and what is its destiny. For example, in the issue of prostitution, it might go something like this.

- **Creation** – Human beings are created to enjoy sex. It's not wrong. But it is a relationship of joy and equality. There is no perversion envisaged, or abuse. That women – or men for that matter – should be even asked, let alone coerced, to sell their bodies has no place in God's world.
- **Fall** – We each have a capacity to abuse others rather than love them. Men particularly are prone in their very hearts to exploit rather than care for women. It is lust out of control, and lovelessness in the home. When I visited a ministry that helped prostitutes in Bristol, England, I learned that 95 percent of all women prostitutes had been abused sexually by a male figure in their lives. Prostitution is not a bit of harmless fun. Life is not a French film, in which bored housewives take an interesting career turn. The whole phenomenon has its roots in what is universally dreadful.
- **Redemption** – Christ gives every person the ability to value the other, not to exploit them. Indeed, our Lord models it. The true Christian parent will not abuse their child, and will help them lovingly if they take a wrong turn. The true Christian will not abuse someone else's body, because they are sacred. Churches are often the only context that can provide the long-term love and forgiveness to help prostitutes into a new life. That is what will reduce prostitution much more effectively, not only condoms and

flexible policing. It's not easy, and it takes years to help a person break free, but it is possible with the help of God.

- **Consummation** – The ultimate goal is to live together in mutual joy and peace, valuing each other. That vision is what motivates us. That aging female prostitute is still a child of God who could have a destiny as a beautiful being in the new creation, the eternal kingdom. We have a hope that motivates us to make a difference now.

The whole issue can be reframed away from how to manage a social issue into seeing prostitutes as children of God and intervening in a way that is loving and supportive, offering a way out of destructive behavior patterns through the forgiving love of Christ. This is most often through rehabilitation programs, half-way homes, basic-skills training, and vocational counseling, but it is Christ that gives them the motivation to start and complete these programs, and very often, at least in places like St. Paul's Bristol, it is the church and not the government that run these programs. Notice that we have not just talked knowledgeably about the problem. We place all problems and issues into a great biblical drama of four acts – creation-fall-redemption-consummation – which are the true dimensions of reality. Don't let others shrink reality down to material dimensions. The preacher's job is to stretch the canvas of reality back out to its full theological frame, and connect human life to God, without whom it is a shrunken, foolish thing.

To be credible then, the preacher has to talk in such a way that the audience feels like they know how to live as a Christian in the real world. This credibility is gained through an authentic description of reality in all its ambiguity, complexity, and even stupidity. But we are not just describing the difficulties of living. Any modern novelist does that. Our job is to connect the reality of God's reign to the messy reality of life. Most of us are trying to be faithful Christians. Most of us are failing at it. God loves us anyway, but we'd rather please him. Exploring how we please him as we fail him is the key to the reality test.

Letter 15:
The exegetical test –
"with the word"

Or, Am I preaching the divine insight from the Bible?

It's funny you should mention your dream, because last night at a particularly boisterous meeting of the PAAP club we were sharing "preacher's nightmares." Bad dreams I mean. I must not break anyone's confidence, though there were some doozies in there. Personally, I love nightmares, because they are so wonderful to wake up from. Waking up is normally a ho-hum kind of activity, but when you wake up from a surreal world, where the walls of the church are made of sea waves and the sky is raining purple semolina, whew, what a joy to return to the reliable predictabilities of Newton and Einstein's laws of motion.

I have two preaching nightmares. One is where I am up in front of an expectant audience and I can't find the passage I'm supposed to be dealing with. Sometimes the Bible melts, other times it just stubbornly is the wrong passage even though I have turned up the right page, and my cheeks sting painfully with embarrassment as I run out of repartee to cover for my ineptitude. The other variety is where my tongue grows fat and furry, like an anaconda is trying to get out through my mouth. I try to speak, but the more I try, the more I just spew vomit sounds like Ionescu's mute in *The Chairs*: "grooocch, bllaarrrgggghhhh." Joy inexpressible waking up from those. I was frankly surprised that everyone in the meeting last night had recurring nightmares. Just shows how much nervous exhaustion is involved in taking preaching seriously. Anyway, thank you for sharing yours. I covenant not to psycho-analyze yours if you will leave mine well alone.

Briefly, the matter of feeling that your words lack power when you preach. Every preacher feels that way regularly enough, or ought to. Preaching is warfare, so there are always going to be voices from the pit: "you're not worthy; your words are unclear; God's wasn't in it or there would be revival," etc. Take a leaf from that good ex-soldier Ignatius of Loyola and talk sternly back to the bad spirit. Also, and I admit this is a theological reality that is hard to inhabit, maybe our words are powerful not because of what they do, but because of where they go! Remember Hebrews 10:19: "So friends, we can now, without hesitation, walk right up to God, into the Holy Place. Jesus has cleared the way by the blood of his sacrifice" (*Message*). Is it true that the preacher's words, uttered in the name of Christ, pass through the throne room of the universe where Christ sits to the heart of the listener? Have we got the focus wrong? Not, what do the words do, but where do the words go! Our words become *his* words, and we can relax somewhat, since the effects are in *his* hands, not ours.

Too highfaluting I hear you say? Easier said than done? Amen.

Onwards… to the exegetical test.

All sermons – well, the better ones anyway – are composed of three insights. First, and most importantly (for this is what makes it preaching) there is the *divine insight,* a truth that cannot be derived from any other source but the speech of God. Christianity is, after all, a revealed religion. Hear Helmut Thielicke preaching on Genesis 1. What's the divine insight that he majors on?

> …that everything that happens in the world – my little life with its cares and its joys, and also the history of the world at large extending from stone-age man to the atomic era – that all this is, so to speak, a *discourse enclosed, upheld, and guarded by the breath of God.*[37]

This is what I mean by "the word from above." You cannot derive from any other source of information that the world is created and sustained by a word from a divine mouth. That information – bizarre at a first hearing – has literally come "from above." This is why the preacher's task is to preach the Bible, the repository of these essential insights from God himself.

There is a second level of insight operating in the sermon, the wisdom insight. The Bible contains a huge tranche of teaching that is just good old solid wisdom. "Go to the ant, you sluggard!" "Don't commit adultery." "Don't bear false witness." These are principles of behavior that do not require a divine insight to be discovered. They can be deduced from a careful observation of life and history. In that sense they are natural principles. Yet they surely have their place in a sermon. How often do we preach the virtues of keeping a clean conscience, hanging on when the going gets tough, staying honest when everyone else is fiddling their expenses? In the modern world of the therapeutic, managerial, and scientific revolutions, many preachers incorporate valuable insights from these contemporary "wisdom traditions" with great effect. A sermon I read recently on marriage told the congregation that psychologists had discovered that the number one reason for marriage break up was financial mismanagement and misunderstandings in the first five years of the relationship. She gave methods and advice to guard against this marriage wrecker. That's useful. Thielicke, in the Genesis 1 sermon, muses on the futility of asking questions about creation that cannot be answered – an insight also expressed memorably in the writings of Confucius.

A skill a preacher does need is to relate the wisdom insight to the divine insight. This is modeled for us in the Bible's wisdom literature. Proverbs 22:22 says "Do not rob the poor because they are poor," but verse 23 goes on to say why: "For the Lord pleads their cause." The point of being wise is not to be wise, but to please God, or to avoid displeasing a God who intervenes in the running of the universe still. Natural principles do not necessarily commend themselves by themselves. For example, why work hard? Why not just drop out and sponge off society? It makes more sense to sponge than work if God is not part of the equation. If life is just about surviving until we die, then let others pay for my survival. Practical wisdom is always dependent upon a grander paradigm of divine insight, which defines life's purpose and meaning.

Thirdly, there is the *personal insight* of the preacher. Of all the divine insights on offer in the Bible or in a particular passage, which one am I going to take and put to work for this group at this moment in time? This requires a personal insight. The divine insight has to be taken from above, and made to work down below. That's the task of the preacher.

Stick with Thielicke to see what his personal insight was. How did he make the insight that the "world is run by the breath of God" work for his particular audience in the Germany of the 1960s? Thielicke realizes that many in his audience are struggling with a view that the world turns an indifferent yawn to their fate. He identifies ways in which this manifests powerfully – in nihilism, in an atheistic version of evolutionary theory, in the aftermath of a terrible world war, and so on. Then, he says:

> My life too is fashioned and guided by the same hands that beckoned the stars and the flowers at the world's dawning and make the day and the night… If a thousand years in his sight are but as yesterday, then in his eyes even my little cares will weigh no less than the immensities of Sirius; then for him the tiny stretches of my daily journey, for which I ask his blessing, are just as important as the light years that measure the reaches of cosmic space.[38]

Thielicke's personal insight is to apply the divine insight to the crushing sense of insignificance in his listener. A single person's collection of atoms matters more to the one who holds everything together than an entire galaxy. This is why the preacher's experience is such a large part of the exegetical process. We take ourselves to the text, and the experience of our listeners too. We query, fight, scream, and shout at the text in order to find out how this divine insight could actually help us. We have to ask questions like, "Can I believe it? Is it credible? Does it really work?" The answer should show up in the life of the preacher: she knows that the divine insight will work for her audience because it has worked for her!

In sum, the exegetical test involves three questions: Is my personal insight in line with the divine insight? Am I really preaching a divine insight? Have I linked the wisdom insight to the divine insight? The preacher has to develop a nose for the divine insight, a kind of exegetical antennae.

How? For me, it's a two stage process – *gripping* and *checking*. Exegesis begins with being gripped by the passage, and continues with checking that the truth we have been gripped by is in line with the author's intention.

I'm concentrating here on the discovery of the divine insight. That's commonly regarded as the task of exegesis, which was defined at my seminary as "the art of articulating the meaning of a passage as it was intended by the original author." We were taught an array of tools for unearthing the author's intent – grammatical analysis, textual criticism and lexical study, source criticism, form criticism, redactional analysis, historical cultural background, and theological synthesis. Quite a heavy tool bag all in all. Cost me the best part of US$20,000 in fees to learn those skills. But I've got to tell you – the tools don't give you the nose!

In fact, there is a daft idea that you need to be a "Greek geek" to have any chance of unearthing a divine insight through the author's intent. If you don't know Greek and Hebrew, then you have no chance of acquainting yourself with the basic tradition of interpretation of any single passage. True, but then the question is: why do I have to? Exegesis is a spiritual activity before it is a technical one. The best exegesis starts with stillness. There's a wonderful paragraph in Walter J. Burghart's autobiography. Worried that he was not an expert in scriptural interpretation, he wondered if he had the right to preach at all. Then he writes

> What I did discover, for my homiletic consolation, is that I did not need to be. What is necessary? God's written word must take hold of me as God's spoken word took hold of Isaiah and Jeremiah, of Ezekiel and Hosea; as the spoken word of Christ mesmerized Matthew and Magdalene, captured Simon Peter and the Samaritan woman. How? Basically, the word I study has to be the word I pray, and the word I pray has to be the word I live.[39]

Let me share how I start on a text. First, I do twenty minutes of centering prayer. I am just trying to still the body, trying to stop the riot of my own life, so that when I come to the text, I will not just bring my busyness, or my usual issues. Don't get me wrong. We want to take all of ourselves to the text. It's nonsense to talk of the personality just falling away, and becoming a clay tablet on which the Holy Spirit writes. No, all of ourselves is what God writes on, and the more of ourselves we bring to the text, the more he has to speak to.

Second, I do forty minutes of *lectio devina*, an ancient way of reading Scripture that probably came from the first real preacher of church history, Origen of Alexandria. I take the passage and read it slowly in about five versions. If it's from the New Testament I have a stab at it in Greek. For the first ten minutes, I answer this question aloud: what is this passage about? Just describe the events, characters, and issues. For the next ten, I go through the passage with my five senses. Say I am taking the passage of Jesus stilling the storm in Mark 4:35–41. I would see the awful wave walls, hear the cries of terrified men, grip the rough wood of the bulkhead, smell the sweat of the men at the oars, and taste the tang of the angry sea. I would strain every sensual sinew to be right in that boat. For the next ten minutes, I would try to enter into each character in the passage and ask, "What would they be feeling?" The idea is to get into the emotions of the scene. To feel the sharp sting of rebuke in Jesus' words following the amazement of the stilling. Finally, I spend the last ten minutes on the question: what is God saying to me through this passage?

This method can be expanded of course. There are times I have spent hours on each section. I find it useful because it provides a way to engage my whole self with the passage. I don't just treat it as intellectual information. I am part of the action. My whole imagination is involved, and soon I am gripped by an aspect of the truth that I begin to fashion into arranged thoughts. The sermon is underway. I then use some exegetical tools – investigating the background of key words, or the literary context in more depth. The most valuable exegetical questions in my experience are:

- What does this passage say about God?
- What was this word supposed to do for the original readers?

- In addition to what does it mean, what is it between? The clue to the meaning is so often in the placing.
- Track the word through three layers of reception. What did this passage mean to the author(s)? What did it mean to the original reading and listening community? And, finally, could it work in the same way for us today as it did for the original characters and readers?

Whatever skills you have, you put them to use as you are gripped. The hands of the text grip you by the spiritual lapels, and you are bound to preach its truth. You are involved. Committed. Under conviction.

After the gripping, it's time for checking. I find that the best and shortest way to check my interpretation and application is to consult about three or four commentaries. If they confirm that I am on track, good. If they suggest that I'm not really getting at the heart of it, then I will start again.

A preacher's relationship with commentaries is a crucial one. My two rules are: don't ignore them, and don't consult them too early. Don't ignore them is obvious enough. Consulting them is a way of checking whether or not you have fallen off the exegetical beam. Going to them too early, however, is equally disastrous as it robs you of a primal encounter with the passage. It becomes harder to have your own thoughts and feelings about the truths as you tend to be more impressed with those of the commentators. The commentator cannot tell you what to preach from this passage to your audience. They don't know your audience. Also, commentaries are narrowly focused. The prime consideration is usually, what did this text originally mean? We do not preach solely meaning. We preach the contemporary implication of the meaning.

There is a version of expository preaching which maintains that the main task of the sermon is to explain the meaning of the passage, and largely to let the congregation make the application. This often results in a sermon that is a verse-by-verse structure. I always think that if the aim is clarity and getting one's personality out of the way, why not just read the commentary from the pulpit? The commentator has more skill in expression, more experience in interpretation, and more time to interact with the entire tradition of interpretation than the average preacher.

I've always inclined to Ian Pitt-Watson's equation of expository preaching with biblical preaching. He wrote that "all authentic preaching is expository preaching because it derives its substance from Scripture and is an 'exposition' of it."[40] He goes on to restate the heart of the exegetical test:

> We must preach biblically, or not at all. If what I am saying is not rooted in Scripture, then, however interesting or edifying it may be, it is not preaching. Preaching is *kerygma*, the proclamation of what God has done in Jesus Christ. The sole source of our knowledge of what God has done comes to us through the text of Scripture under the guidance of the Holy Spirit. We neither have nor require any other authority.[41]

I agree. If you don't preach the divine insight, then you are not preaching. Preach the divine insight, and the power and authority of God is released. Don't you agree?

Letter 16:
The grandeur test – "from above"

Or, Am I preaching the greatness of God and addressing the universal questions of life?

Yes, making an impact as preachers is never really about us, though we can sabotage the clarity of the communication. In this connection, I must share Brother Bao's story, a man I met on a trip inside Vietnam in 1996.

Conscripted by the Kymer Rouge in 1966 while only 17, he became totally dehumanized by the war. He saw his best friends shot; his girlfriend raped then strangled. To get by, Bao chewed a jungle leaf prized for its narcotic qualities, and would lapse into dreams of a perfect world, then waken to the hell of war.

One day, his troop ambushed a Southern Vietnamese patrol, and after a fierce skirmish only one of the enemy survived. They lined him up to be shot and gave him a last request. Bucking the usual custom of asking for a last cigarette, the prisoner asked that a portion of a book he had in his top pocket be read to him. Bao began to read the words out loud, "And Jesus said…" But he got no further. Suddenly the air was full of thunder and the trees around them shredded with bullets. He dived for cover and just managed to escape the destructive path of the helicopter gunship.

Next day, he asked his troop leader, "What did Jesus say?" The troop leader looked shocked. Bao said, "Look, it must have been something important for that guy to want to hear it before his death." His leader was furious, and told him he was reporting him to the political commissar. Bao knew he was in serious trouble. On the march back he was struck with painful diarrhea, and the troop waited by a tree for him to go a little distance and relieve himself. There was a loud boom, and Bao returned to the tree to find his companions hanging in bits from the foliage. They were all dead. He continued as a soldier for four more years. Every day he wondered *what Jesus said.*

Finally, when he reached Saigon and his side was victorious, he found a Bible on a dead person, re-covered it with brown paper, and read it all the way back to Hanoi. He said, "I finally got to read what Jesus said, and I decided I wanted to die to those words too." But he added, "I was spared by God even when I was in my sins. The diarrhea was what saved me, and that was God. Otherwise I would have been in bits like the rest of my troop. But God wanted to save me, and he spared me to hear what Jesus had to say."

What a testimony to the power of God and the power of his word – to intrigue Bao for four long years with the phrase "and Jesus said." I told another preacher friend of mine about that story and he said, "It reminds me of what preaching really is… speaking words that God takes, sears them into someone's brain, then preserves that life to hear them and understand them. And I see how little I have to do with it. That's what humbles me. I used to think preaching was about how well I spoke. But now I see what God really does through the words that come from my mouth, and that blows my mind."

I'm not saying don't worry about the impact of your teaching. Just don't excessively brood on it, because impact is primarily God's business. There are so many factors involved that the preacher is simply not in control of – the state of the heart of the listener, the experiences they have had which make them react certain ways, even whether they have taken the right pills that very morning, and so forth. Leave some of the worry in the capable hands of God.

Right, onto the next test – the grandeur test.

Not that I know from experience, but one of the nice things that comes from being famous is that a lot of clever remarks get attributed to you that you never in fact uttered. Though I've never seen it in print, John Paul Sartre was once said to remark that life was like arriving to watch a complex play after it had started, being asked to act on stage without a script, and then having to leave before it ended. As he drank his hot chocolate in a Parisian café he concluded that the essential condition of existence was never having enough "information" to figure out life's meaning.

Contra Sartre, who can only return his cup to his saucer, the preacher's job is to tell the audience the *beginning* and the *end*, to locate them in the whole drama, providing a script, and to help bring meaning to their lives.

We are the custodians of *the plot*.

God gave it to us in his word.

This is an inkling of what I mean by the grandeur test. Am I preaching the greatness of God? Am I addressing the universal questions of life? Am I "staying grand," keeping the focus on life's most important issues and God's presence in them? Am I reminding people that this is God's world, and their life is not their own, but lent to them by God?

For example, where else can a person go to hear this question raised and answered... what is the world for?

Elizabeth Achtemeier has a wonderful answer to that. She says that it's because God likes music![42]

Nature abhors a silence, and choruses back to God all the time this tune: "Indeed, it is *very good*." So with us. Our job is to praise. Do that, and at the most fundamental level of life, we are alive with purpose.

That's good. Achtemeier writes elsewhere, "Great preachers talk mostly about God."[43] That sermon of hers – "God the Music Lover" – is all about how much he loves creation and rejoices in its praise music, from the croak of a terrapin to the banshee wails of a blue whale. The icing on the cake? Why, the Sunday morning congregation warbling through "Lo, He comes with clouds descending."

What a world! What a life! What a God! That's what we want people to experience when they hear a sermon. If they do, then the preacher has passed the grandness test.

* * *

Remember I told you about preaching on the book of Daniel? I said that years ago, I would have looked at chapter 6 and preached three points on God's deliverance. I'd have listed a set of lions in the congregation's lives, and promised that God could deliver them. I'd be right of course. He can. And occasionally does. But I would have missed the grander truth that the book of Daniel is really about.

Instead, I got up into the pulpit with a multicolored piece of modeling clay, round like an orange, and said:

> Once upon a time there was a beautiful orb. It was round and perfect. Suddenly a great hand descended and slapped it flat. Other fingers emerged and began to stretch it out till it resembled a snake. Soon it began to break in parts as it was rolled too thin. Then, just as it was about to lose all shape and fragment, something amazing happened. A new pair of hands emerged and joined the two ends of the snake together. This was amazing. The circle was drawn together until – at the end – the original ball was restored, a perfect orb once more. Only this time it was better, because it was now cradled in these hands that had made it perfect. Never again would it be slapped flat.

I acted all that out with the clay and finished with these words: "That's what the book of Daniel is about. That's what the world's about. That's what our lives are about."

The grander story is that God put the world back into shape for Daniel. His world had been flattened. The God of Israel has been defeated. He was faced with the sick notion that the God he worshiped was a little deity among a pantheon of more powerful gods. But through deliverances, and through dreams, the God of Israel becomes the God of the whole world, and the exile of humiliation becomes the means of salvation to the nations. Daniel's God gets bigger, and the world is remade and restored.

God often does that for all of us. Our world gets flattened. We lose our way. We fear that God is impotent, our faith misplaced. Yet the word puts it back together, and though we may still be exiles in Babylon, our eternal citizenship means far more. We have broken through to what is most important. More important than being delivered from that cancer, terrible though it is. More important than being released from that prison of addiction, horrible though that is. We see our lives as held in God's hands, infinitely precious, and the world as an arena of his loving agency. We have our hope extended into eternal dimensions.

Stay grand, because the gospel is grand!

* * *

I was recently helping a friend prepare a sermon on James 5:1–12. He began brilliantly. The first six verses mention all the injustices of the world, and he affirmed how it was right to feel outraged about it, even to the extent of having very little time for the Christian who would say, "Be patient Bro, the Lord's coming."

Then he said that we must do three things in the face of this overwhelming injustice: plant a mustard seed (v.7), keep going (v.11), be honest (v.12).

He didn't stay grand.

Was that how the prophets stayed patient in the midst of a world full of injustice (v.10)? No, they became inspired by a vision of a world-on-the-way where there was perfect justice. They were patient because they saw that in the meantime, God was giving humankind – in Newbigin's beautiful phrase – a "space for grace" to find the mercy of God before judgment. Outrage is replaced or at least joined with an assurance that perfect justice will be done on an eternal scale. For now, judgment is tempered with mercy lest we all perish.

How much greater is that than the prosaic "keep going and be honest"? Keeping going and being honest are useful, but frankly you don't need to be a Christian to do either. There's nothing *Christian* about this solution to the world's chronic injustices.

* * *

It's easy to stray from the grand line. We don't live there. Most preachers do not set out to be trivial, but often they end up giving us coping skills to deal with life, instead of giving us God who is life.

It's partly the age. Preachers feel bad that they are not respected experts any more, so they offset this sense of irrelevance by playing surrogate therapist or management guru. But remember, people don't come to church to hear modern woes dissected, or learn some coping strategies. What they want to hear is: where's God in all this? And that's where the role of the preacher comes in.

Perhaps the biggest culprit is the preacher's rush to sound *relevant.* "Preach on the topics that people are dealing with," we are urged. So if dads are bad, then you give a talk: "Five ways to be a great dad!" I don't want five ways on how to be a great dad from a preacher. I can get that from Anthony Robbins, the Dalai Lama, or watching the "Oprah Winfrey Show." What I want to hear from a preacher is – is God a great Dad? If so, why?

Practical steps have their place of course, but ground them in the grander story. Relate those five ways to be a better dad to the fatherhood of God. Tell me about God the Father. Tell me why God is a great father! Defend him convincingly from the charge of being an absentee dad. Show me the elements of his fatherly care and love for this world and its people.

Get this: the gospel doesn't have to be relevant. The preacher's goal is to reorient all of life around God and his ways in the world. Not all of that is going to pitch up as a five-stage strategy to get the kids up on Monday morning with more than the usual lack of grace. Give the listener some credit. They can set their own goals. They can manage their own day. Don't worry about being relevant. Catch them up in how much God loves them, cares for them, frets over them, works for them, stretches out a life of joy beyond the grave for them, pours grace upon grace into every nook and cranny of this bizarre adventure we call living, and you have made God relevant to everything. How can he not be, if you paint him in his true dimensions?

* * *

How do we stay grand? Ask four questions of the sermon:

1 Does it talk mostly about God? Does it really exalt the specialness of Christ? Ask where the focus really falls. Is it on practical strategies, or on the greatness of God? Great preachers talk mostly about God! Not about their church. Not about themselves.

2 Does it address the universal issues of humankind? Great preachers deal with great themes. When Dr. Billy Graham visited the old Soviet Union and told seminarians the

secrets of his preaching impact, he said he always majored on four omnipresent problems – emptiness, loneliness, guilt, and fear of death. And he also stressed that the solution to each was to proclaim the gospel of Jesus Christ, simply and authoritatively. Make sure you are really tackling a major existential issue of life. You can't preach a great sermon without a great subject.

3   Does it contain a Christian worldview? There are four questions in the worldview approach: Who am I? Where am I? What's wrong? What's the solution? Ask of the sermon, "Would the listener be able to answer those questions with the Christian worldview as a result?" Preaching seeks to restore a true perspective on life. We are reminded of the *grand scheme* within which we live our lives.

4   Does it have a Christ-centered resolution? Does it exalt Jesus Christ as the fullness of God and the grand distinctive of Christianity? This past Easter there was a series of sermons preached at my church on "the power of powerlessness." The sermons contained good descriptions of the evil people do in crowds, which has an obvious Easter bearing. However, the answer to this evil was put in these kinds of terms: "He met extravagant hatred with extravagant love/ love is the most powerful message of the cross/Jesus defeats death by the resolute persistence of his love." The preacher gave examples from Mandela and Gandhi. But this is a sub-Christian resolution. Jesus didn't defeat sin and death by performing an act of helpless love. It was because of his status as the divine substitute that his act of love could put our sin away. Jesus is not simply a first-century Gandhi. If he is, then there is nothing distinctive about Christianity. Fortunately, this was a church where the liturgy knew the meaning of the cross, even if the preacher didn't, and so we affirmed a theology in the hymns and ritual language that was far grander. For example, consider the fourth verse of "There is a Green Hill Far Away."

There was no other good enough
To pay the price of sin.
He only could unlock the gate
Of heaven, and let us in.

What a far cry from Jesus as moral exemplar. Or Jesus as a Nelson Mandela figure. We were bidden to the Eucharistic feast with these words: "Eat and Drink in remembrance that he died for you, and feed on him in your hearts with faith." Think how uncomfortable we would be to be asked to "receive the body of Mahatma Gandhi, which he gave for you, and Nelson Mandela's blood, which he shed for you?" It's blasphemous, but the preachers did not mean to be. They just failed to remember how grand and how unique Jesus Christ really is!

*   *   *

Tuning in to this grand dimension is not natural. I think that life contains three levels of hope. The first level is *surface hope.* These are the hopes that take up most of our lives. How to succeed in a career, how to have a family, how to have a better house, how to *leave a legacy* as the management gurus put it. These hopes are superficial, however, because they are governed by chance. Not everyone will succeed in a career. Some will not manage to have families, or bring up nice children. Often it will not be their fault. The world of work, for example, is pyramid shaped. Only a few get to the top. The rest have to deal with being below. It's OK, just nature's way of showing us that these hopes are superficial.

The second level is *foundation hope.* These are hopes that we take for granted to build our superficial hopes upon. We hope for good health. We hope to fall in love. We hope a bomb does not go off on our bus. We hope our country does not go to war. Without these foundational hopes, we cannot plan to succeed in anything. I knew a friend who retired from decades of teaching to write his masterpiece. No sooner had he sharpened his pencil and begun to write than he had a massive stroke and was unable to fulfill his lifelong ambition. Illness is so often the way that nature reminds us that we cannot take this foundation level of hope for granted.

At the deepest level is *eternal hope.* These hopes are secret and deep. Often they are hardest to articulate. If you live in the West, the education system will deliberately attempt to keep these hopes suppressed, dedicated as it is to keeping society focused on achieving the superficial hopes. But eternal hopes always come up. Will I find out who I am? Does God care about me? Does this world make any sense? Will I last, or will death swallow me and all my progeny?

Humans are foolish. Often it is only the collapse of the first two levels of hope that allows us to find any hope in life's deepest layers. Preachers have been put on earth to counteract this tendency. They must raise these eternal hopes up to the surface. It isn't easy. It isn't pretty. Nietzsche once warned, "When you look into the void, be warned, because the void looks back at you!"

Same with God. When we see the face of God in a sermon, it is a gaze at once loving and fearful, we attempt a thousand instant evasions. But life is to be lived around the pole of his love and care. We may not be happier, for this is not a happy world, and to swim against the stream is tough. But this is the only way to live. We start living in a world of grace and suffering, and move on to a judgment seat where – thank God – judgment does not have the last word. Jesus has the last word about everything and everyone. It will be a loving word.

Keep life mythic. The preacher must not allow life to be shrunk down. Keep it grand. Keep the gospel grand!

*   *   *

Great men and women know how important this is. May I namedrop for a wee bit? Well, it was an accident really. I was visiting a Russian Orthodox priest at his house in Washington DC in the early 1980s. He was well known to the Orthodox community in Russia by his radio broadcasts. We had been talking for an hour when he rose up with a sly smile and said, "Come next door, there's someone I would like you to say hello to." I walked through the door and looked into the face of Alexander Solzhenitsyn! What a man. I was a big fan. Still am! He had the courage to denounce Stalinism and be hounded out of the USSR for it, and he then had the courage to denounce Western decadence and be hounded out of America for it. He wasn't friendly, however, and we had an awkward few moments with niceties. Then my friend told him I was a preacher. Solzhenitsyn's face lit up and he began to talk rapidly.

After what seemed like three minutes my friend turned to me and simply said, "He says preachers are the world's most important people, because the word drives the world."

I love that. Next time I preached, I told myself, "Rejoice in this privilege. For thirty minutes, the word will *drive the world.*"

You can't help keeping it grand if the word is that great, and God that wonderful, and your task that magisterial!

Letter 17:
The tenderness test – "in love"

Or, Do I really love those to whom I am speaking?

What a beautiful experience you have had recently, and I love the way you concluded – I even copied it out – "One of the great delights of preaching is to get continually shocked that the grace of God is always bigger than we imagine."

Mind you, it doesn't always come to everyone as a shock of delight. Witness one of the most successful preachers of the Old Testament, Jonah, so delighted he wished to die after God's grace was extended to the Ninevites. He thought he was preaching a word of judgment. In God's providence, he was preaching a word of grace.

And while we're on Jonah, he does go to show that God is not limited by a preacher's poor theology. Jonah was a bigoted nationalist preacher whom God "fooled" into using to save those horrible foreigners that Jonah hated so strongly. So don't feel so bad that all those volumes of *Church Dogmatics* are sitting unread on your shelf. The good Dr. Barth probably wrote far too much. Profitable reading it is, but few of us have the time to work our way through all his six million words, and even if we did, think of all the other theologians we would have to forgo reading just to get through Barth's bloated corpus. I will say this though – he was one of the few modern theologians who preached. What a disaster when the theologian moved out of the church into the university. The discipline of preaching keeps a theologian fresh, forcing them to make their ideas intelligible and inspirational. So much of what passes for theology today is just a load of abstruse and badly expressed ramblings read in ever-narrowing circles of interest... But, I rant and digress. The bitterness I tasted at some recent seminars is still on my tongue. Forgive me.

Jonah is an interesting case though, because he clearly didn't love those to whom he was preaching, yet they heard his word gladly. I'm about to argue in this "tenderness test" that we should really try to cultivate love for those to whom we are speaking, and that this love is an essential arrow in the preacher's quiver. But I will admit, as with all the tests, God is always greater than our inadequacies, and to fail in some of them – or even in all of them – is not necessarily to fail as a preacher. We strive for perfection not because we know we will attain it, but in the striving we will get better. There is a saying in Scotland, "In honest error there is hope, in icy perfection there is none." And so, the tenderness test.

* * *

"Do you love them? Do you really love them?"

It was the summer of 1986, and an old Bristolian man with hair like Absalom was earnestly leaning toward me asking me these questions. I was a young preacher at the time. Eager and energetic, I had plans to take my church into the big time, and… er… if my own reputation soared in the process, well, God was good wasn't he? In more carnal moments, I would catch myself dreaming of seeing my sermons in print, hearing them on the radio, having a full international diary, and (if I had been dreaming these days) launching the "Dr. Boyd-MacMillan Study Bible" to a packed bookstore.

"Do you *really* love them?" He pressed me again. He was talking about my congregation.

"Well, yes, of course," I answered, a bit quickly. Then curiosity overcame defensiveness, and I asked, "But how would I know?"

"Do you weep for them every week?"

"Why should I weep for them?"

"Because they don't know Christ as well as you do, and it breaks your heart!"

* * *

Not that I agree that the preacher has to know Christ better than anyone he is speaking to. That's probably an impossibility and – thank God – not a necessity. Rather, it was the emotion required to love a group of people that I realized was not in my tank. It wasn't that I didn't care about them. I did love them, after a fashion. But not with the kind of compassion that old man was asking for. And the older I get, the more I realize that the attitude of the preacher toward their listeners impacts far more than the content of their sermon. Even in secular speechmaking this is recognized. Aristotle isolated three elements of persuasive speech:

- *logos*, the rational content;
- *ethos*, the credibility of the speaker;
- *pathos*, the passion of the speaker.

Crudely, that makes the attitude of the speaker twice as important as the content of the talk. Nothing communicates the essence of the gospel message more to an audience than the preacher's love of the listener.

It's not exclusive to the pastor-congregation relationship either. I remember sitting in the press gallery in Hong Kong during a Billy Graham Crusade. A warty, world-weary old journalist, who didn't have a religious bone in his body so far as I was aware, turned to me during the sermon and said, "Gor, what a terrible name-dropper he is, but he doesn't half love us – that's for sure!"

The tenderness test. What is it? It's when the preacher's heart bursts with an unmixed desire to see everyone who hears his or her words experience the fullness of Christ. It starts with sorrow over the lostness of human beings without Christ, it continues in grief over the ways that we all evade this fullness, even as believers, and reaches out in a winsome fashion to recommend this fullness. Ask yourself, "Do I really love these people? Do I really want the best in Christ for them? Will I pay any price to help them receive the fullness of Christ?"

* * *

This tenderness isn't natural. Remember that beautiful incident when Jesus steps off a boat after days of healing and teaching and finds yet another crowd? The text says, "He had compassion on them, because they were like sheep without a shepherd" (Mark 6:34).

That's not a portrait of someone who loves a crowd. The last thing Jesus wanted to see at that moment was another crowd. But unlike today's celebrities, who court our attention by whatever means and then scream "clear off" when we intrude, Jesus had a love response, and it was supernatural.

It's because he sees not just a hungry crowd, but a *lost* crowd: "sheep without a shepherd." It's the sheep-like nature of this crowd that draws out his compassion. It is instructive that his first act is to teach them, and only later to feed them.

Mark doesn't want us to lose the point that Jesus is *the shepherd* for the human flock in a way that would be blasphemous for the average preacher to contemplate becoming. But in Jesus' reaction there are two great features for the preacher to emulate.

First, *to see well is to teach well*. We see the need. This is what draws out our compassion. We see people as desperately needy who do not have Christ, or do not have enough of him. We see beneath to the deep, existential lostness of being human (even as believers), where we feel adrift in a cruel world. We are frightened of this world, this life. Inside every one of us is a little lost child crying, "Where's my mommy and my daddy?" Behind the most bravado exteriors sitting in the pew, or the most successful faces, is that little child peering up at us saying, "Help me!" Tenderness has a theological dimension.

Second, *to love well is to teach well*. It is the greatest act of social compassion to teach. The text has it, "He began to teach them many things." That's love. Not to arrange a miraculous feeding first, but to give them teaching about the truth, so that their lives may be connected to God. Next time you struggle in your study, wishing you could do more social good, well, think too that perhaps your greatest gift to a needy, hungry world is to teach the truth. That is a love gift in itself. Tenderness has a faith dimension: the faith to see that to teach is to act. Without that teaching, no social problems can be solved. R.S. Thomas, that irascible Anglican in Wales, wrote

The priest's cure, not on prescription, is
that love's casualties must be mended by love.

It's our basic message for the social problems of the world. The political plan pales into insignificance. There will be no peace in Kosovo or Palestine unless ordinary people find it in their hearts to "love their neighbors as themselves." Africa will not recover simply because its debt has been forgiven, but only if its leaders can find it in their hearts to be honest, and not to incur more debt by stealing from their "neighbors." All solutions are in some way therefore spiritual, but the "priest's cure" has the edge. And the priests only speak of what they know: this love of Christ has broken them and changed their lives!

*   *   *

Surprisingly, preachers, and especially pastors, are not renowned for their tenderness. An Australian friend of mine was asked to start a ministry supporting the persecuted church. He visited church after church in his home country, preaching his heart out on the needs of the persecuted, but garnered only a meager response. He was clueless until one day, visiting a sheep farm, he witnessed the farmer call the sheep toward him with a word. "Is that all it takes to bring the sheep running?" he asked, astonished. "Try it," grinned the farmer. My friend spoke the same word that galvanized the sheep. One, out of a flock of two hundred, looked up vaguely at a cloud. The rest kept on munching. "The word has to come from the mouth of the shepherd!" declared the farmer.

This rang a bell. My friend said, "It's because I'm not the shepherd that the people are not giving. I need to get the pastors on my side, and let them speak to the flock. That's the answer. They need to hear the message from the voice they trust and love."

My friend traveled around the length and breadth of Australia having meals with pastors. He told them of the terrible torture their counterparts were enduring in places like Sudan, China, North Korea, and Columbia. The idea was to get the pastors to challenge their congregations, who would be moved by the voice of the shepherd. But nothing changed. The pastors made sympathetic noises, but they didn't take up the challenge. He paid them on trips to the persecuted in China, Vietnam, Laos, but they came back unmoved.

Finally, in despair, he spoke to an elderly retired pastor whom he revered. He explained his strategy and asked his venerable friend to point out where he might be going wrong. This is what the old man said: "Your strategy will work only if you invite the pastor's wife along. Pastors are hard hearted. It's an occupational hazard. But if you tell these stories of suffering to the pastors and their wives, she will be touched with compassion and your ministry in each church will be underway. The spouse will ensure it."

Sure enough, that was it. The logjam was broken. And the ministry prospered after that as the pastors, forced into action by spouses that were broken hearted, addressed their congregations with the urgency required to bring action.

Sad, though, that the hard heartedness of pastors would constitute the logjam. The old retired pastor ruminated on this: "It's just that in our line of work we get inured to suffering. We have to. After all, we have to get through the funeral of the nine-year-old child even though every one else can cry all the way through. We have to cope publicly. And so we gain a deadly familiarity with tragedy and sorrow. If we are not very careful, we end up not feeling in private, or in public."

* * *

There are ways to overcome "compassion depletion." One method was used by a pastor in Eastern Europe. He once showed me his list of church members. Beside each name were penciled initials, one of four sets: GS, FC, AH, SE.

GS stood for "government spy." Fortunately we don't have to worry about that category in the West as a rule, though who is to say that those days may not come. The rest were "fan-club," "apathetic horde," and "sworn enemy" – three sections of any congregation the world over.

"Why categorize them this way?" I asked.

"So I get my love strategy right," he replied.

Every preacher has a few sworn enemies: people who see their main function as leading the "oust the pastor brigade." This pastor explained, "You have to love them enough to remember the reasons why they have such an excess of negativity, and reach out to them with winsomeness, not vindictiveness." He added, "Even if they win, the point then is to glorify God more in your going, than in your staying."

As for the fan-club, the danger here is that we accept too much adulation, and play to the gallery. Love in this situation is to have the courage to challenge them on what they may not wish to hear, and to jeopardize your fan-club status. The pastor didn't mince his words: "American preachers are the worst by far in this. They love being worshiped, and prefer to forget that the gospel – at some point – will end up offending everyone in the church." Love in this context is fidelity to the message in all its facets, so that everyone is brought into contact with the entire message of Jesus Christ, not just the popular bits. In practice, this often means querying some darling distinctive of your denomination. As a friend of mine put it recently, "I'm only popular here so long as I sound like Calvin. The moment I start to sound like myself, I'll be in trouble with my fan base."

Lastly, the apathetic horde, perhaps the majority of any church congregation: people who know God, but seem unable to get close to him. Life succeeds in creating a distance from God and they don't have the "Oomph" to swim against the tide to get to the shore. Said the pastor, "People are weak and lost, and they don't know how to find their way to Jesus. The danger is that we harangue them toward him, or offer ourselves as the guide and take away their freedom and responsibility. Stay winsome, and resist the impulse to be coercive."

*   *   *

I suggest that every preacher create an exercise to increase their tenderness. My own exercise is to preach to my study wall on which hang two large Coptic icons from the Desert of Scete. One icon is of the glorified Christ, reminding me that when I preach, I preach to him, for him, of him. I ask him, "Are you pleased by what is said? Am I giving you enough glory?" Somehow it punctures carnality to do this.

The other icon shows Mary holding the baby Jesus. Mary, for me, represents humanity. A confused teenager when the angel came, still she said, "Yes." She represents ordinary people. If I know members of the group I am speaking to, then I will pretend that I am speaking to them. I ask, "How will you feel the love of God in this sermon? Am I feeling love and compassion for you? If not, why not?"

Then the baby Jesus. For me this speaks of the vulnerability of God, and also of the fact that we are all children in his sight. Some of us are stubborn like children. Some lost and clueless, like children. I ask, "Am I having enough mercy on these children of God? Is this sermon speaking to my own little child inside?"

Create your own method. Some swear by disciplined visitation of the flock, although that does not necessarily induce compassion. Some of us struggle to get to know people even as we interact. Preachers often have big egos. Visitation for them is just another opportunity to pronounce. Or, preachers may feel at ease in front of a group yet be chronically shy one-on-one. Whatever the exercise, it has to produce feelings of compassion. One preacher I know works a morning each week at a home for the severely handicapped. "It makes me softer in my soul," he says. *Get something,* lest a certain callousness become a default setting.

*   *   *

The best way to have compassion is to submit to God. Was it Maimonides that said, "God will grind you till your grains are small, and then the color will show." The act of love that really communicates to an audience is when we have allowed ourselves to be broken by the word of God, led into the wilderness, and put together only by the Spirit of God. If that brokenness is given out, then it automatically comes from a place of compassion and tenderness, because it is the offering of a tenderized soul. I dare not say any more. As an old Brethren divine, Harold St. John, once warned, "Preaching is a happy labor, but I must give blood every time."

*   *   *

Brother Andrew was once preaching in Sri Lanka. "What's the saddest verse in the Bible?" he asked.

He answered his own question: "Psalm 142:4, '...no one cares for my soul.'" And he shared that when he first read the verse in his Bible, he wrote in the margin, "I don't want to be *no one*."

Neither does the preacher want to be *no one*. There cannot be many greater ambitions for a sermon than when the preacher sits down, for the listener to murmur, "That preacher cares for my soul."

Letter 18:
Testy bits and bobs

Or, Why the preacher should sound different to the Dalai Lama!

No, I'm not saying that performing these six tests guarantees greatness. Only God guarantees greatness. OK, sorry, that was below the belt, but you get my meaning.

Think of these tests as drills. You only gain mastery over anything by drilling yourself in the basics. It doesn't matter whether it's learning to paint, to play an instrument, or to make successful investments. What I noticed over the years was that preaching was taught in such a way that these basics were covered but not *drilled into* the preacher. They were overshadowed by a vast array of extraneous or less important material. In the end, the trainee preacher was left with a task list of 150 tips on preaching, instead of being trained in a master list of key drills that gave them the basic competence from which to develop an individual style.

The tests can be self-applied, though I do encourage others to assess the preacher under these headings. What's most important is that each test tries to deliver the preacher from a major failing. Passing the oral test might save you from being too complicated. It will deliver the gift of simplicity, which is the foundation for memorability. The experience test may deliver you from the curse of presenting information to an audience, and merely engaging their minds – it enables people deep in their very nature to feel the power of the gospel solution occurring as you preach; the reality test should save you from irrelevance; the exegetical test protects against the substitution of your own opinions for a divine message; the grandeur test is there to protect against triviality; and the tenderness test is a good defense against an icy perfection in the pulpit.

* * *

Like any teacher, I can't overemphasize the importance of drilling. Every great preacher has either been a relentless self-driller or (more often) has experienced personal drilling sessions with a mentor. Take Martin Luther-King, Jnr. It wasn't his homiletics professor that was his primary influence, but a black pastor called J. Pius Barbour, of whom King wrote, "He made the Gospel live for me."[44] Barbour would gather young men around him each weekend. On Saturdays they would go round to his house and practice their sermon in front of his mirror, where he would give them tips. On Sundays, after the sermon, Barbour would ask them to analyze his own sermon under three headings: content, delivery, and audience reaction. He would also grade himself under each heading, and urged those in his homiletical court to do the same. In this way, one of the defining voices of American black preaching, and also the clarion voice of the American Civil Rights Movement, was drilled and formed. There is no greater tragedy for preaching today than the senior pastor who claims to be too busy to mentor preachers.

* * *

Have I any other tests you ask? You're a glutton for them aren't you? Well, I sometimes slip in a couple of others in individual tuition.

One I call the *foolishness test.* The gospel is foolish. It's insulting – we can't attain salvation. It's crude – faith in a crucified God/Man will bring salvation. It's crazy – that one man writhing on a cross puts the world back in balance. But Paul didn't mind that. He preached the gospel in all its foolishness to an Athenian elite who sneered at the crudeness of it all. So, I occasionally ask, "Am I presenting the gospel in its foolishness and trusting God to work, or am I trying to make the gospel so rational and sophisticated, relying on the argument to make people believe?" I don't say that there is no place for apologetic preaching, though it is fair to say that the apologetic preacher goes out of date faster than all other types. For example, who reads Hensley Henson or H.H. Farmer any more? But our belief is that God exalts this foolish gospel. Keep it foolish, that God may be given his "nuclear opportunity."

Did you know that the biblical sermon conforms to Einstein's *Special Theory of Relativity*? It states that a large amount of energy can be released from a small amount of material. From our small energy output – preaching a foolish, simple gospel – comes an explosion that remakes the world.

Another one is the *theological test*. Every time we get to a passage, or preach on any subject, we still have to mediate the theology of it. For example, I heard a sermon on angels recently. The passage was Genesis 28:10–22, where Jacob pillows his head on a rock and – perhaps not surprisingly – sees some ladder-dancing angels. The preacher's point was, "Angels come in visions." Well, actually, throughout the Bible, they tend to appear more often in the realm of conscious life. That's where he needed to bring a theological synthesis to the sermon. We preach each passage and also what the entire Bible preaches at the same time. This gets harder the larger the topic. If one's topic is judgment, for example, then the theology is not grasped in an hour no matter what dictionary you have to hand. So, it is important to represent the perspective of the faith. I don't make this a separate point as a rule; I can squeeze it in under the grandeur test.

I've also toyed with adding a *persuasion test*. Though the reality and experience test hint at it, I did not deal specifically with the art of persuading an audience, or, for that matter, reading an audience. Remember how Pius Barbour taught King to make "audience reaction" one of the three criteria for preaching success? It is a skill that can be taught, and we'll go into it in subsequent letters if you wish. It is a remarkable attribute, and all great speakers have to have it. Here's Billy Graham talking to one of his biographers:

> Say I'm preaching to an audience of three or four thousand. I can look straight at them, and I can tell when a man way back in the auditorium blinks his eyes. When he does that, I know it's time for a change of pace, or I'll lose some of the people. That's what I've trained my voice for. It's a change of pace that's the secret. I speak in loud tones – oh, not boisterous, but good and loud – and then I soften the voice. It's that difference in delivery that holds them.[45]

But six drills is enough. Make it more and they lose their value as basics. And these extra skills can be incorporated into them.

*   *   *

You asked which one is the hardest for most preachers to grasp. You'll have your own suggestions, but I think that it's probably in the area where the grandeur and exegetical tests meet: Is what I am preaching significantly a *Christian* truth? Let me give you a short example.

When it comes to embodying a faith tradition, there cannot be many others who embody theirs as attractively as Tenzin Gyatso, better known as His Holiness the Fourteenth Dalai Lama. But in interpreting the Beatitudes, this is what he said, "This passage seems to indicate the simple fact that those who are willing to embark on a path and accept the hardships and the pain involved in it will reap the rewards of their commitment."[46]

Now, what's wrong with that? There is nothing wrong in the actual statement, which is really the ethical principle of you reap what you sow, even in the realm of virtue. A Christian preacher got up and said, "It would seem we are exactly agreed on the message of Jesus."

No. The Dalai Lama's statement stopped short, from a Christian perspective.

The Beatitudes are fundamentally not about the spiritual truth that our effort will eventually pay off in our transformation. In fact, it's the exact opposite. Only when we are absolutely useless, hopeless, can Jesus come in. It's not a natural process. You can't motivate yourself to be "poor in spirit." You can't accomplish that. The Beatitudes must not be reduced to a spiritual self-transformation formula.

As preachers, we often miss the Christ-centered or even supernatural nature of the truth we teach. We all too often substitute a religious truth for a Christian truth. Yet, we don't want only to give people control over life's vicissitudes, or urge them to try faith. We want them to know Christ, and that is a transformation radically different to all other religious truth. It looks, sounds, feels, and is completely different to all other truth in the universe. Covet that Christian distinctive. It's our "product" if you like. God has a face. God can be known. God can enter within and remold our inmost being. Jesus Christ has done this, and it is marvelous. Perhaps Bishop Leslie Unwin put this best: "the Christian is always moving from wondering to wondering." The preacher's task is to wonder aloud.

*   *   *

Right, I'm off to China and India for three months. I know you want to hear about the history of the sermon, and the various sermon types, so I'll send those through as I go, but I won't be able to respond to your missives during this period as I am even off email where I am bound. So forgive me if the next set of letters sounds a bit impersonal.

I'm so looking forward to this trip. China contains the world's largest and longest revival at the moment, though such phenomena are always vulnerable. And India is seeing great church growth also. I'm going to learn so much from them. And I'll be preaching a wee bit here and there too. I love the experience of being told, "Preach to us, just give us the word, nothing fancy, and don't dare to stop after just an hour." Doesn't happen where I live. Bring it on!

Section Three:

The History of Preaching – the Forms

Letter 19:
Biblical hints for sermon formation
– from Moses to Paul

It has surprised me more than it should that contemporary histories of preaching rarely begin with the Bible. There are simple and scholastic reasons for this.

The simple reason is that the weekly Sunday sermon is not really a biblical species. If a sermon is a "Sabbath" speech to a group of believers on the implications of a scriptural text, then we don't find many examples of it in Scripture. Old Testament preaching is mainly episodic. It might be on the eve of a battle, or a prophetic interpretation of the meaning of a catastrophe. Moses charges the Levites to read and explain the law every seven years (Deut. 31:10–12), and after Ezra and Nehemiah re-establish the temple in Jerusalem they have a big ceremony where, "they read from the book of the law of God clearly, made its sense plain, and gave instruction in what was read" (Neh. 8:8, REB). But weekly acts of reading and explaining Scripture to believers came in really with the synagogue, which emerges after the Old Testament period.

In the New Testament also, the preserved sermons tend to be evangelistic one-off speeches given to those outside the Christian community. We know the sermon (in the sense of a talk to a Christian group) goes on in the New Testament, but the single specific reference to it is inauspicious. Paul preaches a sermon so long that one of the listeners nods off on the window seat and falls to their death onto the street below. Handily, the apostle brings young Eutychus back to life (Acts 20:7–12). I wish the Spirit would give all preachers the power to resurrect those bored to death by their preaching. In any case, we don't read what Paul said, or glimpse the content of any sermons in a worship setting. Nor do we find a clear model for the form a sermon should take.

The scholastic reason is well put by O.C. Edwards, Jnr. in his recent history of preaching: "There seems to be little reason to think that the shape of Christian preaching in the New Testament period can be reconstructed – which is to say that, while true Christian preaching began much earlier, the history of Christian preaching cannot be traced back earlier than the middle of the second century."[47] Edwards is referring to the work of the guild of biblical scholars who, after their critical dissection of the texts, reckon the mutilated remains of sermons in, for example, the Athens sermon in Acts 17:22–31 to be more Lukan paraphrase than Pauline sermon, or the so-called "Sermon on the Mount" (Matt. 5 – 7) to be a compendium of Jesus' sayings and stories compiled by Matthew and almost certainly not preached in the form we read it. We have summaries of sermons, rather than sermons.

All right, but so what? If the history of the sermon form proper begins a few centuries after Scripture closes, does that mean that what we tantalizingly glimpse of the great biblical sermonizers should not influence the form of our sermons? I care not a whit where author ends and editor begins in Jeremiah, Isaiah, or Deuteronomy. There are principles of proclamation here that I must regard as authoritative and worthy of imitation. So before we go on to look at the six forms of the sermon in the Christian church, here's a quick rollercoaster ride on how biblical preaching affects my preaching.

There seem to be four elements that recur in Old Testament preaching. I'm going to call them acts, idols, choices, and laws.

Acts

Great sermons in the Old Testament *start with a celebration and rehearsal of the mighty acts of God.* When "Moses" closes the Old Testament's most gigantic sermon (the book of Deuteronomy), he starts off with rehearsing the great story of salvation and love that God has for Israel: "He found his people in a desert land, in a barren, howling waste. He protected them and trained them, he guarded them as the apple of his eye" (Deut. 32:10, REB). And on and on goes the recital. The theme is always the same – our God is incomparable! These prophets and priests literally burst with praise at the great acts of God. These acts are not limited to God's covenant acts of deliverance, such as the Exodus, but include his power and glory displayed in the creation:

> The word of the Lord created the heavens;
> All the host of heaven was formed at his command.
> He gathered into a heap the waters of the sea,
> He laid up the deeps in his store-chambers.
> Let the whole world fear the Lord
> And all its inhabitants stand in awe of him.
> For he spoke, and it was;
> He commanded, and there it stood. (Ps. 33:6–9, REB)

Most speech in the Old Testament starts with this reminder of how great God is, and from this rehearsal of his great acts in nature and in history, we know who we are, and what is required of us.

This feature forces me to ask of my sermons: Am I bursting with the great acts of God? Is that my focus? Am I telling people how incomparable is the God of the Bible? What a wonderful relief it is to know that the person who made and runs the world is also loving and just. His power has not made him arrogant or indifferent to the weak. And the ultimate proof of that concern is the life, death and resurrection of Jesus, his Son. Eugene Peterson has a nice definition of pastoral work. He says it "deals with the difficulty everyone has in staying alert to the magnificence of salvation."[48] Beautiful, and just what we mean here. Great sermons rehearse the magnificence of salvation. As we are alerted to it again, our story gets folded in to his grander story.

Idols

Great sermons in the Old Testament usually contain a *searing exposure of idolatry.* Idolatry is the core sin of the Israelites, given that it violates their "prime directive": "You must have no other god besides me!" (Exod. 20:3, REB). But it's the prime sin of us all, given that idolatry is anything that steals our worship away from God, and becomes the story of how we spoil the template of being human. Secular idols make us choose between God and them, but religious idols are more subtle, where the things we trust to get us to God become the very things that keep us away from God. So when we think we are revering him, we are in fact alienating him. Isaiah is the master prophet at exposing this. In 57:3–13, for example, he outlines the terrible idolatry of Israel, who go to the temple while sacrificing children, hopping into bed with lovers, and all the while thinking God is pleased. Idols blind (v.6), and exhaust (v.10), and even silence God (v.11) for a time. But ultimately they provoke him. The prophets expose idolatry because they want Israel to be Israel.

Again, this is so challenging. Have I identified the great "worship-stealers" in the life of my listeners? At root, what are the things preventing them giving God their all? It might not be only living for a dream house or car, or trying to live one's life vicariously through a rock star, it could be over-venerating a pastor, or substituting a tradition of worship instead of encountering God. It's subtle because it's so basic. We are all worshipers. The question is not whether we worship, but what we worship. I knew a preacher who made an idol out of his voice. He had a magnificent baritone. He trained it until it was a mighty instrument. But over time, his love of sounding wonderful displaced his love of God. He never knew it. It had blinded him. In Western society, I wonder if Isaiah would accuse us of "child sacrifice" as he did the ancient Israelites. The unborn children we have sacrificed to the idol of *I'm not letting my life get screwed up* even exceeds the number of Jews killed in the Holocaust. These biblical preachers had a sharp edge because they went to the root. They were trained to look for idolatry and expose it. So must we!

Choices

Great sermons in the Old Testament usually *offer life or death choices to the listeners.* "If you would live," Amos warns, "make your way to the Lord, or he will break out against Joseph's descendents like fire" (Amos 5:6, REB). Prophets tell their people two things – what will happen if they choose death, and what will happen if they choose life. Jeremiah promises the people devastation from a foreign power: "See an army is coming from a northern land... armed with bow and scimitar, they are cruel and pitiless... they are like men arrayed for battle against you, Zion" (Jer. 6:22–23, REB). He also promises that if they take their stand and follow the ancient paths they "will find rest" (Jer. 6:16). I have a framed print of Rembrandt's *Jeremiah weeping over the fall of Jerusalem* on my office wall. He took no pleasure when the judgment announced came about because the people chose badly.

This element spurs me to examine my sermon: Am I giving my listeners a choice? Am I asking them to make a decision? Are they clear from my words what they have to turn from and turn toward? It's so obvious, yet I've been embarrassed to look over some of my sermons and find that I never really asked my listeners to make a decision at all. People want to know what to do! Give them a choice. At the risk of sounding over-Arminian, I think that is the greatest way of dignifying a congregation. The greatest gospel evangelists make it their bread and butter to call for a decision, but I honestly think teachers should do the same.

Laws

Great preaching in the Old Testament *makes it clear what you have to do and what not to do to please God.* OK, it's not all about obeying the law, but it is pretty central. Malachi tells them what to turn from: "You ask, how have we despoiled your name? By offering defiled food on my altar" (Mal. 1:6–7, REB). And tells them what to do: "Bring the whole tithe into the treasury" (Mal. 3:10, REB). The clarity of Old Testament speech is amazing. The listener is in no doubt about what is expected of them after the prophet or priest has spoken. So it's a great aim for all preachers today – do those who listen to me know what they have to do, and what not to do? Again, it's so obvious, but I've come back from a church service where the preacher never defined what obedience looks like. We received some insights on the passage, but nothing to do. No habit to change. No practical suggestions. An Old Testament preacher would not let us off so lightly.

Of course, there is so much more to say about Old Testament communication. I am always challenged by the sheer variety of literary form – oracle, song, dramas, stories, blunt-speaking speeches, wisdom sayings, acted parables – what a range these men and women had. Also, their dedication to the craft of words is astonishing. They labored long and hard over getting the right metaphors and structures to create maximum impact. I'm awed at the price they paid to speak the word of God, and the agony that was involved. Don't you find it a thrill to stand in their tradition? To stand up and speak the words of the same God that Moses, Isaiah, Amos, and Jeremiah spoke? We may not be a patch on them as craftsmen, but it's the same word we serve, and so we are bound together in the same grand tradition – we are the people God has asked to speak his word into his world, and remake it according to his purpose. Whew!

The New Testament has really helped me as a preacher both negatively and positively. By negatively I mean that I was raised to hear certain truths asserted about preaching that, after a more thorough perusal of the New Testament itself, I realized were overstated to the detriment of good preaching. Take these three.

The first one involves people coming up to me and asking, "Are you a preacher or a teacher? What's your gift?" I know where they got the distinction from. It's an old C.H. Dodd idea and you find it in the more elderly dictionaries. Example: Alan Richardson in *A Theological Word Book of the Bible* writes

> In the NT preaching has nothing to do with the delivery of sermons to the converted, which is what it usually means today, but concerns the proclamation of the "good tidings of God" to the non-Christian world. As such it is to be distinguished from TEACHING (Gk. *didache*), which in the NT normally means ethical instruction, or occasionally apologetics or instruction in the faith.[49]

This is overstated, and although "preaching" and "teaching" are not interchangeable in the New Testament, they are not far off it. In places like Matthew 4:23; 9:35; 1 Timothy 2:7; 2 Timothy 1:11, and Acts 28:31 the two terms are in fact used interchangeably. As for this idea that no "teaching" is done to Gentiles, Peter's speech to unconverted Jews in Acts 5:42 and

Paul's speech to the Gentiles in Acts 17:19 are both described as "teachings." This somewhat bogus distinction has caused harm to the preaching enterprise because often those who quiz you to tick the *preacher* or *teacher* box are really asking, "Are you a passionate outgoing evangelist who brings soul to Jesus, or are you a repressed, didactic, more boring type that just instructs the faithful?" There is often a denigration of teaching with the distinction. Worse, if you are a "preacher" you've got style; if a "teacher", you're dull. Or, it can result in the spectacle of preachers who insert a little "gospel pitch" toward the end of the sermon. When that happened recently one of the faithful turned to me and said, "You see, he's not just a teacher, he's a preacher too."

Folks, just drop it. What use is this distinction? In practice, it isn't there. Jesus was called a "teacher" far more often than a "preacher." The fact is, when you preach, you teach; when you teach, you preach. Think Siamese twins, and to operate to separate them causes death to one or to both. All proclamation has to have a didactic core. Must have, or it would be empty rhetoric. We'd be Sophists, not Christians. Which brings me to my next bleat.

Two, have you heard the view that "the good preacher should never spend too much time on the form of the sermon because the apostle Paul told us that 'Christ did not send me to baptize but to proclaim the gospel, and not with eloquent wisdom, so that the cross of Christ might not be emptied of its power' (1 Cor. 1:17)"? How often has that little phrase been quoted to me (more often in the AV) – not with wisdom of words – to suggest that all I have to work on is content, and that all attempts to put my words together well or even beautifully or persuasively is a detraction from the power of the gospel. It's a misunderstanding of the verse entirely. The context is that there are two gospels – the gospel of Sophia, sophisticated human wisdom, and the gospel of the cross, which is not the product of human reason, but a much less sophisticated yet far more effective gift from God. So Paul is saying, in effect, "I won't preach the human gospel of *eloquent wisdom*, but the divine gospel of Jesus Christ, the *foolish wisdom*." It's about the content of the message, not the form the message comes in.[50]

There's a further reply to anyone who tries to say "Paul deplores the use of rhetoric!" It's this: Don't call Paul a hypocrite! Throughout Paul's letters, he is constantly employing the techniques of secular rhetoric to make his points with effect. So he's not going to turn round to say, "When I preach, I never use rhetoric," if he's using it all the time. Look at his framework in 1 Corinthians 15. It's structured just like a forensic speech as outlined in the canons of classical rhetoric. The *exordium*, which commends the speaker to the listener (vv.1–2), the statement of facts (vv.3–11) marshaled in the classic format of who, what, where, when, and how. He then goes into his exposition, making his main argument (vv.12–34), and then he anticipates objections in a refutation section (vv.35–49), and finally the *peroratio* (conclusion) in verses 50–58. It's just as a lawyer would argue a case in court. Not only does he follow the form of classical rhetoric, you can see him using the three levels of style as taught first by Cicero. The plain style in verses 3–11, short and factual. Then the middle style in verses 12–34, where he employs figures of speech, piles up the "if" clauses, uses dialog, and epigram, all in order to persuade. Finally he employs the grand style in the conclusion in order to inspire, building to a crescendo and a song of victory. Does this draw out an "amen" or not?

> Listen, I will unfold a mystery: we shall not all die, but we shall all be changed in a flash, in the twinkling of an eye, at the last trumpet call. For the trumpet will sound, and the dead will rise imperishable, and we shall be changed. This perishable body must be clothed with the imperishable, and what is mortal with immortality. And when this perishable body has been clothed with the imperishable and our mortality has been clothed with immortality, then the saying of Scripture will come true: "Death is swallowed up; victory is won! Oh Death, where is your victory? Oh Death, where is your sting?" (1 Cor. 15:51–55, REB)

My third bleat is of more recent vintage: *Jesus was a storyteller, so make sure your sermons have a narrative focus*. Well, Jesus was a lot more than a storyteller. You'd think the only technique he used was parables. Have these people not read John's Gospel, where his speeches are dense philosophical discourses on the meaning of the signs? Not a parable in sight in the entire Gospel! And what about all his propositional and proverbial styles of preaching in the synoptics? Don't shrink Jesus down to just a storyteller. And don't shrink preaching to just storytelling. I see what is happening – people who spread this view around are asking preachers to become more vivid storytellers. Right on. But don't overstate the criticism of poor storytelling by misrepresenting the varied communicational methods of the Lord.

So much for negative guidance. The biggie I take from the apostolic preaching (I'll deal with Jesus in a later letter) is a simple one: the form of the sermon is malleable, but the core of the sermon is not. It's all about two Greek words, *kerusso* and *kerygma*.

Of a raft of Greek words that we translate as "preaching" in the New Testament, probably the biggest is *kerusso,* meaning, to herald or to witness. Every time it is used, it refers to the fact of proclamation, not the manner of it. For example, in 2 Corinthians 1:19, "it was Jesus Christ, the Son of God, we preached." Or 1 Corinthians 1:23: "We preached Christ crucified." Or 2 Timothy 4:2: "preach the Word." In other words, it's *what* you herald, not *how* you herald, that is the main thing. The distinction is important because there is a rather silly debate about the sermon in which two sides talk past each other. One is the "anti-monolog brigade." Their view is that the sermon is a boring, outdated, and rather authoritarian monolog, and we should scrap it, or at the very least, set alongside it more effective ways of teaching than the sermon, such as dialog, plays, and interaction. The other side is the "pro-sermon faction," who argue that the sermon and preaching are the same thing, and we must have more of it for the church to grow.

I heard an older preacher last year speak on the topic "Is the sermon out of date?" He took as his text Romans 10:14: "How will they hear without a preacher?" But he made a disastrous assumption, that "preaching" equals "sermonizing"! So he regaled us with a talk warning us of the terrible consequences of failing to preach the gospel, by which he meant an uninterrupted monolog in a church setting. This is all completely beside the point. He hasn't done his homework on *kerusso*.[51] Preaching in the New Testament refers to what is preached, not how. A sermon is a type of preaching. It is not the same as preaching. That is to confuse the form with the content. So he talked past his critics, blissfully unaware that they hold the exegetical high ground because they know that "preaching" really means "witnessing to the truth," not "witnessing to the truth in the form of a sermon." Paul preached by "dialog" at Troas in Acts 20:7, and then "conversed" over their meal (Acts 20:11). He's preaching both times, but it's not a sermon where he monologs to a passive audience *à la* the modern sermon. New Testament scholar turned radical church strategist, John Drane, confessed after reading through the Gospels, "I was surprised that none of [Jesus'] messages could with certainty be identified with the sort of monologs that dominate much modern worship."[52] William Barclay adds, "Early preaching was not a monolog but a dialog. It was not a question of one man telling a crowd of men; it was a case of a group of people talking it over together."[53]

But if the pro-sermon faction have to wake up and realize that "preaching = sermonizing" is overdone, the anti-monolog brigade need to rethink their characterization that "monolog = boring" ! The latter group have tended to let their ire run ahead of their exegesis. The use of *kerusso* almost always involves a monolog of some description. To witness to the truth with one's tongue presupposes that one is being given a time to speak without interruption. That's a monolog! When Barclay states, "Early preaching was not a monolog but a dialog," that's not quite true. It would be more accurate to say, "Early preaching was a monolog *followed* by a dialog." Barclay is making his statement on the basis of the synagogue pattern that set the tone for the early church. A synagogue service had four elements: prayers, the reading of Scripture, the address (the monolog), and the discussion (see Acts 6:9–10; 17:2; 18:29). But the dialog followed the monolog. I take the point that if the teaching ministry of the church is conceived primarily in terms of an uninterrupted monolog then it is bound to be ineffective. The sermon should never be the only means of teaching, and the church has to repent of this if all it offers the faithful is a sermon with no come-back. But the anti-sermon reaction has gone too far in some quarters where there is a misplaced embarrassment about monolog today.

This year I was speaking at a Christian convention in the UK and went along to a couple of "alternative" services aimed at the twenties and thirties age group. Well, we watched useless skits, were pressed into small groups to produce drawings that no one understood, we were directed to wander around the building, tie strings here, tie strings there, and none of us really had a clue what we were doing because there was no one at the front who monologed at us to tell us what was going on.

I remember having a chat with one of the organizers, and she said very firmly, "we have to avoid the talking head – that's too boring." She was wrong though. We desperately needed a monolog to give us content and meaning to take to the other activities, which in the end are *response* activities to the monolog. Without the monolog, there was nothing to respond to. It's like C.H. Spurgeon's famous put down of a Brethren conversational Bible reading, "No one knew anything, so we all taught each other." To teach anything, there has to be two elements: someone teaching and someone listening. That's monolog. Yes give the listener a chance to come back, that's dialog, but it all starts with giving the teacher the space to present a content to which one reacts.

Don't go blaming monolog. Blame *boring* monolog instead! Returning home from this conference I wrote in my journal, "I think the greatest problem facing preaching today is the fear of the monolog." There's a lunatic fringe in the anti-monolog brigade that want to banish the sermon completely. Fat chance. The monolog will always be with us. In large groups and even small, it is a communicational necessity. But the effect of this scaremongering is a bunch of preachers who keep their monolog to an embarrassed minimum and fill up the minutes with film clips, skits, and roving mike questions. The problem is this – if they are poor at the monolog, they are probably poor at other forms of communication too! In this conference I mentioned, one preacher introduced a series of completely banal and boring skits, but you don't hear anyone calling for an end to drama! He also used PowerPoint images that were completely off the point, and he had a person wandering around the audience with a roving mike so that anyone who felt led could interrupt the speaker if something wasn't clear, but it was so staged we were squirming. One question was, "Would you say more about the theology of the book in relation to the historical period?" Well, amazingly, it so happened that this was his next segment of material, with PowerPoints ready to go. A miracle? Come on.

This is the danger: The stampede away from the monolog is just spreading the bore factor to other forms of communication. Let these preachers concentrate on developing a more interesting monolog. A good gospel monolog is an urgent need today because people are so busy: always talking, always rushing, always acting. Their real need is to sit down in silence to listen to an interesting talk that has content, that moves them, and makes them think. Then we use all the other methods of communication to make sure the truth is grasped and grafted in to life as it is lived. Don't give monolog a monopoly, but don't banish it either.

So if preaching is witness, what do we witness to? This is where we come on to *kerygma,* literally, the herald's pronouncement, the content of what is proclaimed. The key here is that the apostles preached a gospel they had been given. It wasn't theirs. It's not our message. It's God's. It is entrusted (1 Thess. 2:4) to us. If I want to preach like the apostles, I have to acknowledge this truth: great apostolic preaching involves a witness to a capsule core of truth that was agreed to constitute the gospel. Without this core, say the apostles, the gospel has not been preached!

I know it will surprise you, but the scholars can't agree as to what the elements of the *kerygma* actually were. Dodd was one of the first to come along and identify it. He isolated six elements, mainly from three sermons of Peter in Acts 2, 3 and 10.

1   The age of fulfillment, the coming of the kingdom of God, is at hand.

2 This coming has taken place through the ministry, death, and resurrection of Jesus.

3 Now, as a result, Christ is exalted to the right hand of God.

4 The guarantee of Christ's living presence is the present Holy Spirit.

5 Christ will soon return to bring this messianic age to its climax.

6 To be a part of this, repent, be baptized, receive the Spirit and be part of the community of Christ.

The trouble was, Peter never preached a sermon with all six elements. Dodd cobbled them together from the three sermons. Another issue is, this was the *kerygma* for a Jewish audience, but when Paul preaches to a Gentile audience (Acts 14:15–17 and Acts 17:22–31), the *kerygma* looks a bit different. More like these six elements:

1 Idols are worthless. Repent and turn away from them.

2 Turn instead to the only living God.

3 God is the creator of absolutely everything, including everything in heaven and on earth.

4 In the past, he let nations go their own way, but he always left a witness to his ways and sent blessings upon all.

5 A judgment is now coming when all the world will be judged in righteousness.

6 The truth of this gospel is proved to you through the resurrection of Jesus Christ.

OK, I've done Dodd's trick, and conflated the six from two speeches. But the common elements of the Jewish and Gentile *kerygmas* can be seen, and if I want to be in line with the apostles I must try to ensure that my sermon has this gospel core I am witnessing to. I want to remake the world in the light of these gospel facts. That's my task as a preacher if I stand in the tradition of the apostles. How? One way I sometimes do this is to take the newspaper during the week before the sermon, spread my hand out over the front page, and at the tip of each finger write these letters: J, R, C, S, R. Each of the letters stand for an element of the *kerygma,* and I ask the question: how does the fact that _____ change my attitude to this news?

"J" stands for Jesus

How does the life, ministry, death, and ascension of Jesus change this news? It's been the week of 7/7 – Britain's 9/11 moment, when four Muslim suicide bombers attacked central London. What does Jesus change? What does the fact of the life, death, and ascension of Jesus do here? Well, I remember that Jesus came to reach out to extremist religious zealots. He can reach out to other young men who are wanting to be suicide bombers too. He will help me to love and to reach them.

"R" stands for resurrection

The point is, Jesus' resurrection changes everything. As the misfit says in Flannery O'Connor's *A Good Man is Hard to Find*, "Jesus gone and thrown everything off balance." So how does the resurrection change things? Well, it helps me remember that even if I die on the tube, I lose nothing, and gain everything. My life goes on past death. Christians need not be paralyzed by the fear that is gripping the nation, because Jesus has risen from the dead. Life is fragile, but in Christ, life is eternal. The resurrection has done this, and it's relevant as you ride on the tube.

"C" stands for coming – second coming

How does the fact that Jesus is coming again change this? It tells me that there is a judgment. Those four bombers are not in paradise. Nor have they escaped justice. God ensures a punishment for their terrible sins. The world – in the long term – is absolutely just. That's a relief as well as a motivation.

"S" stands for Spirit – the Holy Spirit

Christ has sent us the Holy Spirit, so how does the fact of the Spirit's presence change this situation? The Spirit is here to give the church the chance to make this society less decadent. Those Muslim bombers were right in this regard – this society is sadly decadent, where cynicism and selfishness reign, and where sharing one's faith is regarded as an act of bigotry. The Spirit gives us the chance to change this, giving us the power and strength to stand out against the corroding atheism and religious extremism, to show how love of God and love of country can safely go together. The Spirit is here. That's why it's possible!

"R" stands for repentance

This is the response to this gospel that is required. What will repentance change in this situation? It makes us take responsibility for letting society get into such a state. It makes us mourn that we as Christians have not witnessed more to Muslims. It makes us forgive so that we are not consumed with fear or bitterness. We can then be able to refrain from the revenge that will only make the solution recede. Repentance makes the solution possible.

You get the idea. The point is that when you preach, you have a message that makes everything – absolutely everything – different. This gospel core, I hope, keeps my proclamation faithful, so that the full extent of what Christ has done, and how thoroughly he has changed everything for the better, is made clear. That was surely one reason why the apostles were so effective. I stand ashamed that too often I have forgotten the gospel core and followed fads and my own thoughts, instead of remaining centered on the truth of the Lord Jesus Christ.

It's very late. I must stop rambling. Of course there are a million things more in the New Testament for the preacher. One should remember that the best sermon is the preachers' life (2 Tim. 3:10–11). One should remember that the task of the teacher is to make mature believers (1 Cor. 3:1–3). No preacher is satisfied with bringing people into the kingdom. Also, in the early church those who had the gift to teach (1 Cor. 12:28) did teach. How many excellent teachers waste away as pew fodder because of clerical castes, institutional structures, or gender barriers. How sad that we have churches today that would not allow Jesus to preach in them because he didn't have the right qualifications. Another challenge: the mark of successful preaching in the New Testament is evidenced by how many teachers the preacher creates. As P.T. Forsyth said, "the one great preacher in history, I contend, is the church. And the first business of the individual preacher is to enable the church to preach."[54]

So there we are. Perhaps there is no model for the form of preaching in the Bible because, in the providence of God, that is something we reinvent for each age. But the gospel is never reinvented. It doesn't have to be. Something that wonderful is, as Beuchner says, "too good not to be true." Do I believe it? Do you believe it?

If we do, we'd better sound like it, and stand with Moses, Deborah, Jeremiah, Amos, Isaiah, Jesus, Peter, Paul, Priscilla, Timothy, and John.

Then we shall see this same gospel turn the world upside down through our words as it did through theirs!

Letter 20:
The patristic homily form – from Origen to the Plymouth Brethren

The sermon as we know it starts with Origen of Alexandria (185–254). It wouldn't have started at all if it had not been for Origen's mother, who hid his clothes when as a ripe sixteen-year-old he desired nothing more than to rush out and be martyred alongside his father. He got his wish in the end, dying at sixty-nine from the effects of torture in Tyre. As in most eras of history, it always takes courage to preach. After all, this is a gospel that can get you killed, and frequently does.

Before Origen, the sermon was a vague anything-at-anytime kind of speech. Mostly it was a collection of random thoughts, usually full of moral finger-wagging. But in the patristic period after Origen, it became a speech with the specific purpose of expounding and applying Scripture to a group of people in a worship or teaching setting. He gives us the sermon's first form…. the homily. Literally the word "homily" comes from the Greek *homilea*, a verb meaning "a familiar conversation." Origen gave us the first sermonic paradigm with these four characteristics:

- preached in a liturgical setting;
- having a prophetic quality;
- based on a continuous exposition of the biblical text;
- conversational in tone.[55]

By far the most important feature was the structure. The controlling principle of organization was the passage itself. The preacher moves from phrase to phrase, verse by verse, down a selected passage, and usually through a selected book. The first essential sermonic paradigm becomes a kind of commentary with applications upon a particular scriptural passage. That's hardly surprising, since early Christian preaching took its cue from the Jewish synagogue. "You want to know how to preach?" asks Origen, "just take a book of Scripture and go through it a phrase or a verse at a time." I call it the "patristic homily form."

The strength of this method is that it stays very close to the text, and gives most scope to be exegetically correct. Origen was the first to insist that preachers do everything in their power to uncover the *original meaning* of the text. He is the father of all expository preachers. Above all, it's simple. There is no agonizing over creating a nice outline, alliterating points, or fretting over whether the argument is tight enough. I was raised with it in my original church tradition – Brethren – who would have been shocked to realize that their method came from an early "heretic" like Origen! The man who restores the form into common usage in a Reformation setting is John Calvin.

A major disadvantage of this sermon form, however, is that it lacks drama. It is too even in its tone. There is no climax. It often results in the preacher making too many points – far too many for the listener to remember. You run down a passage making a comment here, throwing in an illustration there, dusting it off with exhortation bytes, and hope something sticks somewhere. I have frequently observed preachers making twenty separate points in a half-hour talk using this method. The longer the passage, the more confusing it can sound.

Back in the patristic era, the intrinsically undramatic nature of this structure was offset by two features of ancient preaching not so common today – a three-fold theory of meaning (which came from Origen) and three "gears" or levels of language (which came from Cicero). Indeed, if you look at any verse-by-verse sermon structure, you always find that there is some other imported stylistic or interpretative element that is designed to hold the listener's attention. If anyone wants to use this method – and it has its strengths – then hark at how the patristic fathers "spiced it up."

Three meanings

Origen believed that since every human is made up of body, soul, and spirit, so there is a meaning for each part of the person in sacred Scripture. In fact, for these ancients, that's what made the Christian Scriptures so unique. To the body, the literal meaning; to the soul, a moral meaning; and for the spirit, a symbolic or allegorical meaning. Every text, every phrase even, had these three meanings and it was a test of the preacher's skill to tease them out.

For example, take that passage from Mark chapter 4, when Jesus calms the storm. A literal meaning would be: Jesus calmed the storm for the disciples so he can calm whatever storm is in your life! A moral meaning would be this: follow the teachings of Jesus, keep in the boat, and the storms of life will not swamp you. An allegorical meaning would be: the boat is the church, and the storm is the world, but with Jesus in the boat, no storm can do you any harm.

Today, if you hear a preacher going through a passage verse by verse, then you will probably find that they will concentrate rather exclusively on the literal meaning, and then break off to offer moral exhortations. This is OK. There are entire sub-cultures in the church today that demand nothing more from their preachers. But there's nothing thrilling about it, nothing to put fire in the belly, or make you shout "Amen."

The inspirational element in the patristic era came from the allegorical level. This is why Origen and his progeny, like Augustine of Hippo, are so famous. They were clever men, so unfortunately their allegorical interpretations bordered at times on the fanciful. For example, Origen links Genesis 46:4: "I will go down with you to Egypt and bring you up again," to Ephesians 4:9–10, where Christ descends to the lower parts of the earth. Thus the Egyptian wandering becomes a foreshadowing of Christ's mission: he comes to earth, creates a church, then leads them into heaven. Hmmn, a bit iffy to say the least. Worst of all, snobbery took a hand. The allegorical level became the means through which the clever preacher pitched an interpretation to "superior" Christians over the uncomprehending heads of the plebs who could only follow the literal meaning. It became elitist as well as fanciful – two characteristics that made it antithetical to the gospel message.

The upshot is that most teachers of preaching today will tell you never to allegorize. Personally, I think there is a limited place for typological interpretation. After all, there is a bit of "magic" about the Scriptures. The method wasn't beneath Jesus and the apostles, and we can surely look back with eyes of faith into certain Old Testament passages and see pre-figurings of the plan of God. I heard a Scottish Presbyterian minister deal very solidly with the sacrifice of Isaac in Genesis 22, but he never mentioned that this might be a prefiguring of the sacrifice of Christ. I think that's a pity, not only because I think it's legitimate, but because of its effect – it fires the imagination, creates a great sense of wonder, and highlights God's painstaking and perfect plan of salvation.

It's probably my background. I was raised in a tradition that was comfortable with symbolic interpretation, and I must testify to its inspiring power. I remember an old preacher going through Genesis chapter 1. He dealt with the literal well enough, but then he talked about the moon. This is what he said, and it's still with me thirty years on: "...the moon has no light of its own. It has borrowed light, reflective light. As the moon can only shine by reflecting the light of the sun, so the church can only shine as it reflects the light of the Son of God." I loved that. It touched our imaginations and made our spirits soar. Every time I look at the moon I see a parable of how I and the church must live – not by my own light but by reflecting the light of the Son. Now of course it's nothing to do with the literal meaning of the passage, but it's true – we do live by the light of Christ! The church has no light of its own. It's a beautiful thought. And symbolism, allegory, typology, all discerningly used, can create great beauty and stir the imagination. Its absence is probably why I find so much expository preaching today so worthy, and so dull.

Origen says that Noah is a type of Christ. He takes a Jewish approach to it, starting the symbolism with the etymology, where Noah means "rest." Thus, Noah is a type of Christ, and Christ becomes an ark to protect us from the storms of the last days. As Hugh Oliphant Olds writes, "After a flash of insight into the mysteries of God's redemptive plan like this, who needs a human interest story to keep the congregation awake?"[56]

If you must give up a symbolic level of interpretation of the Scriptures, then make sure you have something else to fire the imagination. We are desperately trying to recover the imagination in today's church. Lately, I was in a church when the preacher gave out modeling clay and asked us to shape the clay according to how we saw ourselves in the parable of the prodigal son. The fact is, imagination is going to squeeze in somewhere. Just because typology requires imagination doesn't make it illegitimate as an expositional method. Of course, it has to be disciplined. But don't reject the typological method until you find the Bible fascinating and the Old Testament a wonderful rehearsal of the salvation plan fulfilled in Christ. Something must take the place of allegory, otherwise there is an imaginative black hole despoiling the sermon. We are out to thrill. We preach for effect.

Three gears

Along with the three meanings, the second reason why the Patristic homily was more exciting than today's verse-by-verse preaching was to do with the three levels of style. These early preachers were steeped in the study and use of words. All had been apprenticed to masters of rhetoric. Some, like Origen and Augustine, made a good living teaching rhetoric. They would all be familiar with Cicero's three levels of speech. The idea was to use a "low" or "plain" style to communicate factual information, so the language is simple, factual, and unadorned. Then you employ a "middle" style to persuade. It's more vivid, with many figures of speech. And then you have the "grand" style, where you are out to inspire. These were like gears, and these guys could switch into them very easily. Whenever they get to a verse of Scripture, they can power into higher gears and with words raise your emotions and spirits.

The apostle Paul is a master of it. If you look at 1 Corinthians 15, the first section (vv.3–11) is a statement of the central truths of the Christian faith, in short sentences, with no emotion and no figures of speech. Then in verses 12–34 he changes gears, as he is out to deal with the arguments of unbelief. He piles up "if" clauses, uses question upon question, dialog, epigram, and strings of contrasts, for example First Adam and Last Adam, natural and spiritual, earth and heaven. In his conclusion he uses the grand style, an impassioned description of the glorious moment of the resurrection, and sings a song of victory over death. You can imagine Paul beginning to shout when he says

> Listen, I will unfold a mystery: we shall not all die, but we shall all be changed. In a flash, in the twinkling of an eye, at the last trumpet call. For the trumpet will sound, and the dead will rise imperishable, and we shall all be changed... And when this perishable body has been clothed with immortality, then the saying of Scripture will come true: *Death is swallowed up; victory is won.* O Death, where is your victory? O Death, where is your sting? (1 Cor. 15:51–55, REB)

Two men represent the high point of this patristic homily form. In the Greek speaking world it's St. John Chrysostom (347–407), nicknamed "Golden Mouth" by his contemporaries, and in the Latin speaking world it's St. Augustine (354–430). Here's Augustine effortlessly easing into a higher gear:

> ... the Word of God, through which all things have been made... which is not hemmed in by space, nor extended by time, nor varied by long and short pauses, nor composed by sounds, nor terminated by silence; how much more could this Word, this great Word... go forth to reveal itself to the eyes of men, and, on the other hand, illuminate the minds of the angels! And appear on earth, and, on the other hand, transcend the heavens! And be made man, and, on the other hand, make men!

It's no trouble for someone like Augustine to shift up like this. These sentences would take us weeks. They can mint them on the spot. It's like watching a Porsche 911 going from 0–60 mph in six seconds while I'm trying to get into second in my elderly Volvo.

After this little peroration Augustine says, "Why have you applauded?" But one can't help it. He lifts the spirit. This was a high point in preaching, and only in African American and some charismatic and Pentecostal churches do they have a clue about this use of language to lift people's spirits. People in ancient times flocked to hear Augustine and Chrysostom with the same excitement that people today go to watch a baseball or football match. Where moderns would Ooh! and Aah! over a great curve ball or a skilful step-over that left a defender for dead, back then they would whoop and yell appreciation for feats of language that would reach right into their heartstrings and elevate them to ecstasy. These preachers made your pulse race, your tear ducts well up, your imagination flame. You would come out of the service shaking your head saying, "Gosh, what an amazing gospel." But remember, it was not the structure that carried the excitement; it was the language.

Chrysostom is frequently placed higher in the pantheon of preachers than Augustine by modern homileticians, mainly because he was not given to flights of allegorical fancy, trained as he was in the more sober courts of Antioch. He must have been awfully good this guy. He started preaching when he was thirty-nine, and died when he was only sixty, but no one with the exception of Charles Spurgeon left more sermons in print than he.

Chrysostom's powers of description are amazing. There must have been some terrible disaster before this homily. He spends about 15 minutes describing the feelings of tribulation, in order that "He may make us more sober-minded by the extremity of this tribulation." He describes the woes, and then shows that such feelings are biblical. What listener would not be moved to hear this:

> This is what the prophet of old bewailed, when he said, "The sun shall go down, and the day shall be darkened." …And wherever anyone looks abroad, whether upon the ground or upon the walls; whether upon the columns of the city, or upon his neighbours, he seems to see night and deep gloom; so full is all of melancholy. There is a silence big with horror, and loneliness everywhere; and that dear hum of the multitude is stifled; and even as though all were gone beneath the earth, so speechlessness hath now taken possession of the city; and all men seem like stones, and this calamity's pressing like a curb on their tongues; they exhibit the

profoundest silence, yea, such a silence as if enemies had come upon them, and had consumed them all at once by fire and sword. Now is it a fit season to say, "Call for the mourning women, that they may come, and for the keening women, and let them take up a wailing... let us call the whole creation into sympathy with our evils..."

He could be describing 9/11, or the Rwandan massacre, or the Chinese Cultural Revolution. He creates amazing emotional empathy with his audience. You listen and think "That's it, that's exactly it." Great preaching surely requires an authentic identification with the attitude of the audience.

Another feature of Chrysostom is his memorable phrasing. This is such a key ingredient of preaching. Take this short passage, when he is arguing that it is more satisfactory to be poor than rich: "What is beyond our wants is superfluous and useless. Put on a sandal which is larger than your foot! You will not endure it; for it is a hindrance to the step. Thus also a house larger than necessity requires, is an impediment to your progress toward heaven." It's like reading a Raymond Chandler novel. The gems really sparkle. My favorite (if slightly sexist) Chandlerism: "She was blonde, so blonde it would make a bishop kick a hole through a stained glass window." But listen, these gems have to be polished. We need to carry a notebook around to capture them. To phrase words beautifully, or select an apt metaphor and simile, is just not part of the modern homiletical package. Preaching today focuses purely on structure or content. This is contrary to ancient rhetoric, where there were five canons: invention, arrangement, style, memory, and delivery. All that is left today is invention, namely the gathering of things to say, and arrangement, the structure. It has left us dull sounding. Chrysostom cries to us across the centuries: "Work on making your words sound beautiful! The gospel deserves no less."

Style is not the icing on the cake; it's the dagger that drives the truth home.

These skills are rare today. We tend to talk in one style... the plain or low style. We do not know how to use words to create emotions or to raise the spirits. Learning how takes a lot of work. Try these three ways to get started:

- One, practice sentence imitation. Write down great and powerful sentences, then write your own in the same style. Get an ear for the memorable phrase.
- Two, get along to a Pentecostal-style church and watch to see what the preachers do to raise the emotional temperature of the people. Sure, there is a lot of manipulative preaching around. Preachers can become histrionic, or scream, or sweat. There are cheap ways to get any audience yelling. But the best of them – Martin Luther-King, Jnr., Samuel Proctor, Gardiner Taylor – do it with words. Watch and learn, even if it's just on video.
- Three, get a metaphor notebook. Write down the metaphors that strike you, and work them into short one-minute illustrations of truths. Teach yourself to notice metaphors. They rarely come unbidden. But they are everywhere. The ordinary is so often the bearer of the extraordinary.

That is the patristic homily form. Just because it started in the patristic era, does not mean to say it is confined to it. It's a good structure, but it requires a lot of skill from the preacher to make it powerful. The power does not lie in the structure. Other structures like liberal-inductive or post-liberal narrative have more power. Perhaps this is why the world's most powerful preachers today on the whole don't use a verse-by-verse format. But it has its place. It's especially good for biblically illiterate audiences who just want to get more familiar with Scripture. It's the form that keeps them closest to the text. I've heard it used to wonderful effect among the Chinese house church Christians, who are desperate to know the Scriptures. Even in the West, we must be careful never to underestimate the average Christian's (or even a non-Christian's) interest in simply knowing what the Bible says.

After Pope Gregory the Great dies in 604 the sermon goes into a nose dive for six hundred years and preaching is largely replaced by homilaries, printed books of sermons that preachers would merely read aloud to the congregation. Preaching your own sermon was regarded as a bit presumptuous. But this all changed with the rise of the Mendicant Orders, many of which – like the Franciscans and the Dominicans – were founded to restore preaching to its rightful place. From the Orders came the Universities, and from the Universities came a more scholarly style of preaching. The academic way of preaching became the norm in the church. So to our next sermon paradigm: the scholastic deductive form.

Letter 21:
The scholastic deductive form – from Aquinas to Spurgeon

Why did the sermon decline from the seventh to the eleventh century? Quite simply, because most priests couldn't read, and the few that could, couldn't read Scripture!

Illiteracy was widespread. Few even thought it was worthwhile learning to read. Most priests saw their role purely as administering church rituals. Many could not recite the Lord's Prayer even if their lives depended on it. As for the few that did read, well, Scripture scrolls were scarce and expensive to produce, and often more effort was put into the decoration of these manuscripts than into the understanding of them. We ogle illuminated manuscripts in museums now, as some of the artists were supreme exegetes, but few benefited from their illumination at the time.

So it's no surprise that when the sermon spectacularly revives in the twelfth century it is among the few that (a) could read and (b) had access to scrolls of Scripture. In other words, scholarly monks!

They are the ones who band together, create libraries, copy manuscripts, and establish universities, bringing the intellectual sparkle that dispels the so-called "dark ages" and light the highway to the Renaissance and the Reformation.

And all because a few fellows – most notably St. Francis (c.1181–1226) and St. Dominic (c.1174–1221) – got so fed up hearing appalling sermons that they decided to found Orders (Franciscans and Dominicans) to teach decent preaching again.

Sound familiar?

Some Protestants have a job swallowing this, but they tend to be those who think that the sermon as we preach it today began with Luther, got sounder under Calvin, and was never bettered after Spurgeon. Sorry folks, but it's the Friars who bring us the kind of sermon that still dominates Protestant preaching today – the scholastic deductive form.

In this form, the sermonic structure no longer follows the thought of the passage, but the themes of the preacher as expressed in deductive logic. The sermon becomes a logical form structured around propositions. You pick your theme – usually a Scripture – and define, prove, and apply it.

Take a text, for example the first beatitude: "Blessed are the poor in spirit, for theirs is the kingdom of heaven" (Matt. 5:3). Define this logically in a proposition. Something like this:

• The repentance paradox: the spiritually poor become the heavenly rich.

Then you attempt to prove it by using various authorities and clarifications. Often what happens here is that preachers use negative propositions to clarify the positive.

• Spiritually poor does not mean physically poor.
• Spiritually poor does not mean permanently fearful for your salvation.

Sensitivity to an audience determines the authorities used to bolster your claims. If you are talking to a Catholic audience you might quote the Pope. If a Presbyterian audience, Calvin. To a Pentecostal audience, Aimee Semple McPherson.

Finally, it's application time. You apply the general propositions to particular situations – that's what makes the logic deductive as opposed to inductive (which moves from the particular out to the general). For example:

• Poverty of spirit in the individual – repentance.
• Poverty of spirit for the congregation – humility.
• Poverty of spirit for the nation – compassion.

Essentially that's the core of the form. Initially it's preached by boffins to boffins (in Latin, *ad clerum*), but it bursts the banks of academia to take the world by storm, especially in the Puritan era.

The form largely owes its genesis to these scholastic friars encountering Aristotle's texts on logic, fortunately preserved for them in Arabic translation by our Muslim neighbors. Logic takes over as the organizing principle of the sermon. The job now was to "divide the word" into discrete and flowing logical units as you expounded it. The "three point" sermon starts right here.

Look at this sermon of St. Thomas Aquinas (1225–74), one of the biggest brains ever in the church and a Dominican friar. He's selected Ephesians 6:13 as his text: "Wherefore take unto you the whole amour of God... and having done all, to stand."

Aquinas' introduction contains a definition of his theme: "The apostle in these words lays down three propositions. Firstly, he exhorts that we arm ourselves with spiritual arms: take unto you the whole armour of God. Secondly, he shows our need of it: that you may be able to withstand. Thirdly, he gives the reason for it: having done all, to stand." Can you see how logic is taking over? Now we have three propositions, arranged in logical relation: exhortation, need, reason. Then he gives each of these three propositions a "head," proving and applying them:

1 We ought to take five kinds of arms:
   * girdle of knowledge;
   * breastplate of righteousness;
   * shield of faith;
   * helmet of salvation;
   * sword of the word of God.

2 There are five days of evil from which these arms defend us:
   * the day of iniquity;
   * the day of temporal prosperity;
   * the day of temporal adversity;
   * the day of temptation of the devil;
   * the day of judgment.

3 Five ways in which we ought to stand perfect:
   * in purity of heart and body;

- in the keeping of the commandments of God;
- in the reformation of the tongue;
- in love toward God and one's neighbor;
- in the praise of God and in the giving of thanks.

So Aquinas is no longer just offering commentary on the verses of Ephesians as they occur. Rather, he is imposing an order upon the verses.

Meanwhile, the patristic homily does not disappear. Generally speaking, it's kept alive by wandering friars, as opposed to the scholarly friars. Remember, these sermonic paradigms always overlap. They are all valid ways of preaching. They don't replace each other like scientific paradigms (i.e. Einstein's paradigm of motion supersedes the Newtonian one). You can preach any of them at any time. They come from various socio-intellectual contexts, but they are not confined to them.

The scholastic-deductive form became the norm, and I suppose is still the dominant form of preaching today – propositional and deductively logical in structure. The Puritans had a fourfold structure that owed much to it:

1 Text announced and "opened" by explaining the author, occasion, and context.
2 Propositions are extracted from the text, and made into doctrines, often called "branch the first," "branch the second," and so on.
3 "Reasons" are given for each doctrinal proposition. The truth of the propositions is proved by example, argument, quoting authorities, and other such strategies.
4 "Uses." Here the doctrines are milked for application.

This sermon form continued long after the Puritan era. A great exponent was C.H. Spurgeon. He interwove application throughout, not confining it to the end. See what he did with the text, "When thou awakest, it shall talk with thee… afterward it keeps man from the strange woman" (Prov. 6:22–24).

1 The word is living… It shall *talk* with thee:
- because it is pure truth;

- because it is the utterance of an immutable, self-existing God;
- because it enshrines the living heart of Christ;
- because the Holy Spirit has a peculiar connection with the word of God.

2 The word is personal… It shall talk with *thee*:
- God's word talks about men, and about modern men;
- it speaks to men in all states and conditions before God;
- as to all your states of mind;
- how very faithful it always is.

3 Holy Scripture is very familiar… It shall *talk with* thee.
- it speaks the language of men;
- Scripture come down to simplicity;
- it is familiar with all that concerns us;
- it has answered enquiries.

4 The word is responsive… It shall talk *with* thee, not *to* thee.
- the book converses with us;
- the book grows with us;
- the book reveals its heart to you;
- the book will love you.

5 Scripture is influential… "afterward it keeps man from the strange woman."
- it soothes our sorrows and encourages us;
- it has a wonderfully elevating power;
- it warns and restrains;
- it will confirm and strengthen you.

At the risk of belaboring the point, you can see that this is no longer the logic of the passage, but the logic of the preacher. Don't be put off by this. Don't think that to go through a passage verse by verse is more biblical than minting propositions about it. The deductive logic method is the most universal type of preaching for very good reasons.

Where the form really scores is in its clarity. Deductive propositions distil biblical truth in a wonderfully dynamic way, linking the specific truth of a passage with the general truth of faith in one capsule and memorable formulation. These propositions reshape the world into a Christian form as they restate scriptural truth. They make the faith universal, understandable, and memorable in a way few other forms can.

People say it runs the risk of being undramatic. The argument goes that the form requires a rather abstract beginning, where the principles are all up front and the really important practical stuff relegated to the back. Bosh! In the right hands, doctrinal propositions can be incredibly exciting. I remember a sermon by the Irish preacher and scholar Alec Motyer starting with this proposition: "If God's power is resurrection power, then it follows that it only works with the dead!" I've lived off that for years. Every time I'm at the end of my tether in fact, I recall it, and realize that God often lets me get into a "dead" situation, so that I turn to him and experience his resurrection power. That's the value of a magnificent proposition – it creates a universe of Christian truth to live in.

And another thing: who says that you have to keep the application to the end? Look at that Spurgeon sermon. He is applying his propositions as he goes.

For all that, I would issue at least four warnings on this scholastic-deductive form. The first is an oral warning. The danger is that preachers multiply points, or they may have three or more separate themes going in an outline. This becomes too much for the average listener to follow and retain, even when the points are cleverly alliterated.

Once I did some informal surveys on sermon retention in the US. The findings were that:

- 51 percent remembered one point, but it was never the main one.
- 10 percent remembered more than one point, but the more points they remembered, the more points they invented.
- 37 percent could not remember any points at all because (a) they found it difficult to concentrate or (b) they didn't like the speaker.

- 2 percent got the main point.

Result: make your theme singular. Use points but keep them clustered around a main point.

The second warning about the scholastic-deductive form is intellectual. Technically, a deductive argument is one whose warrant is strong enough to guarantee the truth of the claim. From Aristotle to Aquinas, deduction was regarded as the tightest kind of reasoning because you can deduce truth from a true premise. Aquinas made much of the existence of God being shown because he was the "unmoved mover," that is, anything in motion must have something first to set it in motion. The assertion that "Our hearts are restless till they find their rest in thee" is a similar deductive formulation.

The problem here, though, is that we live in a world that claims to have rejected deduction in favor of induction. Scientific inquiry begins with the observation of particulars and moves to general hypotheses in a very tentative way (ideally). Deduction is formally rejected because it begins with the hypothesis as a premise and therefore cannot come up with new knowledge: the claim is implicit in the premise. Claims that Thomist thinkers make are revelation based, which are just not regarded as true by many in the first place. Deductive reasoning is always circular. It's fine if you accept the premise, but it cannot command assent if you don't. For example, the whole "unmoved mover" argument took a hit with Newton showing that the universe could have started without an unmoved mover. So you do have to be aware of the limits of deductive reasoning. Certainly for apologetic purposes, it is not so valuable today.

On a more prosaic level, there is a simpler intellectual warning here – don't let your points become pegs! The skill is to ensure the points come from the text. However, many preachers get to a text, create three points, alliterate them, and assume they are preaching the truth. The fact is, it's easy to generate an outline. The question is, is the outline coming from the passage? Alec Motyer humorously illustrated this by suggesting a three point sermon out of the phrase (and it is in the Bible – look it up!) "oh my bowels."

- It was a profound condition – "bowels."
- It was a personal condition – "my."
- It was a painful condition – "oh."

The danger that I am highlighting is that the logic gets divorced from the content. Soon the preacher just creates an outline of pegs on which they hang their latest bugbears. You can really say anything you like under Motyer's points above. The points become general invitations to rant, rather than truths derived and applied from the passage.

Third, there is a spiritual warning with the scholastic-deductive method: don't shrink truth down to intellectual propositions. It can get over-cognitive. There are many kinds of truth and knowing – even emotion is a form of knowing. So beware of assuming that just because truth has been captured in a proposition that it is the best or even the most powerful way of communicating it.

Finally, the scholastic-deductive form comes with a social warning, sounded first by Fred Craddock, who was concerned that the deductive style might sound too authoritarian in a modern "Jack's as good as his master" culture. When the preacher says, "This is what this verse means, let me show you the fruits of my labor, and here's how I suggest it may apply to you," there are many who would react by saying, "Who do you think you are to claim a privileged monopoly on the meaning of this text?" That's why Craddock called his book *As One Without Authority,* a description of the modern preacher, suggesting that an inductively structured sermon might be a more appropriate form for the age. It's a fair point. You do have to watch what Christian sub-culture you are in. Certainly for the mainstream liberal tradition, what Craddock says is true. In evangelical circles, however – especially in the growing two-thirds world churches – a loss of authority for the preacher is simply not happening.

So there it is – the main sermon form of history: introduction, three points, and a dab of application as we go or a big dollop at the end. Many preachers are not even aware that there are other forms out there. But the next sermon form to emerge represented a reaction to excessive logical structuring, when preachers would get into the pulpit and deliver massive lectures, often lasting over an hour, full of deductive doctrines. It was time for a change in some circles. Enter the "moral essay" form.

Letter 22:
The moral essay form – from Tillotson to Williams

Poor John Tillotson. No preacher was more universally feted and admired in his day, nor so universally reviled afterward, than Archbishop John Tillotson (1630–94). How about this for a put-down by C.H. Sisson in, *The English Sermon, 1650–1750*: "Tillotson was one of those ordinary able men, common enough in the world of affairs, who owe their eminence to the utter suitability of their opinions to the political requirements of the times."[57]

Ouch!

Maybe there was too much of the ambitious creep about him. We've met the type: those who make sure that they go to the right colleges, whisper the right things in the right ears, marry into the right family, and make it their life's work to ensure that they are in the right place at the right time when the "big one" comes along. They only call you when they want something. When Tillotson oiled in on the niece of Oliver Cromwell, she sent him packing. But her dad was having none of her coolness. "You shall have him, Betty, for he is the best polemical divine in England."[58] Betty did what Daddy said!

Well, it pays off if you actually buy the myth that position equals influence. Tillotson became Archbishop of Canterbury; an achievement for him perhaps, a sell-out in the eyes of some others.

But Tillotson is not remembered for being Archbishop of Canterbury. Few are. No, he is famous for being the first representative of a new kind of sermon that arose in the seventeenth century – the Protestant moral essay form. This sermon took the style of an essay – lop off the text from the beginning and you are essentially left with an essay structure on classical lines. As for the content, it majored on the moral benefits of Christianity, in sharp contrast to the recondite doctrinal speculations of the preachers of the time. Here are a couple of typical Tillotson sermon titles: "His Commandments are not grievous" and "The Duty and Reason for Praying for Governors."

Negative attitudes toward this sermon-type are partly due to Canon Charles Smyth, a slightly persnickety parson who wrote a classic history of Anglican preaching.[59] See his damning verdict:

> "… as recast by Tillotson, the sermon lost its heroic note, and became a moral essay, the vehicle of a sober, utilitarian, prudential ethic, rather than a proclamation of the Gospel of the kingdom of God. In the hands of his contemporaries it had seemed indeed to belong to literature altogether, rather than to homiletics."[60]

Hmmn. Possibly a bit harsh, and to get a sense of the value of the moral essay sermon, we have to remind ourselves historically of the kind of preaching it set out to replace. First of all, there was a great fatigue with abstruse theology. The scholastic-deductive sermon was hemorrhaging out of control in the hands of many preachers. Their subject matter was entirely to do with theological speculation. A single word of a text might be squeezed and wrung into twenty different logical propositions, and then put to contentious use. The subject was often a diatribe against the latest heresy, even when the average person in the pew had not even heard of it. It became a kind of "art for art's sake" situation with preachers preaching for their own amusement, and for the plaudits of other preachers, with a bemused and bored congregation forced to look on. Moral essay preaching arose out of the desire to make preaching practical again; to take real issues and give the listener something from the sermon that they could actually do. For doctrinal speculation, they substituted plain ethical duties.

Secondly, there was a rejection of stylistic conceit. To follow the sermons of a John Donne or a Lancelot Andrewes you needed a nodding acquaintance with classical rhetoric, a working knowledge of Latin and sometimes Greek, and the concentration span of an Aristotle. Try following this from Andrewes:

This *Immanu* is a Compounde againe: we may take it, in sunder, into *Nobis* and *cum*: And so then have we three pieces. 1. *El*, the mighty GOD: 2. and *Anu* wee, poore wee; (Poore indeed, if we have all the world beside, if we have not Him to be *with us*.) 3. And *Im*, which is *cum*, in the midst between *nobis and Deus*, God and *us*; to couple God and us; thereby to conveigh the things of the one to the other"[61]

It's hard enough to make sense of in print, let alone hearing it in the context of a seventy minute sermon. To be fair, these men were often preachers at Court, where a super-educated audience expected to be entertained with flourishes of erudition. Men like Donne were called "metaphysical" preachers, not meaning of a philosophical bent, but rather something more technical: essentially the more unlike and bizarre the comparison in a simile or metaphor, the more applause it drew. "Buzzard love" would be an example. To the extent that their sermons were mimicked by ordinary priests, the parishes suffered. It was an Anglican called Robert South, in 1660, who called for a return to a form of speech he called "plain style," in other words, speak in a way that is conversational and familiar! So moral essay preaching also arose from a desire to be natural, rather than affected, in the pulpit. Instead of bizarre metaphors, windy delivery, and pompous verbal pyrotechnics, the new look was to be cool, rational, and straightforward. I call it "Oxbridge Don" preaching.

Finally, there was a need to present the faith in an age when scientific rationalism was on the rise. Francis Bacon had struck a blow for induction over deduction, and modern science was on its way. Many preachers felt defensive, fearful that Christianity's explanatory power had been demoted in favor of naturalism, or, at least, an indifferent theism. The task, as they saw it, was to carve out a new role for faith, sealed off from the withering heat of science. Those preachers who felt that they had to respond to this reacted either by going *mystical* or by going *ethical*. The mystical option came from Friedrich Schleiermacher, where the religious experience is located deep within the feelings of the self, far away from the explanatory power of science, which can only deal with empirical phenomena. The other is to go ethical, where the sermon makes the case that Christianity is always relevant because it tells you what to do, how to be honest, and even how to succeed in a new, more prosperous, meritocratic world.

Going the ethical route meant producing a sermon that put the moral element of the gospel to the fore in the simplest possible style. Structurally, it remained indebted to classical canons, flowing according to a forensic speech – exordium, explication, proposition, partition, argumentation, application, and conclusion. The talks were topical, with a text at the front, but lop it off and you had a moral essay. There was little that was exegetical about it, but the form did have its high point in the likes of great stylists such as Newman and Bushnell. In France, there were great wordsmiths like Massillon and Bourdaloue who took it to new levels. This sermon type had the great advantage of being wonderfully readable. Books of sermons by Philips Brooks and F.W. Robertson were virtual million sellers in an age when every good girl and boy was required to read an "improving" book.

In fact, it still sells millions, as Harvard Chapel preacher Peter Gomes will attest.

Don't knock it. It has its place!

Content issues: the moral bit of the moral essay form

Let's face it, there are times when the morality element of Christianity needs to be preached more than any other element. During the ferment of the black struggle for civil rights, Martin Luther-King, Jnr. used the form time and time again in appealing to his audiences to respect an ethic of non-violence. He reached great heights as he made that ethical case on Christian grounds. Desmond Tutu, in South Africa, also comes to mind. I remember a sermon of his against "necklacing" – the grisly practice of burning a person to death by placing a lighted tire over their shoulders.

Context is critical here. In places like China, people know morality is important, but they want to hear what is distinctive about *Christian* morality. In places like Britain, by contrast, people often need to hear why any kind of morality is necessary at all. These are the issues of the age, and whenever the sermon is invited or nudges into the realm of public discourse, it is usually because there is a moral crisis requiring urgent address. The political sermon tends to be a moral sermon. And there's nothing wrong with that.

Once I was at a very posh party in Bath where everyone was starting to snort cocaine to take the merriment into another dimension. I refused and someone taunted me, saying, "It's because you're a Christian you can't have fun." And I remember replying, "No, it's because life is full of beautiful pleasures and dreadful pleasures; Christianity just helps me tell the difference." In that context, that was OK. They didn't want to hear about my prayer ecstasies, or the joys of Christian fellowship; they just wanted to know on the simplest level why anyone like me would still bother with such a passé, killjoy religion as Christianity. My answer was: because its moral guidelines keep me out of trouble. Actually, the reply owed something to the reading of a fine book by John Killinger on the Ten Commandments. He writes:

> In her beautiful novel about Maine, *The Country of the Pointed Firs,* Sara Orne Jewett describes the ascent of a woman writer on the pathway leading to the home of a retired sea captain named Elijah Tilley. On the way, the woman notes a number of wooden stakes scattered about the property in random fashion, with no discernible order. Each is painted white and trimmed in yellow, like the captain's house. Curious, she asks Captain Tilley what they mean. When he first plowed the ground, he says, his plow snagged on many large rocks just beneath the surface. So he set out the stakes where the rocks lay in order to avoid them in the future. In a sense, this is what God has done with the Ten Commandments. He has set out the stakes where the rocks are. He has said, "These are the trouble spots in life. Avoid these, and you won't snag your plow."[62]

So it's no bad thing to have a sermon with the purpose of "How not to snag your plough." We will never rehabilitate the image of Christianity in the West if we cannot make this simple truth stick: Christianity is good for people!

Style issues: the essay bit of the moral essay form

Some complain that the essay form means the tone is too even. It can lack highlights or drama. There is something in this, but then, it's all about audience. I was raised in Northern Ireland, where it was felt that if the preacher didn't have a good shout, then the Spirit wouldn't come down. I don't shout any more myself, because I really dislike being shouted at. Whenever a preacher begins to bellow, many Europeans start to think, "Watch out, we have a screaming fascist here," and the mind projects old newsreel footage of Mussolini and Hitler strutting about in jack boots at their rallies. Educated European audiences want passion, but they don't want ranted at. So a natural, conversational style – well suited to the essay form – has its place.

Maybe it's terribly English, as I said before, very Oxbridge Don, and – all other things being equal – you don't want to hear an Oxbridge Don preach! But there are always exceptions. It's no coincidence that one of the best exponents of the moral essay form is the current Archbishop of Canterbury, Rowan Williams, as Donnish as they come. He speaks in an even, detached tone. Not a hint of rant. His sermons are carefully layered essays of arguments, like chapters of an academic book. Granted, his oral punch is compromised by the density of argumentation and the convoluted phrasing. His institutional platform gives his sermons a prominence that they would not otherwise command. But, he can preach a great moral essay sermon.

Williams' Christmas sermon for 2003 is a good example. He has a short text that he briefly refers to in the first paragraph and that's about it. It's the words of the angel to Joseph in Matthew 1:20: "Fear Not." He moves immediately into a discussion of why religion is feared today by a liberal elite. There is a fear of faith in some circles of British society, which aggressively insists that religion be invisible and private. Essentially, his subject matter is a moral one: what should be the place of religion in public life?

Williams then gives reasons to explain why religion is justifiably feared, including its history: "… alas … religious faith has too often been the language of the powerful, the excuse for oppression, the alibi for atrocity."[63] This admission would have the effect of relaxing people who fear faith. He moves on in the argument to show that this fear is misplaced because of the manner in which Jesus came at Christmas – not by force, but in stillness.

> Here then is the real Christian response to the modern secular person's fear. God is no hostile alien, snatching away what belongs to us. Faith is not either a perversion of human freedom or a marginal and private eccentricity. It is human freedom raised to its fullest by the fact that God has embraced it in love…[64]

If Jesus' followers reflect his "Christmas manner," they will refrain from using religion for coercive ends. Williams ends with a great challenge that Christianity takes human freedom to its highest level. It's a human rights argument, if you like, and as the language of human rights is the only moral discourse allowed in Western public life today, it's a superb contextualization of the Christmas message. Of course, such an argument and style would be quite useless if he were speaking to Latino or Afro-Caribbean charismatics. But his sermon is quite brilliant in the context of a generally skeptical and secular audience, as well as for a Christian audience that may need reassurance about the right to apply their faith to public life.

The form has its place. And please don't label preachers as "Oh, he's a moral essay preacher" or "So-and-so is a scholastic thematic." A good preacher uses all these forms. Historically speaking, people do get stuck in them, but that's because they emerge with such force as a breakaway to the old paradigm. Rowan Williams, for example, usually preaches in an essay style, but he is not always a *moral* essay preacher. He preaches many sermons where the primary thrust is theological, devotional, even prophetic. These forms are categories, not coffins. The good preacher masters them all.

For all that, one has to be suspicious of a style of sermon that reads so well and sells many books. Sermons that read well rarely sound well. The essay is not an oral form!

There's an even bigger problem with the moral essay form to watch out for. It's this: the power ain't in the ethics!

The power of Christian morality lies in the fact that it is Jesus Christ who gives us the power to be good. The ethic only makes sense when you add theology to it. Christianity's essential appeal – and its uniqueness – does not lie in its ethics. The preacher's goal is not to make people better or more successful citizens, but more Christ-like creatures. I am more forgiving toward others when I live in the realization of how much God has forgiven me. As we realize how much Christ loves human beings, we see each human being as sacred. That's why we value people so highly – God died for each one. Indeed, that's the best basis for human rights.

Not long before the end of his life, the great missionary statesman Lesslie Newbigin gave a speech to the World Council of Churches in 1996. In his late eighties and nearly blind, he conveniently failed to see the "time's up" notice and went on (thankfully) to say this:

> It seems to me that in the century that lies ahead of us these are the three major factors which will compete for the allegiance of the human family: the gospel, the free market, and Islam... As to Islam: while the other great world faiths are deeply significant and worthy of respect, none of them makes the same claim for universal allegiance. As to the free market: the crucial question is going to be whether the Christian church can recover its confidence in the gospel in order to be able to challenge with confidence the enormous power of this ideology which now rules us. We are dealing here with an idol, the idol of the free market, and idols do not respond to moral persuasion. They are cast out only by the living God, and it is only the power of the gospel in the last analysis which can dethrone idols and which can create the possibility of a free society.[65]

Preachers are called to smash the idols of the age in the power of God. It's spiritual warfare. But you can never smash an idol through moral persuasion or suggestions of sanctified common sense. No, we have to unleash the mighty gospel of God and embed it into our communities so that we can refuse to worship these idols. The moral essay sermon has too often proved defenseless in the face of an idolatrous foe! You must connect morality to Christ, or the de-supernaturalized faith will surely fall into the hands of the idol.

This is a sobering note to end on, but this is exactly what happened in twentieth-century Germany. Great scholars like

Adolf Von Harnack decreed that Christianity was ethics, and relegated the faith to individual do-goodism. The problem is, people can't worship morals. "Be nice to your neighbor," is all very well, but you don't really have to go to church to hear that, nor does it make your pulse race, or your heart burst. And if the faith won't, something else will! The German liberal church had to come up with another product – one that moved people like the supernatural elements used to. That product was an idol: German nationalism. Being a liberal Protestant in early-twentieth-century Germany became identified with being a "proper German." This unfortunate marriage helped put Hitler into power. And arguably because the moral essay sermon slipped its moorings from the epic grandeur of God's mighty works and acts!

Letter 23:
The evangelical revivalist form – from Whitefield to Graham

Each new sermon form tends to emerge as the old one enters the point of its worst incarnation. The nadir of the moral essay form resulted in a sermon that turned something supernatural into something mundane. It took the gospel and made it prosaic. The evangelical revivalist form, in contrast, set out to take the gospel and make it *dramatic.*

Dramatic impact is the key feature of this form. First, the exponents of the form often experienced dramatic and sudden conversions, moments when God erupted into their lives and turned them upside down. Often called the "born-again" experience, this is the "evangelical" bit. These preachers sought to replicate the same experience for their hearers through their sermons. The aim was to induce dramatic experiences of God. Second, the preachers used their emotions to create impact. It became their trademark. Third, they boldly targeted the feelings and motivations of the listener. They sought to move the audience. If the sermon left you dry-eyed, unmoved, and murmuring, "That's interesting," then these preachers would consider themselves a failure.

It is here in the middle of the eighteenth century that the sermon becomes a dramatic art form, every bit as entertaining and moving as a Shakespeare play. The preacher became a performer of the gospel. The altar recedes into the background, and even the pulpit itself disappears to become a stage. Preaching became entertainment of the best sort. Some of the finest actors of the day would come to hear the gospel preached from the lips of Whitefield, Finney, and Moody to get tips for their art. It is this preaching that launches great revivals such as the First and Second Great Awakenings in the US, and becomes the staple form on a highway of revival preachers running from Whitefield to Finney to Moody to Sunday to Graham.

Often the greatest exponents of any new form are among the first. This must be true with George Whitefield (1714–70), who shared with John Wesley (1703–91), the accolade of Britain's most influential eighteenth-century preacher. Let's imagine what it would have been like for a person coming to hear Whitefield after a diet of moral essay fare.

Shock 1

Whitefield shouted. He was loud. So loud his lungs were said to be made of galvanized iron. Others said that he had a roar like a lion. The extent of his pipes must have been immense because once he spoke to an audience of 100,000 outside Glasgow. It was 1955 before Whitefield's homiletical descendent Billy Graham drew a crowd of similar size in that city. That was at Hampden Park, the football stadium, but with the aid of microphones and mighty amplifiers.

Shock 2

Whitefield didn't use notes. He never read his sermon. There was no lectern. No manuscript. No turning of pages. Whitefield had it all memorized, and frequently improvised. His huge cross-eyed stare was boring into your soul the whole time.

Shock 3

Whitefield was always in motion. He strutted around all the time. Some estimated that he walked a mile and a half in the course of a one hour sermon. He put his body into his sermon in a way never seen before.

Shock 4

Whitefield wept. His emotions were in full play throughout. He was called "histrionic" by many, but he let it all hang out. He wept for your sins. He wept at God's grace.

Shock 5

Whitefield went for your emotional jugular. This was not a man out to tell you about the merits of one doctrine vis-à-vis another in a calm rational fashion. He made your heart palpitate and your palms sweat at the fierce judgment of God, and balanced that by raising your hands heavenward in thanks for God's grace. He made you *feel* the gospel. He made you live through it. Try staying calm through these words coming at you at 80 decibels:

> Oh wretched Man that I am, who shall deliver me from the Body of Death? Are all the Grand Deceiver's inviting Promises come to this? O Dammed Apostate! Oh that I had never hearkened to his beguiling Insinuations! Oh that I had rejected his very first Suggestions with the utmost Detestation and Abhorrence! Oh that I had taken up my cross and followed Christ! But alas! These reflections come now too late. But must I live for ever tormented in these Flames? Oh, Eternity! That thought fills me with Despair. I cannot, will not, yet I must be miserable for ever.

Shock 6

Whitefield acted out the passage. He took all the roles of the characters in a biblical passage, male or female. He had different gestures and voices for each, and by all accounts he was a consummate actor. Perhaps his upbringing as a tavern owner's son gave him an eye for distinctive characterization. Certainly he was experienced in the chatter of all classes, not just the educated elite.

Shock 7

Whitefield never talked much about doctrine. The emphasis fell almost entirely on your feelings about what he was saying. Whitefield preached doctrine all right. He was a convinced Calvinist, and had a long spat with the more Arminian Wesley over the freedom of the will and predestination. But the focus of his sermons was not on the delineation of doctrine, but its appropriation. In other words, "There's the truth, but can you feel it?"

Well, we could probably list more. Suffice to say that the
effect of hearing Whitefield would have been similar to how
someone described hearing Charles Finney: "Like cannonballs
through a basket of eggs!" Harry S. Stout's wonderful
biography of Whitefield, *The Divine Dramatist*, credits him with
the invention of the new form:

> "he transformed the traditional sermon into something different:
> a dramatic event capable of competing for public attention
> outside the arena of the churches – in fact, in the marketplace.
> Whitefield showed that preaching could be both edifying and
> entertaining."[66]

This is important. As P.T. Forsyth once said, the history of
preaching is the battle between the altar and the pulpit. One
effect of the Reformation was to place the sermon so centrally
the altar receded into virtual oblivion. Whitefield took it a
stage further: the sermon *was* the service. He preached mostly
in the open air and a sermon was all he gave them. Liturgical
preachers can tut-tut about this development if they wish, but
Whitefield pioneered open air preaching because churches
closed their doors to his style of preaching. He reached the
multitude who did not darken the door of traditional churches
when it was no longer compulsory to attend services. This
probably explains why the greatest exponents of this sermon
type became, in the main, itinerant preachers, and why revival-
meetings became extraordinary events.

So what is the essence of this type of sermon? If you preach
this type of sermon, you are looking for three reactions from
your audience. First, you want them to feel an emotion. Second,
you want to reveal God through the power of your Christ-
altered personality. Third, you want them to make a decision.

Making a decision

The decision bit came particularly from Charles Finney (1792–
1895). This sermon form targets the individual's will. This
focus comes from the evangelical spirituality of preachers who
all had conversion experiences in which they yielded to God
by a decision of the will. They want the audience to do the

same, as this is the best way to ensure that they will have a similar experience. Billy Graham makes no bones about it. He warns his audience that at the end of his sermon he will ask them to "Get up out of your seats." You make a decision to accept Christ, or to rededicate yourself to Christ. This decision is regarded as vital. It is response preaching. It is direct, in-your-face, and asks for a reaction.

In the later part of the twentieth century, this characteristic of preaching began to be used outside a purely evangelistic setting. In charismatic church services, for example, preachers often ask the audience to stand up and receive healing prayer, or to come forward for counseling if especially touched by the ministry. If nothing else, it can be a useful indicator (if discerningly interpreted) of how successful the sermon is. More profoundly, it ushers the profession of faith into the realm of reality.

Feeling an emotion

Unlike the moral essay sermon, emotion is not feared; it is encouraged. The preacher expresses emotion during his talk, and seeks to use words in such a way that they stir emotion in the listener. Take Graham again. Here's a sermon of his entitled "Are You Getting What You Want?" It's a four-point outline:

- Things will not satisfy.
- God satisfies.
- God's offer is free.
- God's offer is for everyone.

You can tell at a glance that Billy Graham's immense impact is not due to his sermon structure. Within this simple structure, he seeks to awaken in the listener an anxiety about their state before God. He tells harrowing stories, paints pictures of hellfire and torment, and solemnly warns that death can come at any moment. He lists all the ills of the world that occur as a result of separation from God – poverty, emptiness, fear, loneliness, drug abuse. He tells you that all secular remedies will fail, and piles up quotations and stories to back this up.

This is all done at high-octane intensity. Nothing in his manner gives the impression that you can "take it or leave it." He is out to create the emotion of fear. Then having created fear, he replaces it with another emotion – hope. There is a palpable shift as he declares, "The sole and sufficient answer to these problems is Jesus Christ." The sermon will then go on to paint the benefits of knowing Christ. This is all done with passion.

Don't automatically assume that this is manipulative. Our feelings are just as important as our thoughts, and the idea that we make the best decisions when emotions are not around to cloud our judgment is thankfully passing. We think what we feel, and we feel what we think. You can't separate the two.

Revealing a personality

Look at this sentence from Billy Sunday, a former baseball player and sawdust trail evangelist raised in America's deep South. He describes Pontius Pilate as "One of those rat-hole, pin-headed, pliable, stand-pat, free-lunch, pie-counter politicians." Or he ridicules members of a particular denomination as "Those ossified, petrified, mildewed, dyed-in-the-wool, stamped-in-the-cork, blown-in-the-bottle, horizontal, perpendicular Presbyterians." Never in a million years will you be able to say it with the effect of Billy Sunday. In this sermon form, you can't hand someone the script and see them preach it as well, if not better, than you. No, it is utterly individual. The preacher's personality is an integral part of the sermon.

Billy Graham is another case in point. He has enormous charisma. Even his gestures are unique. Earlier in his career, he used a battery of them including a clenched fist, pointing finger, ambidextrous slashes, two-pistol punctuation, and all to assist a rapid rollercoaster delivery. He was Billy Graham. There was none other.

What is important is that these men know that the secret of their impact is to embody completely their message. That is their appeal. That is what really communicates. It is their passionate intensity, their grip on God, that shines through their personality. One of Graham's biographers, William Martin, once asked the famous evangelist's subordinates what the secret was of Graham's impact. They admitted that Graham's actual sermons were "Quite ordinary, even sub-ordinary… but the man just obviously believes what he says, and he comes over as a very human person."[67] For this to happen, preachers must allow their personalities to get across. They are not repressed, but expressed.

It is easy to substitute one's personality for the message, or to let charisma overshadow it. A preacher might not intend this, but it does happen. I remember one preacher who was gifted with a golden voice. It had a deep, rich timbre, soothing and yet exciting at the same time, like Laurence Olivier with a dash of the precision of Alec Guinness. He loved his voice too much and blew his call. Walking the fine line where the personality is the vehicle that channels the gospel, rather than occludes it, is very hard to do. Every preacher, no matter what the sermon type, has to walk this tightrope.

* * *

The form is not confined to the evangelical tradition, nor to evangelistic services. Much Afro-American and Afro-Caribbean preaching, even of a liberal-leaning stamp, is built around it. The preacher uses their personality to the full, and since the congregations (in the past anyway) were often poor and downtrodden, the task was "To give 'em an ecstasy and an epiphany every Sunday morning." If anything comes from this form, it is the challenge to put an emotional lift into your sermon, and see the expression of your own personality as a powerful way to communicate gospel truth.

Warnings? Of course there are many. One problem with this form is that it can be far too individualistic, and it shrinks the demands of the gospel down to personal sins that the individual can repent of and theoretically change right away, like adultery, drug abuse, drunkenness. We live and sin in community. Yet you tend not to find evangelistic preachers berating people for the sins of jingoism, racism, or slavery. Reinhold Neibuhr, who gave us the term "structural sin," savaged Billy Graham in the 1960s for his inattention to the racism of the period.

Another problem is that in a church setting, evangelistic preaching of this sort can displace teaching, with the result that Christians do not mature as they might. As a friend of mine in a Fort Lauderdale megachurch said, "I can't grow if all I get every Sunday is John 3:16 and how God will save me from my sins. I've repented. I'm saved. Now I want to grow. But he's not preaching for me any more." It's easy to grow the numbers of a church with evangelistic preaching, but it's harder to grow the members of the church into the deeper teaching of the faith.

And, yes, it can be manipulative. I'll never forget a Canadian evangelist coming to Belfast in my youth and telling my pastor father, "Oh, I can bring 500 out of their seats every night if I make the appeal long enough." It takes great sensitivity to back off and let the Holy Spirit make the impact through the personality, and not the personality at the expense of the Spirit.

Finally, it comes with a health warning for preachers themselves. It is the most ego-boosting form of preaching. To see hundreds flowing to the front seemingly as a result of your words is a heady experience. To have audiences coming to hear *you* preach the gospel, giving it the individual twists that no one else can manage but you... beware! The front pages of newspapers are littered with the scandals of fallen evangelists, and the faith in some quarters has been disgraced. As Jim Baker once said to a friend, "I thought *I* had the power, not God." All too often it becomes show business, not gospel business. People may be coming to hear you, but the object of the exercise is for them to meet God.

This is where Billy Graham has been so impressive for me. I remember once having to escort him from Hong Kong airport. He was staying at the Sheraton Hotel, and they sent a Rolls Royce for their VIP guest to the airport for his arrival. His aides sent it back. "He won't step into it," they said. The bemused Sheraton staff sent a mere Mercedes, but the aide said to me, "He doesn't want to tie the gospel to luxury." The transparency of his organization's finances, his care not to be alone with women other than his wife, his refusal to accept offers of a corporate jet, have all served the cause of the gospel because no one can reject Christ by saying, "He's just a huckster who wants to get rich on my contribution."

So we gain a newer form of the sermon on our journey. One where the preacher is out to "mug" you into the kingdom. Emotional, in-your-face, and personality plus, it reflects well the urgency of the gospel and makes the greatest demands on the skill of the preacher. Yet it became too often the stuff of con-men, of Elmer Gantry types, who grew drunk on the power of speaking for God and coercing reactions. For that reason perhaps, the evangelical revivalist sermon type tended not to run in the mainstream church. It became the sermon of itinerant and often eccentric evangelists who brought their own tents, choirs, and advertising, and was organized, in the worst cases, in spite of the local church witness, instead of at the invitation of them. Within the mainstream churches, another preaching paradigm was going to emerge as the moral essay form continued to dominate: the liberal inductive form.

Letter 24:
The liberal inductive form –
from Fosdick to Craddock

Being raised in a tradition that was anti-clerical, I was fortunate to begin my preaching career at sixteen. In Plymouth Brethren, if you had the gift, you got the opportunity. It was a wonderful system when it worked. When it didn't, it meant that non-gifted Tom, Dick, and (occasionally) Harriet, all preached regularly as well – a severe test of endurance for some of us. I reminisce because someone was recently asking me how long I had been preaching. I was horrified to hear myself answering "Twenty-eight years!" The same person then asked me a fascinating question: "What are the two most significant evolutions in your preaching?" Why he picked two I have no idea, but I had a good think about this, and came up with these two.

The first evolution has been to develop a more *robust inquisition* of the Scriptures. In my early days I tended to stay within my inherited and perhaps too deferential tradition of interpretation. But the older I get, the more I ask awkward questions of the text. I have quit the magisterium for a more independent line of inquiry. Perhaps being a journalist has made me that way. The story always lies in the gap between the rhetoric and the reality, between what people say is going on and what is really going on. One develops a nose for this gap. So when I get to a text now, I subject it to the same suspicion. Say I was to preach on Samson. Twenty-years ago I would have moved straight to issues of morality and taught his story as one of opportunities forgone through indiscipline. Now, I would ask why the author assumes that God is pleased when Samson's final act is one of religious genocide – killing 3000 Philistines, roughly the same number killed by the 9/11 hijackers. These questions lead me down new paths, to deeper truths, and ultimately, to a bigger God.

The second evolution was to develop a *slower disclosure* of truth. In the past I went for maximum immediate impact. You know, the Samuel Goldwyn school: "Start with an earthquake, and build to a climax." I always started with a ballistic missile of a story, followed up with cannon shots of paradoxical propositions, lobbed over some jaw-dropping illustration grenades, and finished with an atomic bomb of a closing challenge. I still have the bomb, but this is what has really changed: for most of the sermon now, I keep it ticking. It's the best seller principle. The ticking bomb forces the reader to keep turning the pages. In other words, I have become largely an inductive preacher, as opposed to a deductive one.

Induction refers to the specific movement of thought in the sermon from the particular to the general. Say you have a passage to preach on. You don't just start in with general information about the passage, but with a particular issue. It might be a contemporary parallel problem to the text. The rest of the sermon solves that problem gradually, holding the resolution until the latter part of the sermon. A classic inductive structure is:

- What is this?
- Not this.
- Nor this.
- Nor this.
- But this!

The inductive method of preaching came in two waves, thanks largely to the liberal church. There was the Fosdick wave in the twenties and the Craddock wave in the seventies.

Harry Emerson Fosdick (1878–1969) was the senior minister at one of the most prestigious pulpits in the US, at Riverside Drive Baptist Church in New York, from 1926–46. Described as "America's most prominent liberal Protestant preacher when religious liberalism knew its finest... hour,"[68] Fosdick carved out a new type of preaching that was to dominate the twentieth century.

Usually, you want to do a new thing when you are convinced the old ways are no longer working. Early in his preaching career, Fosdick concluded that the two prevailing preaching models of his time were failing the church completely. One, he called the expository preaching method. It wasn't working because, as he quipped, "Only the preacher proceeds still upon the idea that folk come to church desperately anxious to discover what happened to the Jebusites."[69]

The other model Fosdick called "Topical preaching," or what I have called moral essay preaching. This was failing in Fosdick's view because the preacher soon ran out of topics and ended up giving banal bromides that could be heard in any context. He wrote, "If people do not come to church anxious about what happened to the Jebusites, neither do they come yearning to hear a lecturer express his personal opinion on themes which editors, columnists and radio commentators have been dealing with throughout the week."[70] If all that was on offer in the pulpit was a moral perspective on the social issues of the age, then there was no need to come to church at all. Reading the papers on a Sunday morning will do just as well. Millions now do just that. Fosdick was determined to deliver a unique experience to his audience from his pulpit, an experience they could not find in any other medium. Where was that uniqueness to be found?

Fosdick's suggestion was to begin the sermon with a description of a particular need within the lives of the congregation. This need he discerned from his experience of counseling congregants during the week: "Every sermon should have for its main business the head-on constructive meeting of some problem which was puzzling minds, burdening consciences, distracting lives, and no sermon which so met a real human difficulty, with light to throw on it and help to win a victory over it, could possibly be futile."[71] After securing attention because he was dealing with an issue close to the heart of the listener, Fosdick then moved to the Scripture text itself to provide responses. In this way, he predated the focus on inductive logic that was to dominate post-war American homiletics. He pioneered gritty, realistic sermons that sought to allow the Scripture text to speak to specific issues. He is the father of the "therapeutic sermon."

Take Fosdick's sermon entitled "A Fundamentalist Sermon by a Modernist Preacher." He begins by describing a discussion where Jewish and Christian men were saying that although they had left fundamentalist ideas behind, like a flat earth or a 6000-year-old creation, they still missed the passionate feelings of secure conviction associated with fundamentalism. The dilemma was: how do we retain the passion of the old-time religion alongside the cool rationalism of the new-time liberalism? Great question! Great issue! And the rest of his sermon analyzes what the old-time religionists possessed in spades that modern liberals had let go of, namely, "an unconsenting individual conscience, the deep secrets of prayer, and a courageous faith in God that rises above the darkest facts of life." He ties it all up with Jeremiah 6:16: "Stand ye in the ways... and ask for the old paths" (KJV).

Mind you, Fosdick was not a pure inductive preacher. Mostly, he would start with a problem, then switch to a deductive form to provide a suggested solution. Nothing wrong with that! No one gets points for purity.

Fosdick was liberal, and so was his main counterpart in the UK at the time, Leslie Weatherhead, who pioneered a rapprochement between theology and psychology. But the method soon spread beyond liberal enclaves into evangelicalism. One of the best exponents of the form today is Bill Hybels, pastor of the 18,000 member Willow Creek Community Church near Chicago. In fact, most megachurch pastors tend to use a "scratch-where-they-itch" introduction, then shift into deductive gear for the response.

In Hybel's book *The God You're Looking For*[72] you can see this clearly in a sermon called "Are You looking for a God... Who Knows It All?" He opens with a specific experience from his high school days, describing the stress of Friday afternoons, when he and his friends would gather with pounding hearts to see if they had made the coach's list for the weekend basketball team. Most were disappointed. Hybels then shifts to talk of another roster, God's list, and asks whether we are sure that we are on it.

You see how inductive his beginning is? Hybels starts with a specific story describing the stress of having one's self confidence and identity on the line all because of a team list, then relates it to God's list, and creates interest by asking us whether we know that we are on it. Then he goes deductive. God is omniscient, so how does that affect our status on the list? He starts in Psalm 139, using David as an example. David knows that God knows all. Hybels multiplies his points: God follows our ways, God knows what we say, God knows what we need, and so on. Next he has three points:

- **The bad news:** He knows your secrets.
- **The good news:** He also knows your scars.
- **More good news:** He knows your service.

Hybels works through the Psalm, building up to his climax that a generous God knows all and still wants to love us and empower us. We are on God's list. "The omnipresence of God is powerful stuff. It makes ordinary people extraordinary, weak people strong, insecure people models of confidence and courage. There's not much you can't achieve or endure if you know God is walking by your side. Just remember: Someone knows and Someone cares."[73]

As I mentioned, after his introduction his essential structure is deductive rather than inductive. After his introduction, the body of the sermon is a series of specific applications of the general proposition: God knows everything! So the two forms can be blended very successfully.

The inductive atomic bomb went off in 1971. It took the form of a book entitled *As One Without Authority* and was a call for a purer form of induction as the best way to beat the anti-authority mood of the age, which was killing the possibility of a receptive hearing for the gospel. The author was Fred Craddock, at the time a forty-three-year-old professor of Preaching and New Testament at the Graduate Seminary of Philips University. Told early in his career that his reedy voice meant that he would never become a great preacher, he went on to become the most influential homiletician of his generation. From 1979–93, he held the Bandy Professorship of Preaching and New Testament at the Candler School of Theology at Emory University.

Craddock's book had a major impact for two reasons. One, it was superbly written. He was a master stylist, with gifts of verbal invention worthy of a novelist. The book reads like a dream. Two, he identified and spoke to a *zeitgeist*. The essence of the age, argued Craddock, was the coming together of two crises: A language crisis, we had lost our faith in the power of words: and a knowledge crisis, we had lost our certainties. He wrote, "Rarely, if ever, in the history of the church have so many periods slumped into commas and so many triumphant exclamation points curled into question marks."

If this is the issue of the age, then how do we preach to it rather than past it? Craddock felt sure that the older deductive format was sure to be ineffective. A deductive sermon started with the conclusion – an unnatural form of communication in his view. It presupposed that preachers had discovered the truth and were dishing it out as a result of their study. But if they were not trusted any more, either because people had a problem trusting the Scriptures, or trusting the clergy, the sermon wouldn't work. Craddock's suggestion was to move to pure induction because it was a more natural form of reasoning. It meant that the preacher enlisted the audience in co-discovering the text, rather than risking a negative reaction by "talking down."

The key idea here is a purer form of induction, meaning, keep the resolution until the end. There is a perfect example of this by John Claypool in a sermon entitled "Life is a Gift." His passage is the sacrifice of Isaac, but he begins by telling the harrowing story of his daughter's death from leukemia when only ten years old. The experience is four weeks old at the time of his sermon, and he is still dazed. But he sees enough to suggest that, in moments of grief like this, he could take three roads, two of which were unsatisfactory to him. The first was the *road of unquestioning resignation*: just accept that suffering comes, we can't understand it, and God has a right to inflict it. But he rejects this because it is human to question, and, furthermore, God welcomes it. "There is more honest faith in an act of questioning than in the act of silent submission, for implicit in the very asking is the faith that some light can be given."[74] Second, there is the *road of total intellectual understanding,* where it is believed that we have all the answers. No, he says, I couldn't find it to be anything more than a mystery why a good and all loving God would not heal my daughter. But it is a relief – you don't have to explain a mystery! These are the roads he has not gone down. The one he finally recommends is the *road of gratitude.* He turns to the passage, teaching that God's purpose in asking Abraham to sacrifice Isaac was to teach him that life was a gift. God had no intention of taking Isaac's life. He wanted Abraham to see that everything – the promises, the land, even the life of his son – all came from God's hand. He applies this to the loss of his daughter, Laura Lue.

> I do not mean to say that such a perspective makes things easy, for it does not. But at least it makes things bearable when I remember that Laura Lue was a gift, pure and simple, something I neither earned nor deserved nor had a right to. And when I remember that the appropriate response to a gift, even when it is taken away, is gratitude, then I am better able to try and thank God that I was ever given her in the first place... I have two alternatives... I can dissolve in remorse that all of this is gone forever; or, focusing on the wonder that she was given to us at all, I can learn to be grateful that we shared life, even for an all-too-short ten years."[75]

What a powerful sermon! One great advantage of such a form is that you have to stay tuned until the end. You want to know how he used his faith to cope. It is perfect inductive structuring to keep you waiting while he goes through the false roads. And notice how honest he is. There is no "Right, here it is, so listen up!"; just a normal Sally or Joe, like those in the pews, trying to make sense of a terrible tragedy. We fall in step with him. We co-discover and we have to stay tuned – the great twin advantages of the inductive sermon structure!

Don't let me oversell it. Craddock may have identified an anti-authority mood in the liberal churches, but that does not necessarily extend to all church cultures, where a regard for the truth of Scripture may not have been so seriously eroded. The deductive method can still work in that setting. Also, pure induction does have its limitations, especially in less skilful hands. It's possible to shrink down the truth of the passage too much to an individualistic need in the quest to find a relevant starting point. And, what if the passage may not seem to be immediately relevant to the audience? After all, the gospel has an utterly unworldly element too. It's also tricky to ensure that your solution not only solves your presenting issue but applies beyond it. It is easy to narrow down the teaching of the passage overmuch. Great care needs to be taken in selecting the presenting issue.

For example, if I was asked to preach on Abraham's sacrifice of Isaac, then I might start in with a recent experience attending a scriptwriter's conference. The speaker was a famous story doctor called Robert McKee, who confessed to being a "recovering Catholic," though whether *from* or *within* Catholicism I could not tell. He told us that the one biblical character he would have loved to write a script about was Abraham, because "He's the guy who tries to murder his own son out of love for God and starts the insanity of religious conflict that led straight to 9/11." It's a common view and a good inductive starting point: "Religion just starts wars, we'd be better off without it!" And one could argue against it by taking Claypool's "gift-theology" line, which would create a striking reversal to end with: God is not the God who takes life, but gives it!

But to take that line results in two crucial limitations. One, many people listening may not share McKee's negative view of religion at all, and therefore the question would not grab them. Indeed, some may be quite offended by it. Two, in answering the issue, you have to leave out an awful lot of the passage's teaching. You have homed in purely on whether God is a cannibal or not, but there's a lot more to the sacrifice story than that.

Well, it can be done, but, like every form, it takes great skill to bring off in its purer form. That said, I do not know a form which holds an audience's attention better than this one, except maybe the narrative form, but then that also relies on the inductive principle in a more extreme form, as we shall see.

Letter 25:
The post-liberal narrative form –
from Lowry to ?

I discovered narrative preaching through an experience of terror. Two years into a Masters of Divinity degree, I found myself in a communications class with only three other students. That meant more time for individual participation. The professor warned us that we might find it "a bit intensive." She wasn't joking. I lost two pounds from the first assignment. You'll laugh, but all I was asked to do was to go out of the classroom for five minutes, then come in and deliver a two minute sermon on the beatitudes.

You have to understand that I have an extreme fear of being under-prepared. I read ten more commentaries than I need to, write a sermon four times as long as required, and still the night before have nightmares that I'm up in front of the congregation and they've changed the topic, or switched the verses, or that I can't find the passage.

After our professor gave us the assignment, I shot into the corridor. Trouble was, I didn't have my own Bible, and was given an old dog-eared King James. Took 35 seconds to find the blasted passage! I looked off into the quad, frantically racking my brains for a wee nugget or two on the *Sitz im Leben* of Matthew's Gospel. Nothing came. Right then, the class next to ours spilled out on their break. Friends came up to me, "Hi, Ron." It was all I could do to shoo them away without snarling.

One minute thirty in. I'm starting to count the beatitudes. Cripes, there are eight. No wait, nine? Oh gosh, is it eight or nine? There might be quite a bit hanging on that. Should I see if there are fewer in Luke? No time, it's two minutes twenty now. Get going, Ron! Come on! I decided that the best thing to do was to go through them one by one, saying what they meant and applying them. I know it was crazy, but I couldn't help myself. I was rustling up an eighteen point sermon. I started shaking. The professor put her head round the door. "Ready?" I managed a dry bark, "Eh, just a little longer..." I was only on the twelfth point. "Just come on in with what you've got!" she said.

If they ever make speed speech an Olympic event, then the gold medal will go to me every time. I rocketed through the points, tongue trilling, and sat down dripping with sweat. I had managed to get to the sixth beatitude before time faults applied. The other students looked shell shocked from the pounding. I sat shaking in my puddle, making "whew" sounds as I mopped the brow. The professor said very gently, "That was fine, but why did you feel that you had to tell us everything about the passage? In a two minute-talk, you might want to make your aim a bit more modest, maybe just take one beatitude and tell us a story."

I stared at her in disbelief. Could it really be that simple? Could a two minute story really work as well as an eighteen pointer? Where did that insane desire to tell them absolutely everything about the passage come from? I crossed a Rubicon that morning in my preaching life. I began to embrace narrative preaching.

I know why I had packed the sermon with so much material. I felt that you always had to precede application with information. Context first, challenge second. But then it struck me – story does both at the same time: it brings information and application together in a seamless form that makes twice the impact. Also, I felt under a particular obligation to be "thorough" with my passage, which for me meant tackling everything. But even here, I began to understand story as a means to express the whole truth. I was reading the ancient mystic John Cassian at the time. Cassian urged Christians to use short verses of Scripture to make unceasing prayer because by doing so we were "folding the recollection of God into the little space of a meditation upon one verse." Story has a similar capacity to enfold infinite truth into a finite form. It's more than an illustration, which is just to make the proposition more vivid. It is the proposition and the illustration in one.

To cap it all, someone in the same communications class did precisely that, and something more. She started in by saying, "All the beatitudes say is, 'if you put God first, you'll put others first, and if you put others first, you'll find yourself.'" Then she told us a story about "Blessed are the meek, for they will inherit the earth." A young man gave up a fine education to support his brother, who went on to become a famous professor. The young man then became a priest, and during the Second World War ran an underground network to get Jews and anti-Nazi Christians to America. After the War, his bravery was recognized, and he became a minister of education in a new interim government. He became his academic brother's boss. "The meek will inherit the earth," she finished. "Put God first, and see God give you the earth." She showed me the something more – story makes you *feel* the truth. I had given them eighteen points *about* the truth. She had given us one point that we *experienced* as the truth.

I started to read up on storytelling and preaching. There were a whole slew of books, some fluffy, some superb, like Walter J. Bauch's *StoryTelling: Imagination and Faith.* I also began to realize that narrative preaching had come from narrative theology, though a grand old theologian called Walter J. Hollenweger once warned me, "Most narrative theologians can only talk about narrative, they can't use narrative." Still, this does give us a clue to the theological address of the form.

One might argue that there are three essential projects in theology: orthodox, liberal, and post-liberal or narrative It could be that a mixture of all three is what we need, but humans being stuck with a need to polarize, it hardly happens. The orthodox project is the first, roughly the way we believed up to the Enlightenment. It rests on the belief that language is analogical, so doctrines can state what is objectively true, and therefore cast light on what is false. Our faith is embedded in the acts of God in history, reliably witnessed to in the Scriptures, and authoritatively proclaimed by the church. This unchanging truth must be believed and proclaimed in every age.

Liberalism's project is to recast belief in the light of modern knowledge. Liberals believe that our understanding of the world has changed so radically that the worldview of the traditionalist is no longer able to cope. Bultmann, for example, says that science shows the silliness of believing in a three-storied universe – heaven, human, hell. Their answer is to believe, with Schleiermacher, that the foundation for faith should no longer be in history, or facts, but in experience. Religion shifted its foundation, from history to intuition. Faith is about what we feel, and how we work out a relationship with God. For liberals, the people who came up with this reconciliation were the scholars, not the church. There is no magisterium (except of the scholastic "in-group"). When it comes to Scripture, for example, liberals use scientific and historical insights in order to extract a time-transcendent core. The disposable husk may include miracles, supernatural beings, and primitive apocalyptic theology. Remaining is the idea of an ethical life of selflessness with which to invite the reign of God in the world.

Narrative theologians believe liberals made a terrible mistake in trying to reconstruct the truth behind the narrative and make it into a proposition. Hans Frei, one of the narrative pioneers, said that the truth lies not in what is underneath the narrative but within it. That is, a narrative is a way of seeing and interpreting the world. It is a world-view, a grid, through which one lives. It's a story. Your tradition, and your community, instruct and reinforce your life as part of that story.

This perspective is a major break with liberalism for a number of reasons. One, it denies the whole enterprise of "hunt the kernel" and pours scorn on the idea that there is some common experiential core at the heart of all religions. The stories are simply too diverse. Two, historicity questions are sidestepped. What matters is how the story shapes your world. Three, narrative theologians believe that your religion is the product of your linguistic story. Liberals tend to say that religion is the product of experience. You have an experience and then you find the words to express it. "No!" say the narrative theologians. The story gives you the categories and grammar, then you have an experience consistent with that story. The ideal should be that, when it comes to the Bible, we are given a story in which the text absorbs the world rather than the world the text, to paraphrase George Lindbeck.

Well, as we have seen in our trawl of sermon form, the sermon babe is quite comfortable breaking away from its theological parents. You don't have to be a post-liberal to be a fine story preacher. In fact, most of the best story preachers are not post-liberals, and many of them, for example Eugene Lowry, would just see narrative preaching as an inevitable development of the shift to inductive preaching. Both views are probably right.

On a practical level, you have two options. First, you can try pure narrative. Your sermon essentially becomes the performance of a short story. I've seen this done well about twice in my life, and it is way beyond the competence of the average preacher. Unless you are phenomenal with words, have received a Nobel prize for literature, and are an Oscar winning actor, don't try it! Have mercy on the listeners.

Second – and this is much more doable – you can *structure* the sermon like a story: starting with a conflict, complicating the conflict to raise tension, and ending with a resolution to resolve the tension, and then give closure. The methodology of Eugene Lowry, in his little classic *The Homiletical Plot* is probably the best on offer in this regard. He argued that the experience of the truth could best be felt if the sermon was constructed like a plot. He outlined the five stages of this plot.

- *Upsetting the equilibrium,* where the equilibrium of the listener is upset by introducing a conflict.
- *Analyzing the discrepancy,* where the conflict is made to count with the listener. The problem is described in all its ambiguity and complexity, creating tension in the listener.
- *Disclosing the clue to resolution,* where the principle of reversal is used to shine a light on the coming resolution of the conflict.
- *Experiencing the gospel,* where the resolution is actually felt by the listener. Needless to say, this is dependent on whether the first two stages have properly engaged the attention of the listener.

- *Anticipating the consequences,* where closure takes place as the preacher outlines the changes that can be expected.

I just simplify the process to what I call TCRs: tension, complication, resolution. Take God's speech to Job. Here's one tension – how does God bawling Job out solve his problem? Complicate it. Maybe God was annoyed. After all, Job's complaint was not over whether God was powerful, but whether God was just! God seems to sidestep the challenge. Resolution – the speech actually shows that Job was trying to be God rather than human. He is a creature in a world full of grace, not a God in a world where everything's gone wrong. You can expand a TCR to the whole sermon – T, C1, C2, C3, R – or use them within points. You don't have to make the entire sermon follow a single plot.

Narrative preachers do tend to oversell their product, however. Yes, it does have immense transformative power. It gives an experience of the word, not just information about the word. And indeed, that goes deep, because our lives are ultimately stories. And yes (usually the clincher), Jesus was a master storyteller.

But there is a very big limitation – not everybody gets the point of a story!

Remember Nathan telling David that story about the rich landowner who stole a lamb from the poor man to feed a guest instead of taking it from his own herds? David was incensed, but could he apply the story to his own life? Nathan has to do something that all storytellers will tell you never to do: point the moral! "You are the rich man!" Nathan thunders, and he's probably jabbing his index finger at David, too. The metaphor is so subtle that it needed the assistance of a simple proposition to hit home. Even a brilliantly told story sometimes needs a little help. In fact, it is amazing how often Jesus explains the meaning of the parable. When Matthew gives us a little parable shower in chapter 14, the parables of the sower, the weeds, and the net all are followed by interpretations.

There is so much more that we could say about story – and many have, at great length – but you get the feel of the story structure in the swim of sermonic history. It's hardly a late-twentieth-century development in the sense that all the great artists of the past were storytellers. The principles of narrative have been around since Genesis. All the more odd, then, that it is so minor a key in the sermonic symphony for centuries.

I must confess though to a real love of narrative preaching for another quite separate reason – it enables me to preach more convincingly the parts of the gospel that sound unpalatable in a propositional form.

Once, while traveling in Israel, I met the British novelist Graham Greene. Over a drink in the King David hotel, he told me – with on-setting inebriation – that the reason he wrote novels as a Catholic was because he found most of the Christian gospel so unpalatable as a proposition, that it could only be explained and appreciated as a story. He instanced one of his early novels, *The Heart of the Matter*.[76] At the root of the story was this proposition: If I lie, cheat, desert my duty, commit adultery, and then commit suicide, but do it all out of love, I will gain the kingdom! Distilled into twenty-five words, the proposition convinces no one. Set in a story of sixty thousand words, embedded into a character for which we feel deep sympathy, we can at least entertain the possibility that he might have lived a life of virtue, even though in the Church's eyes, it was a life of unforgivable sin.

My encounter with Greene stuck with me, especially as I traveled around Eastern Europe and China. In both places, I met persecuted Christians who also embodied truths in their stories that made no impact on Western lives when their lessons were stated propositionally. To say "persecution promotes growth" or that "God's gift to China was the Monster Mao" made no sense to Western Christians. But set in stories, these truths found a space to be contemplated. Stories demand time to appreciate, and may be retained longer in the memory, and in these features may well sit a peculiar transforming power, as we mull them deeper into the soul. I wonder whether a large swathe of the gospel message itself can be appreciated *only* through the story form.

Section Four:

The Preacher's Life – the Issues

Letter 26:
Criticism – What do I do when
I get the bird?

You've had some bad reviews? You want to chuck it in? Yes, welcome to the biggest secret of the ministry... it's not sex that is the number one reason why most preachers leave their jobs, it's discouragement. Poll after poll puts discouragement at the top of the list every time, with sexual indiscretions, or worse, a distant second. And surely criticism expressed against the preacher is the main tributary of that sea of discouragement. The preacher who cannot deal with criticism will not preach for long.

As it happens, I've just had some stinking reviews. I was preaching three times to a group of 400 over a weekend and at the time, inevitably, all I heard were rave reviews. Then I received written feedback from evaluation forms a few weeks afterward. There were a few stinkers. Alongside "That was the most brilliant exposition of Revelation I ever heard" was "I wish I could have taken him aside and straightened out his theology on Revelation." One said I was "easy to follow" but another "far too intellectual." A few described me as "lucid and powerful" and a few as "poor and irritating."

What does one do with this? Let me count the ways...

1 **Accept that it hurts.** Of course it hurts. The few occasional bad reviews upset me far more than the more numerous praises. We can't help it. We want to please everyone, and if someone is upset with our preaching, then it's unfortunate and we take it personally. Such responses to preaching hurts, especially when the feedback is of an anonymous and cruel nature. Christians often express criticism in apocalyptic terms. They don't just write, "I didn't like his style," but, "He betrayed the gospel of Christ." The terms of criticism are often absolute and dismissive, and you can feel deeply

dehumanized because you have just been misunderstood without recourse. Go on, have a wail. It goes with the territory. Like they say about politics in America – *it ain't beanbag!*

2　**Remind yourself afresh that no one is ever everyone's cup of tea.** It's a simple communication fact that there will always be people who will not like your style, or who find that your voice grates, or take exception to your scriptural tack, or take a dislike to your squib features. In any reasonably diverse group of people this is inevitable. Just be thankful if the majority are appreciative. You have to be very careful not to bend over backward to please everyone. Don't let a disgruntled minority change your approach; only a disgruntled majority.

3　**Be aware that much of the ire directed at you is nothing to do with you.** You might inadvertently have squelched someone's pet peeve, or they have some silly hang-up. For example, at this recent weekend I know that a couple of people were upset I did not push a more Dispensationalist understanding of Revelation. I can't spout Hal Lindsay or Jack Van Impe. I don't subscribe to their interpretative grid. Theological disagreement comes out in criticism phrased like this: "The preacher was too ignorant of the biblical teaching of the book of Revelation." While at university, one of my best pals reacted very negatively to a well-known preacher, whom most of us enjoyed. My friend said he was awful, rejecting everything he said. Only months later did we figure out the story. Apparently, the preacher bore a striking physical resemblance to an uncle of my friend, who had been cruel to him as a child. That's why he took a violent dislike to his ministry. It would be insane of this preacher to feel terrible about his awful review from my friend. Insane indeed, but we all do it. There is an insane part of us that accepts responsibility for everyone's wounds. Try not to!

4　**Ask yourself honestly, "Did I preach to the best of my ability, in the time I had available, what I felt God said to me?"** If you can answer yes, then relax. You did your part. You did your best, and you cannot do better than your best. Sure, the *sermon* could always be better – better researched, better reasoned, better delivered, and so on. But you haven't the time to be perfect. You did the best you could before God and before God's people. God asks no more of you, even if some of the congregation do.

5   **Remember again for the thousandth time that a response like "poor and irritating" could be a sign of success.** It may mean you got through to the person, and this is a reaction against you as a means of not looking within at their own issues. You ruptured a veil of false certainty, and planted a foothold for change that may bear fruit later. Sometimes preaching has to take risks and push the envelope. That kind of preaching will poll less satisfaction. Sometimes truth has to disturb as well as comfort. Your gift may be to lead people out to unfamiliar areas. I love that GNB translation of John 7:43: "So there was a division in the crowd because of Jesus."

7   **Treat anonymous criticism with a pinch of disdain.** It's too easy to fire off a few angry phrases. The only really valuable feedback for the preacher is qualitative interaction. Seek that above all else. Find trusted listeners – not necessarily peers – whose judgment and spirituality you respect, to give you feedback in a loving fashion, and value that.

8   **Ask yourself again, "Is Jesus and his message worth this hassle?"** Remind yourself that he is the greatest being in the world, and everyone needs to know him, and his gospel is the only message that can save us. Then decide if the price of proclamation is one you can keep paying. No one will blame you if it is not. Perhaps God is calling you to proclaim the gospel in another way.

9   **Strengthen yourself with the biblical giants.** All of them dealt with carping criticism, misunderstanding, and humiliation. Let the experience lead you to a deeper appreciation of what Jesus endured to bring the gospel to each of us. You might even end up thankful that you are not about to be crucified literally for your messages.

10 **Get out and play.** Anything physical. Fish, garden, cycle, hike, take up tennis, or golf, or ballroom dancing... whatever. You must have a hobby that creates total absorption and

expends aggression outward, otherwise that same energy will turn inward, making you broody. Get moody and it's the end.

11 **Know your issues.** I used to find this phrase infuriating because it was always dispensed by psychologists as if it was the easiest matter in the world to "know one's issues." But it is worth getting clued in on this. Our upbringings have left each of us with wounds and insecurities, and if we are not careful, these feelings of insecurity can be triggered again by criticism, and so we end up with two enemies – an external and an internal critic shouting "You're no good!" The criticism triggers an internal virus of self-loathing which, once launched, can cause more harm than the initial problem. Knowing your issues enables you to recognize and respond when the virus gets triggered.

In practice this is easier said than done. But here's a specific case: a friend of mine failed an intelligence test when he was eleven. Normally he should have gone to a dreadful school, but his parents paid for him to attend a very expensive boarding school. The problem was, they could only afford to send him for one year. After that year, if his grades were good enough, the government would pick up his scholarship and he could remain. If his grades were not high enough, he would be placed back into the dreadful school, humiliating his parents in the process. As an eleven-year-old, he lived in abject terror for a year because no one told him what grades would be good enough to secure the scholarship! He could take no comfort in a 70 percent score; what if the grade was 90 percent? In the end he passed, but the experience left a massive mental scar, where he wondered whether anything he did was ever good enough.

Whenever criticism of this man's preaching was expressed in terms like "We don't think you have the skills to remain our pastor" it would trigger all the feelings of terror, of being a eleven-year-old schoolboy wondering if he was going to make the grade or disgrace his parents. It was a similar situation. He was being assessed, but he didn't know the grade that he needed to get. Over time, he learned to decouple this feeling of terror that came from within and the criticism that came from without. It saved his ministry.

I'm not saying every preacher ought to get into therapy to figure out these internal emotional viruses. I am saying that every preacher does need a level of self-awareness to spot when an old wound has been nicked, and to prevent this from triggering a plague of self-persecution. After all, you don't want to hound yourself out of the ministry.

12 **Ask yourself this: "Did the adverse reaction come as a result of an attempt to make God bigger?"** This is a process that creates resistance. People like to keep God in a safe strongbox, and if you attempt to destroy that box and release God from it, well, God may thank you for it, but God's people may not! Growth is sometimes painful, and the preacher does have a responsibility to grow the spiritual lives of the congregation.

13 **Use the criticism to improve your preaching.** Many of the above stratagems are refusal strategies, preventing criticism from having a destructive impact. But of course not all criticism should be rejected. How does one discern the difference between helpful criticism and destructive criticism? We can't simply say, "I reject all criticism that is anonymously given, or is purely motivated by personal jealousy," because buried under these unattractive skins may be valuable feedback that you can't get any other way. The preacher needs critical feedback.

My method is to listen to the criticisms – no matter how intemperately expressed – wait a couple of weeks, then discuss them with a trusted friend who knows me well and whose judgment I respect. In this way, I have seen some withering suggestions turn into useful insights that have made me a better preacher. Michael Caine once described his acting philosophy as "use the obstacle." He was talking about an incident while learning acting. He had to enter a room, place his foot on a chair, and make a speech. But when "action" was shouted, he put his foot on the chair, and it collapsed. He stopped. The director was furious. He said, "Use the obstacle. You have been given a special opportunity to make this scene extra special and spontaneous. Use that to bring out a deeper acting performance." Caine never forgot the advice, and extended "use the obstacle" into a general philosophy of life. Similarly, "use the criticism" is a way to become a better preacher.

In these ways, criticism will not destroy you. The most unhelpful advice I have heard is "Have the hide of a rhino." Most of us just can't manage that. Indeed, retaining our sensitivity is crucial to our discerning the will of God and carrying out our pastoral duties. I have never met a rhino that preached well.

The greatest temptation of all is to wonder, "Could I not just be completely loving and positive, put the *good* back into the good news." But that's a myth. Preaching the gospel involves judgment, because truth divides. When the brothers of Jesus give him a hard time about being too controversial, he replies, "The world cannot hate you, but it hates me, because I keep telling it that its ways are bad" (John 7:7, GNB). Preachers have to be negative about some things that many ordinary Christians are positive about. Dietrich Bonhoeffer was negative about the Nazis, and many German Christians thought he was overreacting. To raise Christians to a higher awareness of the implications of their faith, and to a more effective repentance, preachers must nail their colors firmly to the mast, not the fence.

Learn to live with criticism. And remember what Rabbi Hugo Gryn used to tell his students: "A rabbi whose congregation does not want to run him out of town is no rabbi. And a rabbi whose congregation does run him out of town is no man."

Letter 27:
Jesus – Can I preach like Jesus?

Or, HWJP – How Would Jesus Preach?

Jesus is overwhelming! That is why we always shrink him down to a size that we can manage. Like that hoary illustration of blind men describing an elephant – one claims it's a rope (he's holding the tail), another it's a flat lizard (he's got an ear), another it's a pillar (he's got a leg), and so on – Jesus the communicator suffers the same fate. Here are three shrinkages overheard in the past six months alone.

One man said that Jesus didn't actually preach, but acted everything out. Jesus' task was to communicate through symbolic action, and according to this earnest man, "never used words much!" Enough said. He's wanting to highlight how Jesus' life was his sermon, but a trunk does not an elephant make!

Another view went, "Jesus is primarily a storyteller!" Jesus would be disgusted, went the argument, to see us using propositions or abstract ideas in a sermon. He told parables that were vivid and interesting. So should we! Though a great storyteller, Jesus spoke in many forms. Proverbs were as prominent as parables in his repertoire. What are the beatitudes but a series of quite abstract propositions? To say nothing of that fierce finger pointing "woe" speech to the Pharisees and Sadducees. Not much storytelling going on there!

A final one (heard just last week) is that Jesus was not only a storyteller, but a *mystery* storyteller. Jesus told stories, went the view, that were rarely self-interpreting, or if they were, they took a long time to figure out. Jesus liked to confuse. He was an artist, telling complex stories that mystified and gnawed away at the hearer until the *eureka* moment came much later. The lineage of the view might date to C.H. Dodd's famous definition of a parable: "A metaphor or simile drawn from nature or common life, arresting the hearer by its vividness or strangeness, and leaving the mind in sufficient doubt about its precise application to tease it into active thought."[77] It's a definition that works well for the parable of the sower, for example, where the disciples are so mystified that they request a private interpretation, but it hardly applies to parables like the wicked vineyard tenants, the meaning of which is so immediately clear that the Jewish leaders want to arrest him. Most of Jesus' parables are not that mysterious. Clever? Always! Obscure? *Not* always!

Well, we could go on, but Jesus the communicator is going to be beyond us as a topic. We always end up "shrinking him." And let's get the "of courses" out of the road as well. Of course we cannot preach like Jesus in the sense that he was perfect, we are not; he had no hypocrisy, we have some; he was divine, we are human, et cetera. Despite these qualifiers, looking hard at Jesus' communication style should be a major responsibility of any preacher of the gospel. Let me offer you nine ways Jesus *the communicator* has formed my approach to gospel proclamation.

1. Great preaching starts with great praying!

I'm always rebuked by how much Jesus prayed! As an observant Jew, he would have prayed regularly in the temple and synagogue (Mark 11:17; Luke 4:16). Yet, he was also fond of retreating to pray (e.g. Mark 1:35; 6:46), taking nights by himself in lonely places before crucial moments, like the choosing of the twelve, or the betrayal by Judas. He goes on a forty-day prayer retreat before beginning his ministry, possibly to consider the implications of his baptism. And his last poignant "upper room" moments with his disciples are soaked in prayer. His prayer experiences are full of intimacy and agony, but it is in prayer that he discovers his identity as a preacher and receives his message! If we want to preach half as well, we had better pray twice as much.

Jesus only spoke words given to him by the Father (John 8:28). He models complete dependence. His power, message, and identity, come entirely from his knowledge of the Father through a life of prayer. This is why he warns his disciples to wait on God after he leaves, until the Spirit comes upon them (Luke 24:49; Acts 1:4). Most of preaching is about waiting!

What it all added up to for me was that I realized that this had to be my number 1 priority as a preacher: learn to love prayer! I have always found it hard. For me, the keys have been to vary place and method. I use a thirty minute daily personal liturgy that involves singing. I take long prayer walks or vigils before important challenges. Each year I take a week-long prayer retreat. I have learned not to swamp my prayer times with too much liturgy. It can give me rhythm, but not intimacy. I have also learned to enlist the senses and be more creative, using music, candles, icons, clay, and seeking specific environments that enhance concentration. I have a set of finger beads that I use three times a day so that wherever I am and however I am feeling, I *will* find ten reasons to praise God. My techniques vary, but they only matter insofar as they create and protect a space to talk to God. Above all, I must make sure that when I am in that space, I do not do all the talking!

From these moments come the reality of knowing a personal God. From that reality come the words to say to a world that is hungry for that reality. Prayer is where you find out first, who God is, who you are second, and last, what God wants you to say. Learn to love prayer, or you will never know if your words are God's words!

2. Be the word you preach!

I'll always remember an Episcopal priest preaching that there was no distinction between clergy and laity, and then proceeding to conduct the Eucharist in a fashion that made it clear that only clergy could. Her actions contradicted her message. With Jesus, there is complete consistency between words and actions. He not only tells us that the kingdom is about welcoming sinners; he eats with them. He not only tells us that he is a suffering messiah; he suffers and dies. In other words, he *embodies* his message. And this gives his words so much more power.

In Hong Kong, I had the privilege of knowing a godly Roman Catholic priest. He had exhorted his flock for years on the theme "Stand up for Christ and you will be persecuted." But he looked at the ministry of Jesus one year, and decided, "OK, I had better *do* what I am saying." He began an outreach to rescue runaway teenagers from the streets. He discovered that the triad gangs were also out looking for female runaways to press gang into sex slavery in Japan. Many times, he would have to fight physically to tear the girls away from the clutches of the triads. He was shot at, and stabbed twice. But his preaching made a lot more impact "because I was suddenly speaking with complete credibility in people's eyes," he said. He added, "I'm only sorry I found out this communication principle in my fifties."

So whenever I preach on a topic, I remember to ask, "Could I *do* it in the context of the sermon?" Or failing that, ask, "Have I practiced this truth so that my speech is coming from the center of an experience of it?"

3. Mint punch lines and master the two minute story!

Sure, Jesus was a genius. But he also must have labored long and hard to come up with so many memorable phrases that distilled his teaching so well. The beatitudes are masterpieces of memorability and economy that delineate his remarkable kingdom in less than 150 words. I'm sure he didn't just shape them on the spot. We know this because so many of his great one-liners follow the patterns of Hebrew poetry, the rules of which he must have learned. T.W. Manson shows Jesus as expert in four types of memorable statement: synonymous (Mark 4:22), antithetic (Mark 8:35), synthetic (Luke 12:49), and step-parallelism (Mark 9:37). They are brilliant. Just think about this: "For everyone who exalts himself will be humbled, and he who humbles himself will be exalted." Or "Whoever wants to save his life will lose it, but whoever loses his life for me and for the gospel will save it." In a single statement, Jesus hands us a huge slew of teaching that will turn life upside down. That takes work, even for a genius. Try to cultivate key statements that put over exactly what you are trying to say.

Have you noticed how short Jesus' parables actually are? "The Good Samaritan" is 156 words; "The Parable of the Sower" just under 200; the parables of the rich man and Lazarus less than 300 words. The lengthier ones, like "The Parable of the Prodigal Son," still don't exceed 500 words. These stories can all be told in less than five minutes!

For me the challenge is not to come up with a story, but one that in five minutes turns the world upside down. Everything can be lengthened for the occasion, but first try to come up with paradigmatic parables or stories that encapsulate the teaching vividly, even draw in and challenge the audience. It is hard, but we must try. Work on impact. Work on form. Jesus did!

4. Try the open air!

It seems terribly simplistic, but when I was a younger preacher I saw that the vast majority of Jesus' speeches occurred in the open air. I said to myself, "Well, if I want to follow Jesus, that's what I should do!"

Jesus does make speeches in the synagogue and the temple, and possibly delivers more actual teaching when he's discussing or discoursing in homes, either with others or the twelve. But big slabs of his preaching are done in the open air. There was a very good reason for this – he wanted to reach the whole nation! Staying within the walls of the synagogue or temple would only have reached the "holy" set. The open air barred no one, and left Jesus freer to perform his unique ministry of preaching and healing without interference. So the "open air" stands for a communicational challenge: Am I preaching in a way that will connect with the majority who do not come into churches? What will project the gospel out into the culture? Am I trying it?

When I first considered this I was living in Hong Kong. I decided to go along to the New Age centers. They welcomed everyone to "explore their spiritual spaces." I reckoned that most of the people thought church passé, and the gospel negative and unadventurous. I was right, but in most cases the contexts were superbly open discussions of people's spiritual experiences. I could gently put a more Christian case in the midst of it. John Drane, the New Testament scholar who has become an expert on Christianity and the New Age, tells of a friend who goes to psychic fairs (which, incidentally, attract numbers exceeding any Christian convention), sets up a booth, and tells people the biblical background of the characters on Tarot cards. That's the open air. Go to where the people are, and address them there!

Then of course there is the *physical* open air. Try open air preaching because, well, Jesus did! I first tried this out in Belfast, twice in Bristol, and a few times in Hong Kong. The kind of speaking you do in the open air forces you to be so different. You must be arresting, vivid, concrete. You realize why Jesus was such a great storyteller, and such a short one: you've got to keep your message rolling in five minute cycles because people usually cannot listen long. The context also forces you to be more interactive. You get immediate responses from an audience, and you learn to defuse anger with wit and grace. It demanded skills I did not have but had to find – fast! The whole experience was terrifying and stimulating, and even if the response was pure abuse, perhaps you know a little how Christ felt as a preacher.

I'm not suggesting that everyone become an open air preacher. There are many parts of the world today where it would be unwise to try. Even in freer countries it can sometimes be a fruitless tactic because few will listen. You have to be smart. You have to gain a hearing for the gospel, and the methods vary from age to age. But I tried it, and I'm the better for it. If nothing else, I grew even more in admiration for the courage and skill of Christ the communicator!

5. To communicate the gospel, don't just preach!

Here I mean don't just *monolog* the gospel! Jesus' preaching incorporates three main styles of communication: monologs to large crowds, dialogs with smaller crowds, roughly twelve to thirty-five people, and apprenticeship-teaching with his intimate circle of the twelve and the women who followed him. This latter type of teaching is where you allow your "audience" access to your daily life, so that they can see in the most intimate way how you connect *word* to *life*. It has to be said that the majority of Jesus' teaching was accomplished in the dialog and apprenticeship contexts. Much debate rages over which of the three delivers the most amount of transformation, and it's quite common to see the monolog rated the poorest of the three in that regard. If I am to influence my congregation or target group, I must do more than talk to them in larger groups.

To dialog requires very different skills than to monolog. Primarily it requires the ability to come up with questions that will allow the audience to discover the truth themselves, and in the context of the discussion, refusing to give an answer, but probing and encouraging the audience to achieve that discovery. Most preachers are poor at this. They like to announce truth. But you can learn so much from this method. The skills are transferable even to the monolog, which at its best is a way of anticipating, raising, and answering the questions that arise in the audience's mind.

Apprenticeship-teaching is even harder, because it is a brave act to let a few people into one's life. Sometimes we are scared that they will "see too much." In my experience, preachers often carry such a low self image that they do not think they have anything to pass on to others. But they are wrong. Anyone over forty has years of reflective experience to pass on.

Senior preachers also need to invite other, younger preachers into their lives. Take walks together. Read books together. And most importantly, prepare sermons together. Let younger preachers learn by osmosis. I think it is irresponsible if senior pastors just preach. All too often they keep clear of people, and instead of discipling other preachers they are jetting off to other cities to preach warmed-over sermons at conferences. It won't do!

Use and master the monolog by all means, but don't assume that it is the only or main communication method for preaching the gospel. It wasn't for Jesus!

6. Remember to be revolutionary!

Jesus really went to the root didn't he? His prophetic critique cut across all the prevailing assumptions. The kingdom of God was thought to be political, emerging with dramatic signs and culminating in the overthrow of the Roman yoke. He said it was within, established secretly, and without spectacle. Everyone said the elect were the righteous. Jesus said the elect were the sinners. Righteousness was defined in his day as keeping the purity laws. He said it occurred only when one observed the spirit that gave rise to the laws – love of God and love of one's neighbor. You name it, Jesus took his axe to the root. What a jaw-dropping experience to hear him reframe and redefine the rule of God in the world.

Of course we cannot hope to surprise like Jesus, but I do ask myself this question: Does this sermon do justice to the *revolutionary* dimension of the gospel? Or have I just given a set of reasons for being successful in, for example, the modern world? What has Jesus to do with being successful? Why not query the whole notion of success? Or don't be so quick to qualify and domesticate the extreme sayings of Christ, like "Go and sell all you have." At least get into the revolutionary spirit of Christ's critique. Don't teach people how to be better citizens! Teach them to be revolutionaries instead.

7. Get over crowds

Jesus drew large crowds, but he never set much store by it. He was never impressed by large crowds. Crucially, he refused to interpret them as an indicator of success in preaching, *contra* those who assume that if a preacher has built a mega church then he or she is automatically hot stuff. They may be, but ask these questions: Have they tried to thin the crowds like Jesus did in John 6:60–71 by preaching the *suffering* dimension of the gospel? Have they preached the hard sayings of the Lord? The danger with crowds is that they can define the preacher, and once the preacher is defined by them, so is the message. In Mark 6:45 Jesus just absconds. I wish some others would join him.

8. It's OK to shock!

Jesus shocked in at least five ways:

- in the way he taught (e.g. with authority, causing astonishment among his audiences, Mark 1:22);
- in the language he used (e.g. calling his audience "children of the devil" in John 8:44);
- in the things he did (e.g. healings and exorcisms);

- in the claims he made (e.g. to forgive sins, Mark 2:1–12);
- in the company he kept (e.g. eating with outcasts, Luke 5:30).

Of course, one cannot be expected to forgive sins or conduct exorcisms like Jesus, but many of Jesus' other shocking actions were quite normal in the sense that anyone could perform them, e.g. eating with outcasts.

Philip Yancey, a white evangelical author, tells of a visit to a restaurant in Mendenhall in 1974, a small town in the American South in the company of a black activist pastor, John Perkins. "When we sat down," recalls Yancey, "the white diners all glared at us and then, as if at a pre-arranged signal, got up and moved away to smaller tables. Except for Perkins and me, no one in the restaurant spoke for the next hour."[78] To shock in certain circumstances with the gospel does not require an array of sophisticated tactics, but the courage to do normal things in unusual contexts.

It's clear that Jesus conscripts the shock tactic for a purpose. He goes out of his way to shock. For example, he doesn't just say "follow me," but adds in Matthew 8:21–22 that following him is more important than burying your father! In the context, what a terrible thing to ask. The point is to awaken people to see that instead of gaining their identity from their family, which was normal, they now have an opportunity to gain their identity from being part of God's kingdom, which was revolutionary. Could it be that the shock tactic delivers a sense of disorientation which affords the gospel a space to create a radical Christ-centered reorientation?

I ask of my preaching: does it shock? Maybe not every Sunday. But if Jesus' gospel is radical, it should shock from time to time, otherwise it may not be the real deal. One does have to be careful. It is easy to be exhibitionist. Few can deliver a shock that contains the gospel wrapped up in it.

I remember seeing Tony Campolo introduced in a very posh church in New York City. He strode to the pulpit, shuffled his notes, looked up and then said a rather rude four letter word that began with "s". The congregation was upset. There was a palpable murmur of disapproval, some intakes of breath, and a hiss from someone near me: "That's disgraceful!" He let the reaction build, leaned over into the microphone, and boomed, "You know what really sickens me? There are kids fourteen years old being pimped as we speak, around the bloc from here, but most of you will be more offended by my use of a four letter word than the sin that surrounds you!"

Whew! It worked for Tony. He created a reaction and then threw it back at us in rebuke. Only the shock tactic can accomplish that. It wouldn't work if I did it. I just do not have his stare-down presence. But there are other ways. Receive permission to be shocking. Jesus was!

9. Preach by dying

Jesus tells his disciples, "When you have lifted up the Son of Man, then you will realize that I am he" (John 8:28). "Lifted up" in this context refers to the crucifixion, and it's staggering to realize that Jesus accepted that only *after* he was crucified would his disciples grasp his message. The words – even from his sacred mouth – were not enough. They would only hit home in tandem with the event of the crucifixion. It is the crucifixion that makes the message clear!

At the risk of being blasphemous, it is the same for every preacher. When we get to the word, we are "lifted up." We have to die to ourselves in order to embody this message, for only when it lives in our flesh can it have power in our words. Sure, we don't die for the sins of the audience. There is nothing vicarious about our crucifixion. But when we begin really to get to the word, God, I believe, arranges our lives so that we have to live the truth, before we preach it.

And that always involves dying!

Letter 28:
Success – Is it so wrong to want to be a Billy Graham or a Luther-King?

Or, The seven characteristics of three super-influential preachers!

Is it carnal to wish to be a world-renowned preacher? Must we condemn the ambition to become a preaching giant?

The fact is, if we do, then we condemn as carnal the most influential preachers of our age.

Billy Graham stated his ambition was "To take the Gospel to every person in the globe." Martin Luther-King, Jnr. wanted to "make America a better nation" through his sermons. Robert Schuller declared that his ministry came out of the sudden thought that "The greatest churches in the world have yet to be organized." He sought to organize them, fathering the mega-church in the process, which Peter Drucker called the most significant movement in the twentieth-century church.

They all *became* influential preachers. But they all *wanted* to become great preachers. They were not modest in their desire for influence, nor bashful in the way that they sought to extend their influence.

* * *

Of course not every preacher is called to be influential in the same ways. Not every preacher is called to be "successful" in the same ways. Not every preacher wishes to be either.

Yet, it does no harm to look at the ingredients that made these three preachers influential, not only in the church, but in society at large. We are all anxious to extend the gospel out beyond the walls of our churches, and these three men managed that. Each, in their own way, created a profile for

the gospel in the culture that the secular media noticed, and
became household names – no mean feat in a Western context
anxious to eviscerate religion from public life. In examining
how they attained this influence, we might find useful ways
to create a similar extension of our presentation of the gospel
message. Rick Warren, whose best-selling book *The Purpose
Driven Life* has been on the *New York Times* Bestseller list
for over a year, learned his skills partly at the feet of Robert
Schuller. There is a structure to success that can be patented in
certain circumstances.

So how did these three great preachers turn into hugely
influential preachers? The success-factors seem to cluster in
seven distinct areas:

1. The sermon

All three were superbly gifted communicators who worked
on their sermons with obsessive zeal. They all shared the
same attitude of wanting to be the best preachers they could
possibly be. As a young seminarian, Billy Graham took a book
of sermons every afternoon into an old shed near his dormitory
and preached to oil cans and lawnmowers for hours, honing his
voice and gestures, and memorizing umpteen master sermons.
This was a commitment to learn the craft of preaching that
far outstripped any of his contemporaries at Florida Bible
Institute.

All target the motivation of listeners. All are able to read an
audience and identify with them – skills not taught so much
today. They do not fuss over structure, keeping their outlines
generic and simple. All focus on universal human issues, like
the need to find God, the loneliness and injustice of the human
condition, the loss of self esteem in modern life.

Having said all that, they were not the greatest of their
breed. Gardiner Taylor and Samuel Proctor were regarded
as better black preachers than Martin Luther-King, Jnr. Even
Billy Graham's most loyal henchmen admit that the content
and structure of his sermons are often muddled and ordinary.
There were more gifted gospel preachers than Graham around,
but they did not achieve his influence. To know why, we have
to look at other factors.

2. The person

All three men have gifts, personalities, and experiences that give their sermons great impact and influence. Sometimes these gifts are physical. Graham has a voice of great beauty, and in the words of a film producer friend of mine, "a Hollywood head" – noble brow, piercing blue eyes, and a mane like a lion. Like it or not, he has a charismatic presence no one can imitate. Likewise, King possessed striking features and an effortless baritone capable of great power and pathos. These are simply *charisms* that are poured into the sermon, but transcend the sermon itself.

Non-physical characteristics are even more important. All possess incredibly high energy levels. By the time King is twenty-eight, he travels 4000 miles weekly, and in each 24 hour period in a major city delivers two or three formal addresses, a press conference, and several media interviews. He kept this up practically until his last year, dying from an assassin's bullet at the tragically early age of thirty-nine. All three were excellent self-publicists, knowing the value of marketing.

Perhaps most interestingly, all experienced a moment of transforming emptiness which gave them their passion.

One night in 1956, King told God that he could not go on. He was weary of the death threats and the exhausting responsibilities of being catapulted into the leadership of the black civil rights movement. He sat in the kitchen pouring out his doubts to God:

> I am here taking a stand for what I believe is right, but now I am afraid. The people are looking to me for leadership, and if I stand before them without strength and courage, they too will falter. I am at the end of my powers. I have nothing left. I've come to the point where I can't face it alone.
>
> At that moment I experienced the presence of the Divine as I had never experienced Him before. It seemed as though I could hear the quiet assurance of an inner voice saying: "Stand up for righteousness, stand up for truth; and God will be at your side for ever." Almost at once my fears began to go. My uncertainty disappeared. I was ready to face anything.[79]

When these men preach a sermon, the effects of God on their personality shines through, giving the words a whole extra level of power. They achieve a complete embodiment of their message. When Robert Schuller challenges his audience to "make your thinking big enough for God to fit in," he only has to point up to the ceiling of his Crystal Cathedral, tangible evidence that his philosophy of action works. When an audience listens to King, they hear a man who by his jail terms and his scars embodies the struggle for civil rights. People invariably report that what impresses them about Graham is not his sermon, but the fervor of his faith: "He completely believes in his message" is so often the amazed verdict of his hearers.

3. The wave

Each preacher was part of a longer, more significant tradition that created a space for their type of preaching. They are the products of, and articulators of, a tradition of ideas that defines their preaching. Their style, even, to an extent, their significance, is given to them. To put it another way, they are surfers. They surf a wave. They do not *make* the wave. The wave makes them.

We have seen in a previous letter how Graham, for example, is a product of American revivalism. He is part of a tradition of preaching stretching back through Moody, Finney, Whitefield, and even Solomon Stoddard. He does not invent it. He masters it. King is a product of the philosophy of Boston personalism, which stressed the value of the human personality, *and* the "black" preaching tradition, which gave him his distinctive *sounding*. Schuller's wave is the combination of Reformed theology and the positive thinking tradition articulated by one of his preaching mentors, Norman Vincent Peale.

To do these preachers justice, however, they not only ride the wave; some *redefine* it. No one marries Reformed theology and positive thinking before Schuller. King is not a typical black pastor. Watch him deliberately eschewing the emotional pulverizing of the black preaching of the time. His face is virtually expressionless. His topics are intellectual. His movement is minimal. Yet his language and sounding remains black, the way he manages to massage and milk every word for sound and meaning. He blended "white" philosophical content with a refined "black" style – a combination which enabled him to gain a universal hearing in a country as diverse and divided as the America of the 1960s.

Everyone is given a style. Those who master it find that it parts the waters for them.

4. *The moment*

They are successful because their sermons contain a powerful contextualization of the Christian message. They discern a *zeitgeist*. They speak to the age in a way few others do. Schuller discerned that it was a therapeutic age matched by a fall in self-esteem, and determined to present the gospel in terms of empowerment. He writes, "I was convinced that psychiatry and religion were merging and blending and that I could do my part to bridge the two and become truly impacting to the entire secular world. Could my preaching become a form of therapy for both the secular and the religious in my community?"[80]

Schuller may have his critics, but no one can deny that he has created a successful contextualization of his understanding of the gospel in modern America. He was awake to the opportunity of his time.

Graham says that there are four issues of the age he constantly addresses: emptiness, loneliness, guilt, and fear of death. In the 1950s and 1960s, he preached much on the themes of anti-communism, but later, in the eighties and nineties, pioneered a gospel that sought to bring an end to the Cold War.

King's challenge was to convince weary and increasingly angry blacks that a non-violent Christian gospel was the only solution to their ills. He managed it because the people were ready to hear it. He also crafted the perfect prophetic metaphor to give them hope in the struggle: daybreak!

The times gave each man a unique opportunity to craft the gospel for the age. These men saw it and took it.

5. *The movement*

They all build movements. They do not stay as mere preachers. Yet, paradoxically, they are careful never to evolve beyond their primary identities as a preacher. Graham gave

American Evangelicalism its defining institutions, like the magazine *Christianity Today*, and the *Lausanne Movements*, and became a political emissary to Communist lands. King played his part in organizing a new Civil Rights Movement, and saw his words enshrined in laws dismantling racist structures of injustice. Schuller's therapeutic insights have had a surprisingly major impact on the medical profession, where his trademark *possibility thinking* is seen as a positive healing message, and his *Institute for Successful Church Leadership* is attested by alumni such as Hybels and Warren in the US, and Cho Yongi in South Korea, the latter leading the largest mega-church in the world, the 500,000 member Full Gospel Church of Seoul.

All three realize that if they are to project their ideas into society, even into churches, then they must organize movements that carry the message out.

6. The network

Each preacher is propelled to prominence and sustained by forces that are not necessarily of their own making.

Sometimes they are catapulted into the culture at large.

Graham was an ordinary traveling evangelist until his 1949 Greater Los Angeles Crusade. One evening, he arrived at the tent to a cluster of reporters and photographers from the secular press, who had hitherto taken no interest. He asked one of them why the fuss. The reporter replied, "You have just been kissed by William Randolph Hearst." Though hardly a Christian, the newspaper magnate had decided that Graham was preaching a message America needed to heed. The next morning, Graham was a national figure as his face beamed out from the front pages. He told a friend on the East Coast, "You'd better get back out here real fast, because something has broken out that is way beyond me."

Graham kept himself in the public eye by the cultivation of celebrities and political heavyweights, writing books, television specials, and radio programs. The patronage of rich industrialists was essential to the extension of his ministry.

It's Graham that gives Schuller his break, suggesting a move into television and introducing him to a key backer. Suddenly, Schuller's audience changes from a few thousand to tens of thousands, overnight. Both were to become regulars on Larry King's nightly chat-show on CNN.

Even more dramatic was King's catapult. He had served less than two years in the southern backwater town of Montgomery, Alabama, when an elderly and weary seamstress in the city, Rosa Parks, refused to move to the back of a bus and let a white person have her seat. Her arrest on December 1, 1955, ignited the black community. A boycott was organized and a mass meeting planned. Though there were twelve other black pastors in the city, King was chosen to lead the movement and do the speaking. That very evening, in Holt Street Baptist church, he gave a speech that resounded throughout America. At twenty-six, he was suddenly the premier spokesperson for black civil rights.

What if Rosa Parks had lived in Memphis? Or Randolph Hearst had picked another evangelist? Would King or Graham have been catapulted to national and international prominence? A secularist would say that you need luck to be successful. Some Christians might say the same. Others would choose to see these incidents as God-orchestrated.

Whatever explanation we plump for, the fact remains: influence was handed to these preachers by forces beyond their control.

7. The event

All three ensure that the sermon is part of a carefully organized listening experience. It is an event within an event. Graham does not preach into a vacuum. Months of preparation go into the creation of a crusade, and the night has a carefully built up atmosphere, with celebrity music, and large choirs, all carefully choreographed to provide maximum impact for the sermon itself.

King preached to crowds of great expectation. Often he was careful to arrive half-way through a rally, creating pandemonium on his entrance. It all added to the drama. His famous "I have a dream" speech was given at the Washington

Monument to a million people ready to be lifted and cheered.

Schuller built a Crystal Cathedral to give his services a special atmosphere, as well as a landmark that draws thousands out of curiosity.

These men leave nothing to chance. They speak to a moment that is brimful of expectation. They labor long and hard to ensure the word will not return void. Insofar as this is a natural process, they do all they can.

* * *

Well, from this quick and personal trawl of some of the factors that turned three great preachers into influential preachers, what is to be learned?

Obviously, the degree of influence each exerted was not ultimately of their own doing. As the Teacher wearily says in Ecclesiastes 9:11, "the race is not to the swift, nor the battle to the strong... but time and chance govern all" (NEB). Luis Palau for example is a great evangelist, but he has never been profiled in the secular media like Graham, and thus his fame extends only to the Christian world, not the culture at large. So be it.

But we can take a leaf from St. Ignatius. To misquote his famous dictum – accept that influence is in the hands of God; act as if influence is in your hands!

If there is one thing I take from the example of these men it is this: *if you want to be an influential preacher, then don't just preach a great sermon!*

These men do not just focus on proclamation. They put as much effort into the *reception* of the word, and the *reverberation* of the word. Reception – ensuring their words are heard optimally. Reverberation – ensuring their words go on being heard long after delivery.

To proclaim the truth is only half the battle. These men fight on a broader front.

So should we!

Letter 29:
Multimedia – to PowerPoint or not to PowerPoint?

Or, The preacher and the communications revolution

It's understandable that when it comes to the communications revolution, most preachers home straight in on the skills question: How do I use multimedia techniques to enhance my preaching?

It's a new communications world. Confusing too. If the average person spends 50 percent of their waking life in front of the television, how is that changing us? The frightening fact is that no one really knows. We only know that the change must be profound.

Preachers feel panicked into competing for the attention of audiences used to "faster" languages that splice words with image and sound, or even dispense with words altogether. "Am I a dinosaur if I keep my twenty-minute monolog?" frets the modern preacher.

An old joke (first applied to creative writing) comes to mind: There are three indispensable rules to great multimedia preaching, but nobody knows what they are!

In my experience, preachers typically respond in four ways to the communications revolution:

> **"Images are now as important as words,
> so let's go multimedia."**

This usually results in lots of preachers using Microsoft PowerPoint, and projecting the points of their outline onto a screen. In fewer cases, the presentations include images. The old adage is wheeled out that people remember 20 percent of what they hear, 60 percent of what they see, and 80 percent of what they hear and see. The implication is that putting your outline on a screen creates an 80 percent chance of retention, 60 percent more than if you just said it.

Yet this may not necessarily follow. For starters, a PowerPoint presentation tool tends to make preachers multiply points, causing more and more to fail in their primary communicative duty to have one primary thrust! You start with an empty computer screen, and the tendency is to fill it up with more points than you need.

Another problem is that PowerPoint takes the attention away from the speaker, which is unfortunate because preaching is **embodied speech.** Consciousness is split, and often the impact is halved. The audience doesn't know whether to look at the screen or the speaker. Instead of reinforcing, the two different media detract from each other.

A speech expert who taught multinational CEO's how to speak asked them if they wished to go multimedia. He was surprised at the vehemence of their reaction: "No, keep the focus on me – *I am* the company!" said one typical respondent. It was not purely ego. One of them explained:

> I need the shareholders to trust me, and standing to the side in semi-darkness while snappy graphics show wonderful results just does not create enough trust. We live in days when everyone distrusts glowing statistics and slick graphics. I need them to look into my eyes, and I want to look into their eyes. Then we know whether we can trust each other.

The preacher too needs this eye contact. The gospel cannot be shared without trust.

Finally, and this has to be said because it is so easily forgotten, a preacher is *already* a multimedia event! A preacher is not just a mouth, but a body that sends literally hundreds of non-verbal signals that attract (or detract) from the message of the words. Never underestimate the power of presence. I once watched the great missionary statesmen, Brother Andrew, startle his hosts when they asked him to put his talk on PowerPoint. "No," he shouted, "because this is where the message comes from," and he pointed slowly to his eyes. "From here," he whispered, and pointing to his mouth and heart, "And here, and here!" He added, "A screen can *tell* them, but it's my life that *shows* them!"

Don't underestimate the power of the environment either. To speak in a historic church has a particular power, as the symbols reinforce your message, and the quiet space calms the heart for deeper concentration. Liturgical preaching is always multimedia and interactive, especially when the climax is the Eucharist.

Even a plain non-conformist chapel can add its voice. As a boy, I once accompanied my father to hear him preach in a tin chapel in Portavogie, Northern Ireland. It was a fishing village, and it was a wild night. Halfway through the service the claxon went off to launch the lifeboat. The rain thundered against the tin, but all fifteen listeners roared out the hymn "Eternal Father, Strong to Save, Whose arm doth bind the restless wave." The sermon came with remarkable force that night because of that amazing atmosphere of expectation. After all, the word must be special for people to leave their cozy homes on a terrible night and cluster around an old wood-burning stove in a leaky chapel. I can still remember all my father's points.

I'm not knocking PowerPoint. Particularly in classroom situations; and for putting over larger amounts of information, PowerPoint is a boon. This is just to caution that putting one's outline on a screen, or even showing images, does not automatically enhance one's sermon. Indeed, it has the capacity to kill it. There are special skills to be learned to marry words and screen, and the textbook that tells us how to do it has not yet been written!

And if you are still not convinced, take Richard Lischer's challenge; he asks us to imagine Martin Luther King delivering his "I Have a Dream" speech with PowerPoint.[81] Would PowerPoint detract or enhance the power of that speech? Surely the answer is – PowerPoint would ruin it!

> **"Television has shrunk the attention span**
> **to a few minutes, so we have to make our**
> **sermons shorter, or use short modules of speech."**

David Buttrick's massive Homiletic is taken up with teaching preachers how to construct twenty minute sermons out of a few "moves." Each "move" is four minutes, containing a statement, development, contrapuntal, image, and closure. His entire method is based on research that the attention span has shrunk to four minutes. While the method is useful, the whole idea of (a) an attention span and (b) a shrinkage in it, is surprisingly hard to prove. Jolyon Mitchell, a theologian and media expert who wrote a book in 1997 relating preaching to changes in radio presentation, warned that little empirical data has been found to support the idea of a shrinkage in the attention span as Buttrick suggests.[82] With storytelling on the rise throughout the church as well as the culture, which often takes more time and is less modular, one must be careful not to railroad preachers into changing their whole style.

> **"The communication revolution has created an expectation of involvement on the part of the audience, so we must be more interactive in our preaching."**

Thus some abandon the monolog in favor of dialog, or have drama segments and more audience participation. By all means supplement the monolog, but why go overboard? After all, the most dominant inventions of the communication age – television and film – are completely non-interactive, though no less popular for that. Another relevant argument here is that since we all have different learning styles, the sermonic monlog is only going to work for specific types and not others. There is a nice cartoon where a person says to the preacher, "I thought your sermon was fractionally off today, minister." To which the minister replies, "Well, I can only please one-sixteenth of the people all the time." That's a reference to the 16 learning profiles of the Myers-Briggs Type Indicator (MBTI). But while useful, any good psychologist will warn that the types should not be taken as determinative. After all, you don't catch movie directors throwing up their hands in despair saying, "Well, we're only going to reach a sixteenth with this one anyway."

Good communicators always go for universals, and can hold almost everyone through mastery of the techniques of being interesting, being clear, being persuasive, being memorable, and being practical, and in so doing covering the five basic communicational domains of attention, comprehension, yielding, retention, and behavior. It's not rocket science.[83]

> **"Because the media is so all-pervasive in everyone's lives, they are the providers of the new meta-narratives and metaphors that we preachers have to use to communicate effectively."**

In Britain, for example, preachers watch soaps and films in order to find points of connection with their audiences. This can be hazardous, however. At the time of writing, *Eastenders* is Britain's most popular soap. Yet only 10 million out of 57 million people actually watch it. And soaps have just been replaced in the popularity stakes by the *Big Brother* series. The problem is that television segments its audience while the preacher tries to speak to everyone. If you deliberately watch very little television, you can get quite alienated when the preacher keeps making references to actors and series you have never seen. A little voice begins to whisper, "Why is this preacher wasting so much time watching stupid television programs?" Too many references to mass media can undermine a preacher's credibility.

* * *

There is one overarching principle to be learned in this area of multimedia preaching, and each preacher has to answer this for themselves: *what can my words do that images cannot, and what can images do that my words cannot?* Great multimedia preaching grows out of a sensitivity to the unique and discrete impact of words and images, so that when they are put together, the sum becomes greater than the parts.

One night, I was listening to the famous actor Peter Ustinov. An audience of over 4000 had each paid more than £15 to hear this remarkable raconteur. The stage was bare. It just contained the chair his bulk sat in. There were no props save some subdued lighting, and he wore a lapel microphone to catch his incomparable baritone. For two hours he held us spellbound with his stories. I remember asking myself, "Would Ustinov – a master storyteller – benefit from the use of images?" This was not asked out of any sense of dissatisfaction with the evening's performance – more as an experiment. I reckoned even Ustinov (and by extension everyone else) would have benefited from the use of images because of two qualities inherent in them – concision and emotional impact.

- **Concision.** This is a technical term referring to the ability to convey a message more swiftly than words – a principle all road signs rely upon. Ustinov took five minutes to describe a Hollywood set he was working on. A picture could have said it in five seconds. With preaching it might work this way. Once I was giving a sermon on suffering. I showed a picture of a starving child: distended belly; crying face; a tear stain on a cheek shining under a fierce sun. We all know that the child has not long to live. We also know that the child never had a chance. And we know it at a glance. I don't have to say, "Look at this. Isn't that terrible?" I don't have to expend time in description. It's done. In an instant. A well-chosen picture can create paragraphs of exposition in a twinkling. But then I asked, "Why would God allow this? Has God the power to save that child? Why doesn't He?" The picture *cannot* verbalize those questions. It takes a preacher to do so. And so image and speech interweave and dialog, each doing what only it can do.
- **Emotional impact.** Ustinov told us of a particular film in which he was playing Nero. He wanted the audience to feel sorry for Nero – no mean feat as he was, Ustinov admitted, a callous monster. A picture or film clip of his movie character would have let us be the judge. We could have asked ourselves, "Well, do I feel sympathy?" Similarly in preaching, a picture like the one of a starving child moves an audience. It creates an instant emotional response. The preacher must then key in to this response: "You felt shame and compassion, but why doesn't God? Or if he does, why doesn't he do something about it?" You can respond to the

emotion that the image engenders in the audience, and move the sermon along in reaction to it.

The key to this kind of communication is to make sure that you are using words in dialog with the images. Two things can go wrong in this regard. One, either the preacher uses words to explain the image, which is unnecessary because the image is eloquent enough. Two, the preacher is saying one thing while the image says another, which is distracting. The trick is to let the image speak on its own terms. An image cannot interpret itself. That's where the words come in. Having a sense of what words alone can do, and what images alone can do, is the key to all multimedia presentation.

The same principle holds for the moving image. I once spoke on the story of Job and puzzled over how to get across the baffling nature of God's speech at the end of the book. How does God's "Let me introduce you to my pets" speech actually solve Job's complaint that God has made the world so unfair? Derek Kidner puts the dilemma nicely: "That a discourse which began with the cosmos should end in praise of two aquatic monsters, however fearsome, may strike us as eccentric; and that it should ignore our burning questions altogether may be a bitter disappointment."[84]

Job has a problem – the world is a mess, and as a devout believer who believes God is ultimately responsible, God appears incompetent at the very least, unjust at the very worst. God answers in thundering tones, describing the queer habits of ostriches, the origins of rain clouds, and seemingly goading Job that he is unable to walk on the ocean floor. Job is baffled. How does God's answer deal with Job's complaint?

To help with this, I showed a five-minute extract from David Attenborough's *The Blue Planet*. It was footage of deep-sea creatures, mainly shrimps and copipods with spectacular and explosive escape mechanisms. Attenborough's sparse commentary accompanied the clip.

Now that clip did three things my words could not.

• It created the visual wonder that Job must have felt from the speech. My powers of description simply could not match the astonishing sights.

- It created the perfect emotional perplexity that Job also felt. How could deep-sea red shrimps and flashing copipods be the answer to the suffering of the universe? The moving images actually delivered to us, temporarily, the experience of being as nonplussed as Job.
- The images matched the landscape of the speech. God lists creatures that Job cannot see. The clip contained footage of deep-sea shrimps human eyes had never seen before. We walked for a moment on the ocean floor, just like God. God is the only audience for these creatures.

The images set up the verbal explanation, which is that if God takes so much trouble over creating an amazing escape mechanism for an insignificant creature 4000 feet down in the cold ocean, then he must also care about us. More. It also gives us a clue to the answer to Job's complaint. Shrimps cannot know whether the universe is worth it because they are creatures. Neither can we. But when we see that the world is full of grace – as exhibited in the care God takes over the life cycle of a shrimp – we can trust that God extends this grace to us also. And trust is the only proper posture of the creature. I hope that the clip enabled the audience to grasp the teaching of the speeches better because they saw and felt the wonder and the grace of the creation far beyond the reach of humans. Of course, it's not a full answer to suffering and injustice. Job gets a reply, rather than an answer, to this problem, and we are in the same position.

I am trying to develop a sensitivity to the general principle of ensuring that I am conveying with the image what words cannot convey, and vice versa. One also needs a sensitivity for the unique impact of sound, which is immensely important, though I have not yet had occasion to try all three elements together. The day will come, however, and how exciting it all is. There are new languages unfolding before our senses. No one has the floor. We are all experimenting.

In a lot of the multimedia presentations I have seen, there is a desire to blend music and image, and not use words at all, even afterwards. But there is a problem with this for the preacher. As Umberto Eco writes, "The ability of a visual language to express more than one meaning at once is also its limitation." An image never interprets itself! In the wider artistic world, this is acceptable because no one wishes to be "preachy." You cast the watcher adrift into their own sea of infinite interpretation. God forbid that the artist should actually have a cognitive intention! But the preacher is required to present a particular content that does contain exclusions. For example we don't want people to think that God is cruel, or that God is impersonal, or that Christ is just a gifted human. We want them to connect with the revelation content of the gospel. So speech will always be necessary to make this clear. Who knows, maybe the monolog will stick around longer than some technophiles think.

So we must not let the complications and challenges of the communications revolution rob the preacher of the conviction that their words do three things uniquely:

- The preacher's words rescue the image from the curse of infinite ambiguity. Sure, an image carries the advantage of infinite suggestibility, but infinite ambiguity is the price that is paid.
- The preacher's message is individually applied in time and space to a specific audience. Often by someone who knows the audience intimately.
- The preacher's message is physically embodied. The gospel is enfleshed in human tissue, representing the most exciting features of our message – that God is a personal Being who loves to communicate directly with each of us.

Preachers relate to the multimedia world primarily out of a desire to imitate it, garnering communication techniques to help their own presentations. But we also relate to it – paradoxically – by critiquing it. William Fore, for many years the media watcher for the World Council of Churches in the US, argues that the mass media actually push a materialistic worldview that gradually substitutes for the Christian gospel. Analyzing programs from secular television, he concluded that the world-view was:

1   that the fittest survive;
2   that power and decision-making start at the centers, i.e. Washington and multi-national boardrooms;
3   that happiness consists of limitless material acquisition.

Fore concludes that "the mass media… tells us that we are basically good, that happiness is the chief end of life, and that happiness consists in obtaining material goods."

The preacher is not to stand for this terrible shrinkage of life's dimensions, which is all the more deadly because mass media is our virtual wallpaper, and its influence seeps in unnoticed.

Once I freeze-framed a clip from a recent remake of *The Thomas Crown Affair*. It showed Pierce Brosnan leaving a fabulous New York house and getting into a front seat of a Bentley. I asked the audience to react to the clip. This is some of what they wrote:

- This is what success looks like, big homes, flash cars.
- This is what handsome is.
- I hate my life, I'm driving an old tiny Ford.
- I wish my man was gorgeous and wealthy.
- When is my life going to happen?

And so on. Look at the unspoken impact. Look at the worldview it pushes down one's throat. Look at the dissatisfaction it engenders. Do you really want to stand for a medium that says you are nothing if you are not (a) drop-dead gorgeous, (b) independently wealthy, and (c) smart and able to control the fate of other people through your decisions?

I replaced the image with one of Meryl Streep from *Sophie's Choice*, the still of her face just after she has made her terrible decision to send her daughter to the ovens of Auschwitz to save her son. The reactions were very different:

- What choices in life have I made that I cannot face?
- That's life… it's suffering… it's full of hard choices.
- I'm so glad to have my freedom and not be forced to give up what I love.

- Did God feel that way when he sent Jesus to die?

Those reactions could lead to more spiritual empowerment than the ones coming from the first clip. They illustrate that we must not be against the technology, but against the way that much of the mass media has been manipulated to portray distorted values.

This leads us to the huge and murky area of the whole impact the communications revolution is having on our unconscious lives. There is that fearful insight of McLuhans: "First we shape our tools, then our tools shape us." In an era when the chip has replaced the book as the prime means of storage, and the digital revolution has expanded to all aspects of life, the way our brains process information is quite possibly changing, and thus so is the way people hear our sermons. Clearly there is no limit to the preacher's relationship with the communications revolution, and we haven't yet mentioned cyberspace. Whole new questions are being raised. Do we need a physical preacher? Can we have virtual church? Could the digital revolution ultimately reshape human nature itself, where a semi-cyborg existence beckons?

It ain't just about PowerPoint folks!

Hold on to these two principles. First, *words are not finished, but they will increasingly form part of the sermon, rather than constitute the sermon itself.* Don't think that the monolog is over. If you – like me – embrace more types of multimedia sermon, then appreciate this very non-technical reason for doing so: it makes preaching less lonely! A good multimedia sermon is a team affair. The skills and time needed to put together a quality talk illustrated with excellent graphics, clips, and sound is beyond the scope of most individuals. Good. More people will share the burden.

Film clips are being increasingly used in sermons. They tend to work in four ways:

- **As illustrations.** The preacher makes the point, and the clip shows how it applies, or vice versa. The problem is that the clip can blow the preacher away. Perhaps it's best to use the clip at the beginning and end of the talk. This is the least powerful relationship between image and word.

- **As exposition.** You reveal how a film approaches a theme or issue through a character, delineating the issues and positing various resolutions. This can be very powerful, assisting the reality test because the key characters all have real conflicts in real life (if the film is a good one).
- **As an illuminating dialog partner.** You react to the depiction of the Messiah and the world in, for example, *The Matrix.* This can be very helpful for younger audiences (and never forget that popular films are primarily seen by the under thirty-fives) who may be unaware that a movie has these spiritual themes. The preacher uses the film's artistic take on the subject, and incorporates these insights into the message.
- **As a hostile dialog partner.** You show clips of a film in order to bring to the surface its worldview and then confute it.

Second, *technology isn't evil, but neither is it neutral.* Be aware that when you use PowerPoint, for example, it is asking you to change your sermon to suit it. For example, it will ask you to put up more and more points, or more and more images, and you may choke your own speech and impact in the end. If you have to use it – and some churches do require it now – then prefer images over text, though if you must use text, keep it simple. Better still, project a key sentence permanently that captures the thrust of your sermon. I heard a great sermon on prayer, and the PowerPoint screen reverted between the points to this quote from St. Ignatius: "Pray as if everything depended on God; act as if everything depended on you." It reinforced the central message beautifully, and the preacher made constant reference to it so that we were not puzzling over why it was there.

As we think through the preacher's new and emerging relationship with the communications revolution, however, keep anchored to this thought expressed by the British preacher Stephen Wright: "Preaching can take many forms, but it's most important feature is its simplest – that a *person* does it."

Letter 30:
Habits – The seven habits of a semi-effective preacher

You ask, "What daily or weekly habits have you found are most helpful to becoming a better preacher?"

It's the kind of question we might answer differently every time we were asked. It's also very individual. What works for me may not work for you. But here are seven habits that have really helped me in recent years. I can't claim they have made me a successful preacher. Neither can I claim that I keep them up every week. But I do aim at them, and accept that it's OK to fail a lot. Thank God it's the meek and the weak that inherit the earth.

1. Voyage around your lectern with the giants

Get yourself a lectern. It needn't be fancy. Place it in your study, and once or twice each week – more if you can manage – read, nay, perform, aloud a sermon from a great preacher of the past or present.

I use the series *20 Centuries of Great Preaching*, which preserves three or four sermons of ninety-five preachers, ranging from Origen to Savonarola to Luther to Finney to Marshall to Lloyd-Jones. Take a voyage with the greatest preachers in history. There is nothing quite like it to realize that (a) all great preaching is about speaking to the age, and (b) great preaching demands the highest in eloquence, excellence, and insight that a human being can muster. It makes me take the craft more seriously. It helps me to revere the Bible. Above all, it enables me to see the worth of my profession as I speak the words of these great men and women who changed the world by speaking the words of God.

Devise a daily liturgy

Try compiling a daily liturgy. I found existing liturgies did not satisfy me. This was partly because the liturgies were too long, or too denominationally slanted, and left no room for imagination or spontaneity. Also liturgical systems tend to have Bible readings that are lectionary-based. I hate having to read edited highlights of the Bible, especially if someone has taken out what they consider to be the "awkward" bits. I want to read the whole Bible. I use a system which enables me to read it through in a year.

My liturgy is simple. I get through it in an hour. I read four chapters of the Bible in the middle, with a notebook to jot down thoughts. This notebook has become my key preaching resource. The other elements are designed to draw out my praise, remind me of the wonders of being alive in Christ, and stimulate my imagination and my capacity to wonder. You'll see there are various elements: a postcard of a painting to meditate on; a hymn sung at full volume; verses to ponder and questions to answer; and others. Here's a Sunday one.

Opening prayer

> Lord Jesus Christ; Let me seek you by desiring you,
> and let me desire you by seeking you;
> let me find you by loving you,
> and love you in finding you.

*   *   *

> I confess, Lord, with thanksgiving,
> That you have made me in your image,
> So that I can remember you, think of you, and love
>   you.
> But that image is so worn and blotted out by faults,
> And darkened by the smoke of sin,
> That it cannot do that for which it was made,
> Unless you renew and refashion it.
> Lord, I am not trying to make my way to your
>   height,
> For my understanding is in no way equal to that,
> But I do desire to understand a little of your truth
> Which my heart already believes and loves,

I do not seek to understand so that I can believe,
But I believe so that I may understand;
And what is more,
I believe that unless I do believe, I shall not
    understand.
(St. Anselm, 1033–1109)

This great faith

With all this in mind, what are we to say? If God is on our side, who is against us? He did not spare his own Son, but gave him up for us all; how can he fail to lavish every other gift upon us? Who will bring a charge against those whom God has chosen? Not God, who acquits! Who will pronounce judgment? Not Christ, who died, and rose again; not Christ, who is at God's right hand and pleads our cause! Then what can separate us from the love of Christ? Can affliction or hardship? Can persecution, hunger, nakedness, danger, or sword?… I am convinced that there is nothing in death or life, in the realm of spirits or superhuman powers, in the world as it is or the world as it shall be, in the forces of the universe, in heights or depths – nothing in all creation that can separate us from the love of God in Christ Jesus our Lord. (Rom. 8:31–39)

Bible reading

1. The great plan.
   How we were made and what we were supposed to be!
   Genesis chapters 1 – 2; Psalm 8.
   "God created the world out of nothing. As long as you are not yet nothing God cannot make something out of you" (Luther).
2. Yearly readings. (I use the Robert Murray McCheyne method, which enables me to read the Old Testament once and the New Testament twice in a year, reading approximately four chapters a day.)

Scriptural prayer

John 17 and Job 3:11–26; 42:2–6.

Prayers and intercessions

Preacher's verses

Luke 16:10: "Whoever listens to you, listens to me, and whoever rejects you rejects me, and whoever rejects me rejects the one who sent me."

2 Chronicles 18:13: "But Micaiah said, 'As the Lord lives, whatever my God says, that I will speak.'"

Jeremiah 23:9: "My heart is crushed, and I am trembling. Because of the Lord, because of his holy words."

Scripture recitation

John 1:1–14

Question for contemplation

Why is Christianity always the most revolutionary option?

Quote: "The glory of God is a man fully alive."

Primary truth reminder

I am infinitely valuable.

Hymn

Breathe on me, breath of God,
Fill me with life anew,
That I may love what thou dost love,
And do what thou woulds't do.

* * *

Breathe on me, Breath of God,
Until my heart is pure,
Until with thee I will one will,
To do and to endure.

* * *

Breathe on me, Breath of God,
Blend all my soul with thine,
Until this earthly part of me
Glows with thy fire divine.

* * *

Breathe on me, Breath of God,
So shall I never die,
But live with thee the perfect life
Of thine eternity.

Poem

> *In church*
> Often I try
> To analyze the quality
> Of its silences. Is this where God hides
> From my searching? I have stopped to listen,
> After the few people have gone,
> To the air recomposing itself
> For vigil. It has waited like this
> Since the stones grouped themselves about it.
> These are the hard ribs
> Of a body that our prayers have failed
> To animate. Shadows advance
> From their corners to take possession
> Of places the light held
> For an hour. The bats resume
> Their business. The uneasiness of the pews
> Ceases. There is no other sound
> In the darkness but the sound of a man
> Breathing, testing his faith
> On emptiness, nailing his questions
> One by one to an untenanted cross.
>
>   *   *   *
>
> In the chapel acre there is a grace,
> And grass contending with the stone
> For mastery of the near horizon,
> And on the stone words; but never mind them:
> Their formal praise is a vain gesture
> Against the moor's encroaching tide.
> We will listen instead to the wind's text
> Blown through the roof, or the thrush's song
> In the thick bush that proved him wrong,
> Wrong from the start, for nature's truth
> Is primary and her changing seasons
> Correct out of a vaster reason
> The vague errors of the flesh.
> (R.S. Thomas, End of "the Minister")

Picture for contemplation

Belshazzar's Feast, Rembrandt.

Closing prayer

> God be in my head
> And in my understanding.
> God be in mine eyes
> And in my looking.
> God be in my mouth
> And in my speaking.
> God be in my heart
> And in my thinking.
> God be at mine end
> And at my departing.
> (Sarum Primer)

3. Keep a tiny verse book

Each week I write down a single Bible verse that has impressed me in my readings. I preserve it in a hard-bound notebook two inches wide by four high. It slips into any pocket. I carry it everywhere, take it out frequently, and dwell on that verse. I began to do this after meeting an evangelist friend in China.

He moved from village to village, town to town, in the revival province of Henan, central China. He would speak about Jesus, and every week around a hundred people would profess faith in Christ. This was in the 1980s, when Bibles were scarce. He had to keep moving on, otherwise he would be arrested. His dilemma was always, "I've got nothing to give these people, but I must leave them something so they can keep on growing into God."

So he devised this system: out of the hundred converts, he picked five people at random. He said, "You are going to lead a weekly meeting of twenty people." Then he took the five leaders to a stream and picked out five smooth stones for each of them. On each stone, he chiseled a verse of the Bible. He gave them the stones and said, "Each week, give a different member one of the stones. Let them live with the verse, have it with them in the fields. Then, the next week, when you come together, listen to what God told the person about that verse on the stone. As long as that person holds the stone, they cannot be interrupted. I'll see you in six months, to see how you are getting on, and give you five more verses." Whenever he visited the groups, he found that they were going on in the faith. His method was working.

What was really interesting about this was that I met this man again in 1996, when there were a lot more Bibles around. He still used this method for his new converts. In fact, a missions organization was quite annoyed at him for not handing out Bibles immediately to the new converts. I had to take representatives of the mission to him. This was his defense: "I don't want the new converts to encounter too much truth too fast. Otherwise they will get into the bad habit of never using what they know." He added, "A verse a week is the right pace. It slows them down to believe at the heart's pace. It is dangerous to learn truth faster than we can live it."

That really hit me. *It is dangerous to learn the truth faster than we can live it.* My little notebook enables me to learn the truth at a pace that enables me to practice it. What a difference it has made!

4. Find suffering people to teach the faith to you

You will have gathered by now that I am very interested in the persecuted church. I take every opportunity to meet persecuted Christians and read about them. They teach me the faith. They suffer, yet rejoice. They gain Christ in the midst of their pain. They know the faith with a depth I lack from my privileged vantage point. No matter. That's the beauty of the Body of Christ. One person's experience becomes another person's insight. Encounter the persecuted, and you will get to know how the faith works. The suffering, the marginalized, and the lonely, can do the same. Find them, and let their faith teach you. You must get out of the study. I'll always remember the first time I went to study at Francis Schaeffer's L'Abri community in Switzerland. Before I was allowed to go into the library, I first had to nurse a quadriplegic middle aged man in the mornings. I learned more about the God's care for human beings from wiping his mouth and changing his bedlinen than from all the Bible study and reading that week. You must meet people different to yourself. Where faith and trouble meet – that is the place of greatest inspiration. Go there!

5. Read a great book each week

A preacher needs to read. Set an hour aside a day to read a good book. Don't throw the fag-end of the day at this. Schedule a time when your powers are sharp. And don't just stick to reading theology. Read history or a classic. I'm going through Richard Overy's *The Dictators* at the moment. It's the story of Stalin and Hitler. Great books are the timeless and contemporary commentary on the truths we expound from the Bible. If you must read theology, pick thinkers that you are likely to disagree with. I remember working my way through Schleiermacher's *The Christian Faith*. Though the father of modern theology, much of which I reject, it stimulated my thinking in a way a more evangelical volume could not.

6. Use phylacteries for praising

You must stimulate your senses to praise. Otherwise, we don't praise! And when we don't, we are not fully alive. A phylactery, you will remember, is a small leather box containing Hebrew texts on vellum, worn by Jewish men at morning prayer as a reminder to keep the law. It need not be a box, but something physical is needed to remind the senses: praise God or die!

I met a Christian woman in China who kept two stones in her pocket. On one she had carved "I am but dust and ashes." On the other "I am God's beloved child for eternity." During the 1960s, when the atheistic persecution was at its height, she would be forced to sit in front of groups screaming at her and ridiculing her faith. She got through it "By holding these stones in my palms, reminding me that yes, I was nothing, but with

God, I was precious." She said, "The body always forgets God. That's why you need the word in your palms." John Donne put it this way: "The body licenseth the soul."

So I always use something that cues my senses to praise God. At the moment, it's finger beads. There are ten beads, and every time my eyes light on it, I count off ten reasons to praise God. I have used other items also – icons, stones, crosses, knots, and so on. Conscript the senses to praise God. Out of that comes life, and the preacher must have life.

7. Build yourself a cell

In the late 1980s, I met a very great Chinese Christian called Wang Ming Dao. Sentenced to solitary confinement for his faith in 1960, he emerged twenty odd years later with his faith as strong as ever. His endurance became an inspiration for millions. No one symbolized the power of God better in China than Wang Ming Dao.

I interviewed him on three occasions not long before his death. The first time, he asked me suddenly, "Young man, how do you walk with God?" I listed off a set of disciplines like Bible study, prayer. He retorted, "Wrong answer! To walk with God you must go at walking pace." I wondered what he was on about, but the mystery was never solved as he buried his face in a water melon. The interview was over.

On the second visit, I quizzed him about his prison experience. I confessed, "I find it hard to relate to your story. I will never be put in jail like you, so how can your experience have any impact on my faith?"

He thought for a minute, then asked me a series of questions: When you go back home, how many books do you have to read in the first month? How many people do you have to see? How many articles do you have to write? How many sermons do you have to preach?

The more questions he asked – and I answered – the more panicked I began to feel. I thought to myself, my goodness, I've so much work ahead I'll never manage it. At that point Wang Ming Dao leaned forward and whispered, "You need to build yourself a cell!"

He explained. "When I was put in jail, I was devastated. I was an evangelist. I wanted to hold crusades all over China. I was an author. I wanted to write books. I was a preacher. I wanted to preach more sermons. But in jail, I had no Bible, no pulpit, no audience, not even pen and paper. I couldn't even witness to my jailers because they pushed my food through a flap. I could do nothing... except get to know God. And for the next twenty years that became the sweetest relationship I have ever known."

Then he said, "I was pushed into a cell; you will have to build yourself a cell. Simplify your life, so that you have time to know God."

The final time we met, I asked him, "Why did you say, in our first talk, that to walk with God we have to go at walking pace? Surely God can go at whatever pace he likes?"

His answer haunts me still: "God walks because he loves his garden!"

My interaction with this great Chinese Christian reminded me that God works with the heart, and "fellowship pace" is a lot slower than "service pace." It's one thing to serve God. It's quite another to know him. For Wang Ming Dao, persecution put him into a cell where he returned to walking pace, where he could still himself enough to commune properly with God.

The Japanese missiologist Kosuke Koyama talks of a "three-mile-an-hour God." That's the pace at which we walk. God leads the Israelites out into the desert for a forty-year, three-mile-an-hour walk, so that they can learn a nineteen-word truth: that man does not live by bread alone, but by every word that comes from the mouth of God (Deut. 8:3).

So I build myself a cell, a place where nothing is allowed to intrude on a time where there is only God and myself. Occasionally, this has been a literal cell, a hut in the garden. Normally it is a space in the corner of a room, a time when there is only silence.

It has been the hardest fight of my ministry to preserve this "cell." But it is vital. From silence comes the word, and the word needs to be spoken into silence to be properly heard.

Over time, this cell has become a garden, and God has become a friend.

Build yourself a cell.

And *know God*.

Then you will preach from a center of intimacy with God.

And that will make all the difference!

Letter 31:
Afterword – the Chinese are coming!

A couple of years ago I was asked to design a preaching curriculum for the full time teachers of a certain house church movement in China. "Be very radical," they urged. My modus vivendi was to leave out everything I learned in seminary and put in everything I wished I'd learned. We ended up with a full-time, one-year course that the Chinese rather mystically referred to as, "The 66, the 33, and the 1." The goal of the course was to provide every preacher with the facility to preach – at the drop of a hat – the content of every single book of the Bible, and on every facet of the person and work of Christ.

So there were three main modules.

1 **The 66.** Graduates had to prepare sixty-six one-hour sermons on each book of the Bible. Each sermon must contain an outline of the contents of the book and application of its teaching to individual Christians, the local church, and the nation of China. They had to learn each sermon by heart (not by my insistence, but of the house church leadership), and no notes were allowed. In the final examination each preacher stood before a panel of three (and also in front of the whole school) and a card was drawn at random from a pack of 66. The moment the book was announced the preacher was given five seconds to get launched with the appropriate sermon. This ordeal was repeated twice more for each candidate, as the pack was shuffled again. The day I was there I heard three different sermons on Nahum. That's chance for you.

2 **The 33.** Graduates had to preach thirty-three one-hour sermons on the life and work of Jesus Christ. Each sermon must be based on a single verse, of which not more than ten should be drawn from outside the Gospels. Why thirty-three? One for each year of Jesus' life. The whole ministry

of Christ must be covered by the selected verses, starting from his pre-existent state at the beginning of time, to his birth, life, death, resurrection, ascension, intercessory work, and second coming. In a grand concession, I noticed that the examiners allowed the graduates to use one page of notes per sermon.

3 **The 1.** Graduates are asked to imagine that they are sitting at the Great Feast at the end of time, just as it is described in Isaiah 25:6–8. All people groups are represented, as well as all nations and, of course, all the saints from every era, from Jacob to Jowett, from Noah to Niemuller. Although Augustine, Luther, and Whitefield would be in the audience, it would be just like God to invite a complete unknown to preach a sermon on this occasion. The sermon goal would be to exclaim on behalf of all the saved what a wonderful kingdom plan God had wrought. So each preacher in the Chinese seminary prepares their "sermon for the end of time." That one can last as long as they wish, which is only appropriate as it is designed to be preached when time is no more. Of course, the object of the exercise is to free the imagination and consider the whole salvation story from God's point of view.

Yes, I know. We can't ask Western preachers to do this. It would cost too much, unlike in China. Taking twenty people away to a house in the country for a year, with one change of clothes, no books, a few notebooks, a bible, a daily bowl of rice and a few vegetables, costs the princely sum of US$300. They are content. We wouldn't be. Nor would the curriculum be recognized. They don't care. Most crucially, these are peasant farmers, and only recently literate. Because they come from an oral culture, they have mnemonic abilities far beyond the capacities of a Western Christian.

But I must say, as one who shivers to admit spending tens of thousands of dollars to complete a Masters of Divinity I watched a few of these Chinese men and women graduate with a mixture of delight and envy. Delight that they were through. Delight to see a sense of achievement shine in their eyes. Envy too. I envied the closeness to the text they had built up. I envied the way they had built the Bible into their brains. I envied their frontal-lobe knowledge of the whole biblical story. I envied the readiness of their tongues to proclaim the gospel of Jesus Christ.

Quite a contrast with the day I left seminary. I had a really high GPA in my pocket, and in my head, complete confusion about what the Bible was about and where God was in my life.

I had been given the tools to deconstruct the Bible, but I had not been given the tools to reconstruct the message of the Bible in my heart.

I was knowledgeable about theology, and quite uncoupled spiritually.

Tragically, very few noticed, least of all myself.

No, it wasn't a waste of time. But it was some years before I was able to recover the fire. That's another story, perhaps for another round of correspondence. All I can say is, if you want to learn how to work the words of the Bible into your life, pray, oh pray hard, for a wilderness.

But I close with that story, because it hints of the exciting future of preaching. Sure, I provided these Chinese preachers with this curriculum, but they fulfilled it in a way I could never hope to emulate. So both sides of the Body of Christ – free and unfree – stimulated each other to a greater proclamation. I'm so thankful Christianity is no longer a Western religion. The Chinese are coming. And our Indian brethren. And our Indonesian brothers, and our Palestinian sisters, and Columbian pastors, and Iranian Bishops, and northern Nigerian evangelists.

The homiletical loaf is about to be re-baked courtesy of these new preachers from the wider church. It will taste even better than before. I hope I live another forty years to savor it. I pray you will also. It has been a joy to correspond. Preach well, pray hard, and take more risks!

Acknowledgments

Although writing a book is always a lonely labor, the isolation has been thankfully offset by many friends who have taken time to read sections and give comments on the manuscript. If this book is half-way successful in its aims, then their quality feedback has much to do with it.

Special thanks to Cindy Frost, my sister Morag Bryce, and my first preaching mentor, Alan Nute, for reading almost the entire manuscript and suggesting invaluable changes. Thanks also to the Rev. Dr. Stephen Wright for his feedback on behalf of the publisher.

Thanks also to Deborah Kelhe, Jules Gomes, Sandra Giet, Robert Duerr, John Paul Lotz, and another preaching mentor, Eddie Gibbs, for taking time from their busy schedules to read portions of the manuscript.

Without certain friends I would never have been able to develop as a preacher. Thanks to five men in Hong Kong who sent me to seminary to preach better: Steve Phelps, Colin Blair, Henry Craig, Cameron Talloch, and Cyril Ley. I hope this repays some of that investment. In addition to Eddie Gibbs, I received valuable input from a wonderful caste of homileticians, especially Ian Pitt-Watson, Marguerite Shuster, William Pannell, and Mitties McDonald DeChamplain. Other friends were a tonic to talk with about preaching: Fr. Bill Broderick, John Drane, Richard Deibert, Des Philby, Mick Lumsden, and Murray Watts, in whose castle in Freswick, northern Scotland, this book was conceived. Honor should be given to my preacher heroes, especially to St. Augustine, Charles Spurgeon, Helmut Thielicke, James S. Stewart, and Martin Lloyd-Jones, and a small club of preachers I did hear in the flesh and took special inspiration from: Elizabeth Achtemeier, David Hubbard, Lewis Smedes, and Samuel Proctor.

Above all, I was set wonderful standards, and not just in preaching, by my pastor father, J.R. MacMillan, who showed me how to do what mattered most.

Finally, to my wife Eolene, the thanks that can never be expressed fully. Without her support and encouragement, and her acute critique of every chapter, this book would never have been written. We first met in the stress of a homiletics small group, where we had to critique each other's sermons. Perhaps we have never left it.

Endnotes

1   Quoted in *Of Fiction and Faith*, W. Dale Brown, ed., (Grand Rapids, MI: Eerdmans Publishing Co, 1997): 211.

2   *Faith in Life: A Snapshot of the Church Life in England* (London: Churches Information for Mission, 2001).

3   Press release, November 14, 2001.

4   Martin Lloyd-Jones, *Preaching and Preachers* (London: Hodder and Stoughton, 1971): 309.

5   From the poem "The Church Porch," *George Herbert, The Complete English Works*, Ed. Ann Pasternak Slater (London: David Campbell Publishers Ltd, 1995): 21

6   Thomas G. Long and Cornelius Platniga, Jr., eds., *A Chorus of Witnesses: Model Sermons for Today's Preacher* (Grand Rapids, MI: Eerdmans, 1994).

7   Long and Platniga, Jr., *Chorus:* 156.

8   Fred B. Craddock, *Preaching* (Nashville, TN: Abingdon Press, 1985): 61.

9   Donald Coggan, *Preaching: The Sacrament of the Word* (New York, NY: Crossroad, 1988): 31.

10 Ann Monroe, *The Word, Imagining the Gospel in Modern America* (Louisville, KY: Westminster John Knox Press, 2000).

11 William H. Kooienga, *Elements of Style for Preaching* (Grand Rapids, MI: Zondervan Publishing House, 1989).

12 Dietrich Bonhoeffer, *Letters and Papers from Prison*, Translated by R. Fuller *et al* (New York, NY: MacMillan, 1972): 199.

13 Frits De Lange, *Waiting for the Word* (Grand Rapids, MI: William B. Eerdmans Publishing Co, 1995): 26.

14 *The Tablet*, August 23, 2003, "Preacher, be a teacher," by Laurence Freeman: 11–12.

15 P.T. Forsyth, *Positive Preaching and the Modern Mind*, (London: Independent Press, 1907): 54.

16 Paul Ricoeur, *The Symbolism of Evil* (Boston, MA: Beacon Press, 1967): 347–57.

17 Walter J. Burghardt, *Long Have I Loved You: a theologian reflects on his church* (New York, NY: Orbis Press, 2000): 108.

18 Martin Rees, *Our Final Century* (London: William Heinemann, 2003): 61.

19 Rees, *Century*: 3.

20 Helmut Thielicke, *How the World Began* (Philadelphia, PA: Muhlenberg Press, 1961): 238–39.

21 Theilicke, *World*: 240.

22 Theilicke, *World:* 250.

23 Yngve Brilioth, *Landmarks in the History of Preaching* (London: SPCK, 1950): 11.

24 Saint Augustine, *Teaching Christianity* (De Doctrina Christiana), Tranlsated by Edmund Hill, O.P. (New York, NY: New City Press, 1996): 106.

25 Joseph Campbell, *The Power of Myth,* (New York, NY: Anchor Books, 1991): xvi.

26 Martin Rees, *Our Cosmic Habitat* (London: Phoenix, Orion Books Ltd, 2001) xi

27 www.edge.org. See article entitled "Ban All Schools? That's a Dangerous Thought," by Roger Highfield, *Daily Telegraph*, January 3, 2006.

28 Ibid

29 Charles H. Kraft, *Jesus' Model for Contemporary Communication* (Pasadena, CA: Fuller Seminary Press, 1991): 123.

30 D. Martin Lloyd-Jones, *The Kingdom of God* (Cambridge: Crossway Books, 1992): 8.

31 Lloyd-Jones, *Kingdom*: 9.

32 Lloyd-Jones, *Kingdom*: 11.

33 Douglas Adams, *The Prostitute in the Family Tree* (Louisville, KY: Westminster John Knox Press, 1997): 34.

34 Adams, *Prostitute:* 37.

35 See Claude Levi Strauss, *Structural Anthropology* (New York, NY: Doubleday, 1967) esp chapter 11.

36 Literally, spiritual reading, a method devised by ancient monks that uses Scripture texts as a topic of conversation with Christ.

37 Helmut Thielicke, *How The World Began* (London: James Clarke & Co, Ltd, 1964): 14 (italics mine).

38 Thielicke, *World:* 19.

39 Walter J. Burghardt, *Long Have I Loved You* (Maryknoll, NY: Orbis Books, 2000): 110.

40 Ian Pitt-Watson, *A Primer for Preachers* (Grand Rapids, MI: Baker Book House, 1987): 23.

41 Pitt-Watson, *Primer:* 23.

42 Elizabeth Achtemeier, *Preaching as Theology and Art* (Nashville, TN: Abingdon Press, 1984): 62–70.

[43] Elizabeth Achtemeier, *Preaching the Hard Tests of the Old Testament* (Peabody, MA: Hendrickson Publishers, Inc, 1998): 1.

[44] Richard Lischer, *The Preacher King* (New York, NY: Oxford University Press, 1995): 70.

[45] William Martin, *A Prophet With Honor* (New York, NY: William Morrow and Company, Inc, 1991): 114.

[46] The Dalai Lama, *The Good Heart*, (London: Rider, 2002): 54.

[47] O.C. Edwards, Jnr., *A History of Preaching* (Nashville, TN: Abingdon Press, 2004): 8.

[48] Eugene Peterson, *Five Smooth Stones for Pastoral Work* (Grand Rapids, MI: William B. Eerdmans Publishing Company, 1992): 31.

[49] *A Theological Word Book of the Bible*, ed. Alan Richardson (New York, NY: MacMillan Company, 1953): 172.

[50] See Gordon D. Fee's "The First Epistle to the Corinthians" in the *New International Commentary on the New Testament* (Grand Rapids, MI: William B. Eerdmans Publishing Company, 1987): 68–78.

[51] He hadn't done his homework on the word "sermon" either, which comes from the latin *sermo*, meaning "a dialog."

[52] John Drane, *Faith in a Changing Culture* (London: Marshall Pickering, 1997): 134.

[53] William Barclay, *Communicating the Gospel* (Stirling: The Drummond Press, 1968): 35.

[54] P.T. Forsyth, *Positive Preaching and the Modern Mind* (London: Independent Press, 1907): 53.

[55] See Robert P. Waznak, *An Introduction to the Homily* (Collegeville, MN: The Liturgical Press, 1998): 4.

[56] Hugh Oliphant Old, *The Reading and Preaching of the Scriptures in the Worship of the Christian Church, Vol. 1, The Biblical Period* (Grand Rapids, MI: William B. Eerdmans Publishing Company, 1998): 320.

[57] C.H. Sisson, ed., *The English Sermon, Vol. 2: 1650–1750* (Cheadle: The Carcent Press Limited, 1976): 190.

[58] Sisson, *Sermon*: 190.

[59] Charles Smyth, *The Art of Preaching: A Practical Survey of Preaching in the Church of England 747–1939* (London: SPCK, 1953).

[60] Smyth, *Art:* 160.

[61] Horton Davis, *Worship and Theology in England, Vol. 2, From Andrewes to Baxter and Fox 1603–1690*, (Grand Rapids, MI: William B. Eerdmans, combined edition 1996): 145.

[62] John Killinger, *To My People With Love – The Ten Commandments for Today* (Nashville, TN: Abingdon Press, 1988): 13–14.
www.archbishopofcanterbury.org/sermons_speeches/2003/031225.html, accessed 22 February, 2004.

[64] www.archbishopofcanterbury.org/sermons_speeches/2003/031225.html

[65] Lesslie Newbigin, *Signs Amid the Rubble* (Grand Rapids, MI: William B. Eerdmans Publishing Co, 2003): 119–20.

[66] Harry S. Stout *The Divine Dramatist: George Whitefield and the Rise of Modern Evangelicalism* (Grand Rapids, MI: William B. Eerdmans Publishing Co, 1991): xvi.

[67] William Martin, *A Prophet With Honor* (New York, NY: William Morrow and Company, Inc. 1992): 580–82.

[68] Robert Moats Millar, "Fosdick, Harry Emerson," in William H. Willimon and Richard Lischer, eds., *Concise Encyclopedia of Preaching* (Louisville, KY: Westminster John Knox Press, 1995): 154.

[69] Millar, "Fosdick": 92.

[70] Millar, "Fosdick": 93.

[71] Millar, "Fosdick": 94.

[72] Bill Hybels, *The God You're Looking For* (Nashville, TN: Thomas Nelson Publishers, 1997).

[73] Hybels, *God:* 20.

[74] John Claypool, "Life is a Gift," in *A Chorus of Witnesses, Model Sermons for Today's Preaching,* eds. Thomas G. Long and Cornelius Plantinga, Jnr. (Grand Rapids, MI: Eerdmans Publishing Co, 1994): 125.

[75] Claypool, "Life": 129–30.

[76] Graham Greene, *The Heart of the Matter,* (London: Heinemann, 1947). Greene liked to describe himself as a "Catholic atheist," which gave rise to an ongoing debate as to whether he had any real Christian convictions at all.

[77] C.H. Dodd, *The Parables of the Kingdom* (Glasgow: William Collins and Sons, 1978): 16.

[78] Philip Yancey, *Soul Survivor – How my Faith Survived the Church* (London: Hodder & Stoughton, 2001): 35.

[79] Martin Luther King, Jnr., *Stride Toward Freedom* (New York, NY: Harper and Row, 1964): 114–15.

[80] Robert Schuller, *My Journey* (San Francisco, CA: Harper SanFrancisco, 2001): 281.

[81] Richard Lischer, *The End of Words: The Language of Reconciliation in a Culture of Violence* (Grand Rapids, Michigan: William B. Eerdmans Publishing Company, 2005): 26.

[82] Jolyon P. Mitchell, *Visually Speaking: Radio and the Renaissance of Preaching* (Edinburgh: T&T Clark, 1999): 18.

[83] There are very sensible guidelines on how to incorporate learning styles into preaching in the book *Psychology for Christian Ministry,* by Frazer Walls, Rebecca Nye and Sara Savage (London: Routledge,

2002). See especially the chapters entitled "Diversity among Christians" (40-58) and "Teaching and preaching" (121–138). The cartoon referred to is on page 57.

84 Derek Kidner, *Wisdom To Live By* (Leicester: Inter Varsity Press, 1985): 72.